THE SEARCH AND SEIZURE HANDBOOK

David M. Waksman, J.D.

Prosecuting Attorney and Former Sergeant, NYPD

Debbie J. Goodman, M.S.

Chairperson

Miami Dade College, School of Justice

Editorial Consultant

Prentice Hall
Upper Saddle River, New Jersey
Columbus, Ohio

Library of Congress Cataloging-in-Publication Data

Waksman, David M.
   The search and seizure handbook /David M. Waksman; Debbie J. Goodman,
editorial consultant.—3rd ed.
      p. cm.
   Includes bibliographical references and index.
   ISBN-13: 978-0-13-503845-1 (alk. paper)
   ISBN-10: 0-13-503845-6 (alk. paper)
   1. Searches and seizures—United States—Popular works.   2. Searches and seizures—
United States—Cases.   I. Goodman, Debbie J.   II. Title.
KF9630.W35 2010
345.73'0522—dc22

                                                                              2008039177

Editor in Chief: Vernon Anthony
Acquisitions Editor: Tim Peyton
Editorial Assistant: Alicia Kelly
Production Manager: Wanda Rockwell
Creative Director: Jayne Conte
Cover Designer: Bruce Kenselaar
Cover photo: Jupiter Images
Director of Marketing: David Gesell
Marketing Manager: Adam Klosa
Marketing Coordinator: Alicia Dysert

This book was set in 10/12 Palatino by Integra and was printed and bound by Bindrite/Command Web.

Pearson Education Ltd., London
Pearson Education Singapore Pte. Ltd.
Pearson Education Canada, Inc.
Pearson Education—Japan
Pearson Education Australia Pty. Limited

Pearson Education North Asia Ltd., Hong Kong
Pearson Educación de Mexico, S.A. de C.V.
Pearson Education Malaysia Pte. Ltd.
Pearson Education, Upper Saddle River,
   New Jersey

Prentice Hall
is an imprint of

www.pearsonhighered.com

10 9 8 7 6 5 4 3 2 1
ISBN-13: 978-0-13-503845-1
ISBN-10:   0-13-503845-6

OVERVIEW

Until now, many books about the criminal justice system were either novels or dry treatises and textbooks written by scholars with little practical experience. Finally, here is a fast-paced, real-life recounting of what really happens in American courtrooms.

Similarly to *Law and Order*, *CSI*, and *Homicide-Life on the Streets*, which brought police work and trials into America's homes, this book advances the action by explaining, in simple terms, the legal reasoning of Supreme Court decisions, which established the working rules, often called technicalities by the uninformed, that police and prosecutors must abide by. The Bill of Rights is brought to life in a way that dramatizes the need for our constitutional protections.

In this book, the Fourth Amendment to the U.S. Constitution is explained in simple terms. Who can a police officer search and where can he search? What happens to evidence found when the search is later found to violate these rules? Are there exceptions to the constitutional requirement to obtain a search warrant before the search?

The question asked by legal scholars over 75 years ago is still with us—*Should the criminal go free because the constable has blundered?*

These are the issues discussed in this book and no police officer is ready for the street until they are mastered. The investigation—and his or her life—may depend upon them.

Reviews on
The Search and Seizure Handbook

"David Waksman's *Search & Seizure Handbook* is not only good common sense, but it also provides the reader and potential trainer with a good basic understanding of the constitution and the various safeguards that a law enforcement officer must have to be successful dealing with the current criminal justice system."

Wm. B. Berger
Chief of Police
North Miami Beach PD
Past president of IACP

"As a retired police chief from the North Miami Police Department, and now serving as the Basic Training Director at MDC School of Justice, I am impressed with the substantive content matter which is presented in his handbook on the law of search and seizure."

Thomas Hood, Director
Basic Training Academy
MDC School of Justice

"I wish he were around when I was running the Detective Division. They all would have been winners. *The Search and Seizure Handbook* belongs in every squad room!"

Al Seedman,
Chief Detectives, NYPD (ret.)
Nationally acclaimed author of *Chief!*

"More thrills than a great murder mystery. Waksman wrote the book on Homicide. This is how it's done. *The handbook* is required reading for all detectives and those who want to ride with them."

Captain Marshall Frank (ret.)
Homicide Bureau
Metro-Dade Police Department
Author of *Beyond the Call and Dire Straits*

"No one should investigate violent crimes without reading Waksman's tell it like it is—take no prisoners method of prosecuting criminal trials. He's been teaching the cops of America How to Do It for over thirty years. This book is a must read."

Dr. Robert Domalewski (ret.)
Asst. Director of the Southern
Police Institute(ret.)
University of Louisville

"I was engrossed by David Waksman's *The Search and Seizure Handbook*. The information is easily digested in a few pleasant hours. The book comprehensively covers the material presented in an entire term in a Constitutional Criminal Procedure class at the University of Miami School of Law."

Chiara M. Juster
Student of Law
University of Miami

ABOUT THE AUTHOR

David M. Waksman, J.D., is a nationally known homicide prosecutor with vast experience in trying violent offenders. He is a very popular speaker, not only at professional meetings, but before business and civic groups as well. Waksman brings a witty and pointed humor to this oftentimes dry and sensitive area. He has been invited several times to address the Mystery Writers of America, giving them the reality they need for their novels.

Mr. Waksman is well published in police publications. He has had two criminal justice–related Op-Ed articles published in the *Miami Herald* and has been featured numerous times on TV shows such as *Inside Story, Inside Edition, COPS, Hard Copy, 48 Hours,* and *Dateline NBC.* The local TV networks call upon him to comment on current cases in the news. On the 200th anniversary of the Bill of Rights, Mr. Waksman appeared with Justice Antonin Scalia, Judge Robert Bork, and several other distinguished judges and lawyers in a nationally televised PBS segment of Fred Friendly's *The Constitution— That Delicate Balance.* The show featured a hypothetical case highlighting the constitutional problems encountered in investigating and prosecuting a capital case.

Waksman has toiled 35 years in the criminal courts of Miami, Florida, after working the mean streets of The South Bronx for six years as a police officer. He may have tried more first degree murder cases than any other American prosecutor (80 and still carrying a full caseload).

Mr. Waksman's career as a prosecutor began under the legendary Richard Gerstein. He also worked eighteen years as an assistant to America's most popular, and longest serving Attorney General, Janet Reno, when she served as Miami's top prosecutor. During that time period he tried over ninety homicide cases to juries, including twenty in which the death penalty was sought.

Prosecutor Waksman's trial experience spans well over 180 jury trials, primarily for such crimes as homicide, rape, child abuse, armed robbery, home invasion robbery, and public corruption. In federal court, five years before the world heard of Rodney King, Mr. Waksman was sworn in as a Special Assistant United States Attorney to prosecute a Hialeah, Florida, police officer for conspiracy to violate the civil rights of two people, by killing them, after that officer was acquitted in state court of homicide charges, resulting from an off-duty drug robbery gone bad.

David Waksman, not content to fight his battles in Miami-Dade County, has been teaching the cops of America the law and procedures they need to combat violent crimes in their communities. Since 1988 he has taught a monthly seminar on homicide investigation for the *Southern Police Institute* (University of Louisville) in various locations (19 states, 32 cities) across the country. He also teaches new detectives, crime scene technicians, medical examiners, and forensic investigators at the nationally renowned Dade County Medical Examiner's *Police-Medical Investigation of Death* seminar. He has taught classes (one a Fourth Amendment seminar) at the University of Miami School of Law and at several colleges in the South Florida area. Local police departments continually call upon Mr. Waksman to teach refresher courses and in-service training to their investigators.

Waksman is also on the staff of the National College of District Attorneys, at their training facility in Columbia, South Carolina. He teaches newer prosecutors how to be effective advocates in jury trials at the National Advocacy Center.

In September of 2001, Mr. Waksman was invited by the U.S. Departments of State and Justice to participate in a training seminar in Yerevan, Armenia. With two FBI agents and a medical examiner, a five-day class, titled "Major Case/Homicide Investigation," was taught (*during the week of September 11*). The seminar was an advanced-level course designed for Armenian investigators, prosecutors, and medical examiners currently participating in homicide investigations. The class was presented in rather austere conditions, in a former Soviet military installation. As the investigators spoke no English, the class was taught with simultaneous translations, as well as with his collection of rather graphic slides.

His unique experiences and engaging style make him a compelling storyteller, one who can cut through the confusing legal issues that have befallen our modern American justice system. He tells it as he sees it, yet protects himself from the carnage, as most cops do, with humor, albeit away from the grieving families.

The compliment he appreciates most came from a Metro homicide detective: *Waksman, you're nothing more than a cop in a lawyer's uniform.*

ABOUT THE EDITORIAL CONSULTANT

Ms. Debbie J. Goodman is the Chairperson of the School of Justice at Miami-Dade College. She holds a Master of Science degree in Criminal Justice from Florida International University and a Bachelor of Science degree in Criminology from Florida State University.

DEDICATION

This book is dedicated to all the cops I rode with, learned from, worked with, taught, and all the rest I never met—who put themselves in harm's way—every shift—to protect us from the bad guys—and who help those who need our help. You are the true heroes of America.

I must also acknowledge the great lawyers and judges who taught me the meaning of justice.

I love you all.

David Waksman

PREFACE

"A room is searched against the law, and the body of a murdered man is found. . . . The privacy of the home has been infringed, and the murderer goes free. . . . We may not subject society to these dangers."

    Justice Benjamin Cardozo, speaking for the New York Court of Appeals in *People v. DeFore*, 1926.[1]

    The criminal is to go free because the constable has blundered.

    Could it ever happen?

TOPICS COVERED IN *THE SEARCH AND SEIZURE HANDBOOK*

---

[1]This case can be found in Appendix A.

CONTENTS

INTRODUCTION

QUESTION:

If our job is to enforce the law, must we also obey it? Can we disregard the law in our efforts to bring lawbreakers to justice? Do the ends justify the means?

****

Decency, security, and liberty alike demand that government officials shall be subjected to the same rules of conduct that are commands to the citizen. In a government of laws, existence of the government will be imperiled if it fails to observe the law scrupulously. Our government is the potent, the omnipresent teacher. For good or for ill, it teaches the whole people by its example. Crime is contagious. If the government becomes a lawbreaker, it breeds contempt for law; it invites every man to become a law unto himself; it invites anarchy. To declare that in the administration of the criminal law the end justifies the means—to declare that the government may commit crimes in order to secure the conviction of a private criminal—would bring terrible retribution. Against that pernicious doctrine this court should resolutely set its face.

Justice Louis Brandeis, dissenting, *Olmstead v. U.S.,* **277 U.S. 438 (1928)**

In his reasoning, Justice Brandeis relied upon an earlier case from the U.S. Supreme Court, *Boyd v. U.S.,* decided in 1886. That opinion quoted at length from two famous English cases that preceded our Constitution and upon which the Bill of Rights is based:

A sufficient answer is found in *Boyd v. United States,* 116 U. S. 616 (1886), a case that will be remembered as long as civil liberty lives in the United States. This court there reviewed the history that lay behind the Fourth and Fifth Amendments. We said with reference to Lord Camden's judgment in *Entick v. Carrington,* 19 Howell's State Trials, 1030:

'The principles laid down in this opinion affect the very essence of constitutional liberty and security. They reach farther than the concrete form of the case there before the court, with its adventitious circumstances; they apply to all invasions on the part of the government and its employees of the sanctities of a man's home and the privacies of life. It is not the breaking of his doors, and the rummaging of his drawers, that constitutes the essence of the offense; but it is the invasion of his indefeasible right of personal security, personal liberty and private property, where that right has never been forfeited by his conviction of some public offense—it is the invasion of this sacred right which underlies and constitutes the essence of Lord Camden's judgment. Breaking into a house and opening boxes and drawers are circumstances of aggravation; but any forcible and compulsory extortion of a man's own testimony or of his private papers to be used as evidence of a crime or to forfeit his goods, is within the condemnation of that judgment. In this regard the Fourth and Fifth Amendments run almost into each other.'

The following was added by Justice Oliver Wendell Holmes, also dissenting in *Olmstead*:

(T)he government ought not to use evidence obtained . . . by a criminal act. . . . (W)e must consider the two objects of desire both of which we cannot have and make up our minds which to choose. It is desirable that criminals should be detected, and to that end that all available evidence should be used. It also is desirable that the government should not itself foster and pay for other crimes, when they are the means by which the evidence is to be obtained. . . . We have to choose, and for my part *I think it a less evil that some criminals should escape than that the government should play an ignoble part.*

These noble ideas were finally adopted by the U.S. Supreme Court, in *Mapp v. Ohio*, 367 U.S. 643 (1961), which made the Fourth Amendment binding upon the states. They were more fully developed in *Katz v. U.S.*, 389 U.S. 347 (1967), which defined the area the government must stay out of without a search warrant—that in which one has a reasonable expectation of privacy.

CHAPTER 1

10-18—Condition Corrected!

It was a cold night in The South Bronx, early in 1968. I had been assigned to the 40th Precinct shortly before Christmas. That night I was patrolling in a radio car—with a heater, as opposed to my normal foot post. It also had a radio. Towards the middle of the 4 p.m. to midnight shift, we got a job from the Communications Bureau, known as CB.

"See the Lady, 622 East 140, apt 4B, Unknown Condition,"

said the dispatcher. *Unknown Condition* was the most common handle CB put on situations they couldn't figure out. Their theory was: "We're giving it to two New York City cops; they'll handle it."

The NYPD used the 10 code for radio transmissions. If CB had a *Past Burglary* call, they gave us a *10-20* right after the address; a *Robbery in Progress* was a *10-30*. We acknowledged the job with a *10-4*, backed up other units needing help when a *10-13* was broadcast and responded *10-18*, after handling calls that were too complicated to explain.

10-18 meant *Condition Corrected*. CB didn't know what they were sending us to, but when we got there, we corrected whatever the condition was!

This job sounded like a domestic dispute—every cop's most dreaded call. As much as the couple hated each other that instant, they could join forces and attack us in a moment.

It was usually two irrational—probably drunken—people fighting over things you had no control over. Whether he came home drunk, lost his paycheck gambling, couldn't get a job, or one or the other got caught fooling around or just plain flirting, they called 9-11 and we had to resolve their problems.

We usually separated the couple into different rooms and tried to calm them down. If that didn't work, each cop would ask the one he had to spend the night with a friend. Quite often we did that several times during the course of the tour of duty.

This time it was different. A small, disheveled woman opened the door and handed me a .25 caliber semi-automatic pistol—a popular gun for the ladies—fit nicely into the purse. Before I realized what was happening, she pointed towards the rear room.

Her beloved was in that soon-to-become-familiar position—on the floor, leaking blood from a recent opening in his circulatory system. Essie Mae's common-law[1] husband, Whitfield Pratt, had two pencil-sized holes in his chest. He was lying on a rug, which was rapidly turning burgundy, with ever-shrinking borders.

Without knowing why, I quickly looked around for other people with guns, opening all the closets and looking under the beds (and anywhere else someone looking to hurt me could be hiding). Not finding anyone else in need of my rather limited medical abilities, I cuffed Essie Mae and asked CB to have the sergeant respond. That was a rather good call to make when you had no idea what to do. Not hearing the customary *10-18*, the other cops in the precinct asked if I needed *Backup*.

With great confidence (I had almost ninety days in the precinct, as a real cop, having replaced my rookie grays with the blue uniform), I announced that everything was under control and awaited the Old Sarge. He had been in The Bronx so long, nothing fazed him.

"Whacha got, Kid," he barked, as he gasped for breath, entering the apartment. There were no elevators on 140th Street, or for that matter, for several miles around—and the Sarge wasn't fond of climbing stairs. As a matter of fact, the only exercise he ever got was lifting 12 ounce bottles.

"I think I done wrong, Sarge. I searched the apartment without a warrant and seized the gun before I knew what I had."

Having survived thirty years in The Bronx, the Sarge was not about to let a rookie get him killed. He checked out the place himself.

Then the Sarge told me: "This guy ain't goin' nowhere for a while. Take her to the stationhouse, I'll call the meat wagon."[2]

"Don't talk to her before the Squad interviews her."[3]

I asked again, "Did I do wrong?" The Sarge dispelled my fears.

"It was an *exijentzy* Kid, don't worry, you made a nice collar."

It would be four years before I entered law school and learned about the Emergency Rule, which covered exigent circumstances. The professors (in many subjects) would say, "Do whatever you must to deal with the emergency, then apply the regular rules."

Removing a gun from a shooter's hand, searching for other bad guys and victims, and getting first aid to the injured is just what the U.S. Supreme Court would allow ten years later in *Mincey v. Arizona* (1978).[4] We were just *dealin' wit an exijentzy* and didn't know it.

---

[1]Common-law marriage was only recognized in the state of New York for those persons living together prior to October 1, 1938. That rule wasn't very well understood south of Fordham Road in the 1960s and 1970s.

[2]Dead bodies, known to cops as DOAs, could not be moved until the medical examiner, a physician specializing in forensic pathology, examined the body in place. Prosecutors, cops and M.E.'s usually got along well, all being on the same team. The Docs have a bizarre sense of humor. They too, need protection from dealing with death on a daily basis.

[3]We'll discuss why, at length, in the book on Interrogation Techniques, called *Stories From the Courtroom*. The quick answer is that the rookie hasn't been trained in how to get a defendant to waive his *Miranda* rights.

[4]See Chapter #3, *Barry Headricks*.

I'm sure the detectives in the precinct squad never secured a search warrant for the Pratt residence before conducting their crime scene examination. Pratt just went to the morgue, Essie went to jail, and I let it all go to my head. "Great collar," everyone kept saying, except the old Sarge. He told me "Kid, there are times in this job that are very rewarding, but if you want people to love ya, you shuda joined the Fire Department."

About twenty-five years later, the courts of many states began recognizing the affirmative defense[5] known as the *Battered-Spouse Syndrome*. Today, if a jury believes the woman's story of constant abuse (many times difficult for us to refute), they can apply the rules of self-defense and see if she had any place of safety to run to (friends, a job, Mom) and, if not, acquit the battered spouse for her *anticipatory* strike. Actually, it's a departure from the rule of self-defense, which allows only enough force to prevent the *imminent* use of force against a person. Her actions are allowed as the law recognizes that if he is not stopped, he will *most likely* batter her again. This can be a very dangerous situation to live under.

I was never called to court; I'm sure Essie took a plea. The legality of the search of the Pratt residence was not litigated. Had it been, under today's law, the prosecution probably wouldn't have been able to use anything but the gun Essie Mae placed into my shaking hand and the shocking sights I saw as I walked around apartment 4B.

This book will discuss what can, and more importantly, what cannot, be done at the scene of a homicide, or another crime. As we study the rule of *Mincey*, remember that this is a dangerous business that many have chosen as their life's work. Remember also, Police Officer Barry Headricks, of the Tucson, Arizona, Police Department. Despite our dear brother's untimely and vicious death, this rule stands for the proposition that the U.S. Constitution protects us all. As we study the cases that govern our conduct in a killer's apartment, we will see how that same rule protects us as well.

Discussion:

What types of situations are covered under exigent circumstances?

_____

_____

_____

_____

Is looking under a bed, without getting permission from the tenant, permitted?

_____

_____

---

[5]An affirmative defense, argued in court by defendants, admits the crime. "I did it but, it was self defense, I was insane, or entrapped, or under duress. . . ." I call it the *Yeah, but*, defense.

Is there any authority to enter the apartment without the owner's permission?

_____

_____

_____

If Essie Mae knew her husband was going to beat her when he awoke from his drunken stupor, is she allowed to shoot him while he sleeps, under the law of self-defense?

_____

_____

_____

_____

Lesson:

What have we learned about emergencies in this chapter?

_____

_____

_____

_____

_____

Are search warrants always required before entering a person's apartment or house?

_____

_____

_____

_____

_____

_____

_____

_____

_____

_____

Afterthought:

Was there any probable cause to arrest Essie Mae?

_____

_____

_____

_____

Notes:

_____

_____

_____

_____

_____

_____

_____

_____

_____

_____

_____

_____

CHAPTER 2

Roots

The wind may enter, the rain may enter, but the king may not.

The right of the people to be secure in their persons, houses, papers, and effects, against unreasonable searches and seizures, shall not be violated, and no warrants shall issue, but upon probable cause, supported by oath or affirmation, and particularly describing the place to be searched, and the persons or things to be seized.

—The Fourth Amendment to the Constitution of the United States—

Why this fascination with warrants, probable cause, and judges? Why can't cops just do their job of investigating crime and protecting us from those who cannot or will not follow society's rules? They know who is *probably* dirty, what is *probably* stolen, whether a crime *probably* occurred. Isn't that *probable cause*?

The origins of our search and seizure laws began in England, when the king's soldiers searched homes and businesses without court-ordered search warrants, as we know them now. The searches were authorized by orders known as *Writs of Assistance*. Government agents were allowed to make unlimited searches under them. These writs were so named because the customs official to whom they were issued "possessed the legal authority to command the assistance of a peace officer and the assistance, if necessary, of all nearby subjects, in the execution of the writ."[1]

These writs, despite being issued by a judge, were warrants in name only because they gave the customs official *general exploratory search powers* and were automatically issued to the official upon assuming office. They were valid for the duration of the life of the then reigning British monarch. The writs authorized these officials, in the port cities of the American colonies, to search houses, vessels, warehouses, shops, and all other places for goods that had escaped the import duties (because they were

---

[1]Leonard Levy, *Origins of the Bill of Rights* 150, 158 (Yale University paperback 2001).

smuggled into the colonies). No evidentiary showing was required; no description of the place to be searched and no things to be seized were required on the face of the general writ; no return, listing the property seized, was required to be filed with the court issuing the general writ. . . .[2]

The taxes sought were extremely unpopular in the colonies and formed the basis for much of the protest to and open defiance of the Crown. Two U.S. Supreme Court opinions have cited the controversy caused by the general writs as one of the leading causes of the American Revolution. "The [Fourth] amendment was in large part a reaction to the general warrant and the warrantless searches that had so alienated the colonies and had helped speed the movement for independence" (*Chimel v. California*, 395 U.S. 752, 760-61 (1969)). "Historically we are dealing with a provision of the Constitution [the Fourth Amendment] which sought to guard against an abuse that more than any one single factor gave rise to American independence" (*Harris v. U.S.*, 331 U.S. 145, 159 (1947)) (Frankfurter, J. dissenting).

The writs were first seen in England in 1662 and were introduced by Parliament to the colonies in 1696. The demand of the common Englishman that his privacy be respected was summed up best by William Pitt, the Elder, on the floor of the House of Commons in 1763:

> *The poorest man may, in his cottage, bid defiance to all the forces of the Crown. It may be frail; its roof may shake; the wind may blow through it; the storm may enter; the rain may enter; but the King of England may not enter; all his force dares not cross the threshold of the ruined tenement.*[3]

It has been suggested that the spark of the American Revolution was lit in Boston in 1761. Following the death of the British king, George II, on October 25, 1760, all existing writs of assistance expired and had to be reissued. A petition, asking the court to issue new writs, was filed in Boston by the chief customs officer for the Northern District of America. The petition, like those that preceded it, was not sworn to, did not allege that any particular untaxed goods were in Boston or were in any way connected to a particular case or investigation. The customs officer simply requested that the writs be issued to him and his officers, *as usual.*[4]

In February 1761, sixty-three Boston merchants, represented by James Otis, Jr., a leading attorney of the day,[5] opposed the issuance of the new writs of

---

[2]See the exhaustive new treatise by former Chief Judge Phillip A. Hubbart (Third District Court of Appeal, Florida), *Making Sense of Search and Seizure Law* (Durham, North Carolina: Carolina Academic Press, 2005) at pp. 21–22.

[3]This well-known protest of the elder Pitt against the invasion of the home became very well known to all watching the *Watergate* hearings, as Senator Sam Ervin chastised the government officials who ordered burglaries for political purposes. It appears routinely in U.S. Supreme Court opinions discussing the history of the Fourth Amendment. See *Payton v. New York*, 445 U.S. 573, at 601, fn. 54 (1980) and *Miller v. United States*, 357 U.S. 301, at 307 (1958).

[4]Hubbart, p. 24.

[5]Otis resigned his lucrative position as the Crown's Admiralty Counsel to take this case. Hubbart, p. 24.

assistance. Otis, arguing before the Massachusetts Superior Court, attacked these searches as illegal:

> [The writs] appear to me . . . the worst instrument of arbitrary power, the most destructive of English liberty, and the fundamental principles . . . that was ever found in an English law-book. . . . It is a power that places the liberty of every man in the hands of every petty officer. . . . One of the most essential branches of English liberty is the freedom of one's house. A man's house is his castle, and while he is quiet, he is well-guarded as a prince in his castle. This writ, if it should be declared legal, would totally annihilate this privilege. Customs house officers may enter our houses when they please—we are commanded to permit their entry—their menial servants may enter—may break locks, bars, and every thing in their way—and whether they break through malice or revenge, no man, no court may inquire—bare suspicion is enough. . . . *An officer should show probable grounds, should take his oath before a magistrate, and that such magistrate, if he thinks proper, should issue a special warrant to a constable to search the places.*[6]

A young lawyer named John Adams sitting in the courtroom, of whom we would hear much more from years later, observed:

> I do say in the most solemn manner, that Mr. Otis' oration against the writs of assistance breathed into this nation the breath of life. . . .
> American independence was then and there born: the seeds of patriots and heroes were then and there sown. . . . Every man (in that courtroom) appeared to me to go away, as I did, ready to take arms against (the) writs of assistance. Then and there was the first scene of the first act of opposition to the arbitrary claims of Great Britain. Then and there the child Independence was born. In fifteen years, namely 1776, he grew into manhood, and declared himself free.[7]

Needless to say, the writs were issued, and the rest, as it is said, is history.

They were issued, but only after the chief justice of the court, who just happened to be the king's lieutenant governor of the colony, and a merchant, not a lawyer, reserved ruling and sought instructions from England. In the next term of court, November 1761, he granted the petition of the Crown's customs officers and issued the writs.[8]

It was this history of abuse of governmental power, both in England and in the colonies, that caused our founding fathers to place in the Fourth Amendment

---

[6]L. Kinvin Wroth and Hiller B. Zobel, 2 *Legal Papers of John Adams* at pp. 139–144 (1965).

[7]10 *Works of John Adams* 276.

[8]Hubbart, p. 29.

language reflecting their concerns about the sanctity of a person's privacy. When we read the Fourth Amendment, we clearly see the evil sought to be suppressed:

> *The right of the people to be secure in their persons, houses, papers, and effects, against unreasonable searches and seizures, shall not be violated, and no warrants shall issue, but upon probable cause, supported by oath or affirmation, and particularly describing the place to be searched, and the persons or things to be seized.*

What must be appreciated is that Englishmen settled in Jamestown, Virginia in 1607, landed on Plymouth Rock in Massachusetts in 1620, and took over New Amsterdam in 1664 (from the Dutch who settled there in 1612). Upwards of one hundred fifty years later, there was very little loyalty to the British Crown, other than by some of the wealthy landowners. By that time, many in the colonies had come from countries other than England, or were second- or third-generation Virginians, Bostonians, or New Yorkers (of Dutch ancestry). They had little affection for a government 3,000 miles away, which heavily taxed them and put up soldiers in their homes (the reason for the Third Amendment—but that's another story).

A trip to Lexington and Concord brought me to a cemetery containing tombstones dating to the mid-1600s. Having grandparents born on your farm or in your village, and having never set foot in the mother country, easily brings a desire for independence from taxes, soldiers, and the unjustifiable abuse of power that come from an oppressive, distant government. One such "American" was John Adams, one of our founding fathers and a major voice in the Continental Congress making the case for independence from England. Born in 1735, he was the fifth generation of Adamses to live in Braintree, Massachusetts, a farming village not far from Boston. The first Adams came from England almost 100 years earlier with his wife and nine children, as part of a ten-year Puritan migration, which brought twenty thousand Britons to the new world seeking religious freedom. John Adams, his father, and grandfather were all born and spent their lives in Braintree. The four generations before him had all served as officers in the militia and as deacons in the church. John was the first to return to England and Europe in the service of his country and eventually negotiated the treaty ending the War of Independence.[9] These were the people who yearned for a Fourth Amendment to protect them.

Did the Framers, not the *farmers*, as I thought when first reading that phrase in junior high school, but the guys who debated and wrote the Fourth Amendment and the rest of the Bill of Rights, expect them to be obeyed by government officials? Was this Bill of Rights to have any teeth, or merely be a set of highhanded admonitions for government officials to aspire to in their discretion? The need to protect the people was eloquently discussed in the letters and speeches of James Madison, Thomas Jefferson, and several other heavy hitters of the day—Patrick Henry, John Marshall (later to be chief justice of the United States from 1801 to 1835), and

---

[9]David McCullough, *John Adams* (Simon & Schuster, 2001) pp. 29, 127, 414.

George Mason (friend and law teacher to Jefferson), to mention a few. One legendary legal historian wrote:

> They (the Bill of Rights) were intended to be absolute legal guarantees to the citizens strictly binding upon every agency of the new government, including Congress and the Executive himself. They were declarations which were to be enforced. The radicals of 1788 knew full well that only through the Courts of law could these rights be enforced.[10]

A more modern scholar expressed a similar view:

> Although it is uncertain what precise measures the Framers had in mind for the courts to utilize to enforce the Fourth Amendment in particular, it is abundantly clear that they intended these remedies to be extremely effective. They had just fought a revolution, in part, to guarantee Fourth Amendment freedoms to the individual and certainly they were in no mood for pale measures when it came to giving these freedoms the force of law. . . . (This) can be gleaned from the thirty-year history that led up to the Amendment.[11]

We now fast forward to twenty-first-century police work (phew, so much for the history!). There are two parts to the Fourth Amendment: the clause prohibiting *unreasonable*[12] searches and seizures and *the warrant clause*. Warrants are not always required. Several exceptions have been allowed by the courts, based primarily upon necessity and danger to police officers. These exceptions have been specifically limited to the situations facing the police at the time. Almost all of the situations involve police–citizen encounters where it would be unreasonable to stop the action and run to the courthouse to apply for a warrant. When these situations are present, the cop in the street has more authority than a justice of the U.S. Supreme Court. Why, you ask?

Before a judge can sign a warrant and order a search of a home, what must he/she have?

_____

_____

_____

_____

_____

---

[10]Charles Warren, *Congress, the Constitution, and the Supreme Court*, at p. 91 (1935 ed.).

[11]Hubbart, at pp. 80–81.

[12]Notice how *reasonable* searches are not prohibited.

So long as police officers are expected to be doctors, lawyers, clergymen, and everything else, let's discuss some cases that established these exceptions. When the following situations, *exijentzys*, are present, the cop on the scene just does his thing. Even a judge can't do that. However, efforts to enlarge the scope of these necessary searches have always been met with resistance by the court. Let's see why.

a. A search pursuant to a lawful arrest and the area within the arrestee's immediate control:

Chimel v. California, 395 U.S. 752 (1969)

In 1965, three police officers in Santa Ana, California, armed with an arrest warrant, went to Ted Chimel's home to arrest him for burglarizing a coin shop. Mrs. Chimel invited them in and they waited about ten minutes for Chimel to arrive. When he did, he was arrested. He then objected to the officers' request to "look around." They did not have a search warrant. The entire home was searched anyway, including the attic, garage, workshop, and his *upstairs* bedroom dresser drawers. Some of the stolen coins were found during that search. The police seized them and other items. It was argued that this was a search *incident to a lawful arrest*. This exception to the warrant requirement, as are most, was intended to protect arresting officers—and to prevent the destruction of evidence on the arrested person's body, or within his reach. However, the right to search, incident to a lawful arrest, is limited to its purpose. That purpose is, once again, to protect the arresting officer and any evidence of that crime that is on or near the subject. Along with that authority, goes the right to search the area within the arrested person's reach, where he might get a weapon or destroy the nearby evidence. *Chimel* is known as the *arm's reach* or *wingspread case*.

Here the police officers exceeded the limits of what was allowed. There was nothing in the rest of the house that might hurt them while making the arrest. Nor was there any danger that evidence beyond the immediate area would be destroyed. If they had any probable cause to believe that any of the stolen coins were there, they could have applied for a search warrant.

This rule was intended to assure the safety of the officers and to prevent the destruction of evidence. It allows for nothing else. These officers went too far.

Question:

What happens when you arrest him, and he wants to change clothes in his bedroom, or use the bathroom?

_____

_____

_____

_____

What if he wants to kiss the kids goodbye?

_____

_____

_____

_____

Can you search those areas you allow him to enter?

_____

_____

_____

_____

To what extent?

_____

_____

_____

_____

Plenty of cops got killed being nice guys by allowing that.

Discussion:

_____

_____

_____

_____

_____

_____

_____

_____

_____

_____

_____

After the court discussed the reasons why the officer should be allowed to make those *immediate area* searches, it issued its ruling. In legal circles, it is known as *the holding of the case*. Lawyers and judges like to say, "The case held. . . ." or "The court held. . . ."

There is no (good reason), however, for routinely searching rooms, other than that in which the arrest occurs—or for that matter, for searching through all the desk drawers, or other closed or concealed areas (in that room). Such searches may only be made under the authority of a search warrant . . .

We are not dealing with formalities. The presence of a search warrant serves a high function. Absent some grave emergency, the Fourth Amendment has (placed) a magistrate between the citizen and the police. This was done neither to shield criminals nor to make the home a safe haven for illegal activities. It was done so that an objective mind might (decide when a home should be searched) in order to enforce the law. The right of privacy was deemed too precious to entrust to the discretion of those whose job is the detection of crime and the arrest of criminals . . . . And so the Constitution requires a magistrate to pass on the desires of the police before they violate the privacy of the home. We cannot be true to that constitutional requirement and excuse the absence of a search warrant without a showing by those who seek (exception) that the exigencies of the situation (require it).[13]

What happens when you have a lawful arrest, and you conduct a search pursuant to that lawful arrest? What can you do with what you find? The dope and guns are easy. So is the property he stole. But what can we do with his wallet, address book, other papers on his person or in these modern times (not contemplated by the writers of the Fourth Amendment), his cell phone and pager? What do they have to do with protecting the officer or the evidence? Are they yours to examine?

The ability to search the person of an arrestee for fruits of the crime and/or weapons has been traced by the Supreme Court to the common law of England. The authority of the police to expand the search to the area *around his person* was decided in *Chimel v. California*, above, in what is referred to as generally the area from which the arrestee could obtain a weapon or destroy evidence.

In *State v. Gustafson*, 258 So. 2d 1 (Fla. 1972), *affirmed* 414 U.S. 260 (1973), the Florida Supreme Court rejected as reversionary and restrictive, the concept that there must be a nexus, or a connection, between the offense and the object taken in the search, for the search to be truly incident to the arrest, at p. 4. Accordingly, in *United States v. Robinson*, 414 U.S. 218 (1973), decided simultaneous with *Gustafson v. Florida*, the Supreme Court likewise rejected the assertion that a search incident to a valid arrest was limited to either a pat-down for weapons or to evidentiary fruits, stating:

. . . A police officer's determination as to how and where to search (a person he has) arrested is necessarily a quick (decision) which the Fourth Amendment does not require to be broken down in each instance into

---

[13]*Chimel*, at 761.

an analysis of each step in the search. The authority to search the person incident to a lawful custodial arrest, while based upon the need to disarm and to discover evidence, does not depend on what a court may later decide was the probability in a particular arrest situation that weapons or evidence would in fact be found upon the person of the suspect. A custodial arrest of a suspect based on probable cause is a reasonable intrusion under the Fourth Amendment; (and) that intrusion being lawful, a search incident to the arrest requires no additional justification. It is the fact of the lawful arrest which establishes the authority to search, and we hold that in the case of a lawful custodial arrest a full search of the person is not only an exception to the warrant requirement of the Fourth Amendment, but is also a "reasonable" search under that Amendment.[14]   *Robinson,* at 235.

The authority to search includes any clothing or containers within the arrestee's possession. *New York v. Belton,* 453 U.S. 454 (1981). Such a search may be conducted at the scene of the arrest or at the station house as part of the booking process. *Illinois v. Lafayette,* 462 U.S. 640 (1983); *United States v. Edwards,* 415 U.S. 800 (1974). In accordance with these concepts, courts have had little difficulty in upholding the search of an arrestee's wallet, notebook, address book, or other papers, found on or about the person arrested. *United States v. Rodriguez,* 995 F.2d 776 (7th Cir. 1993); *United States v. Molinaro,* 877 F.2d 1341 (7th Cir. 1989); *United States v. Vaneenwyk,* 206 F.Supp. 423 (W.D.N.Y. 2002).

Likewise, following the rationale of *Robinson, Belton* and/or *Edwards,* the federal courts have had little difficulty in upholding the search of a **cell phone or pager memory device** incident to a valid arrest. *United States v. Finley,* 477 F.3d 250 (5th Cir. 2007); *United States v. Hunter,* 166 F.3d 1211 (4th Cir. 1998); *United States v. Ortiz,* 84 F.3d 977 (7th Cir. 1996); *United States v. Mercado-Nava,* 486 F.Supp.2d 1271 (D. Kan. 2007); *United States v. Parada,* 289 F.Supp.2d 1291 (D. Kan. 2003); *United States v. Reyes,* 922 F.Supp. 818 (S.D.N.Y. 1996); *United States v. Lynch,* 908 F.Supp. 284 (D. V.I., 1995); *United States v. Chan,* 830 F.Supp. 531 (N.D. Cal. 1993). In addition to rejecting the Fourth Amendment challenges, the courts have rejected claims that such retrieval was a violation of the federal wiretap statute. *United States v. Mercado-Nava,* supra; *United States v. Reyes,* supra; *United States v. Meriwether,* 917 F.2d 955 (6th Cir. 1990).[15]

Another, similar rule is:

b. Hot pursuit of a fleeing felon:

Warden v. Hayden, 387 U.S. 294 (1967)

This case involved the armed robbery of the Diamond Cab Company in Baltimore, Maryland. The robbery occurred on St. Patrick's Day, 1962. Two passing taxi drivers, hearing the shouts of *Holdup,* followed the robber to a nearby house. The police

---

[14] Keep in mind that it is only *unreasonable* searches that are prohibited by the Fourth Amendment.

[15] Special thanx to Assistant State Attorney Joel Rosenblatt, Legal Division of the Miami-Dade State Attorney's Office, whose legal research has always made me look good in court.

were given that information, as well as a description of the robber and his clothing. Within minutes, a number of patrol cars arrived. The officers told the lady who answered the door that they believed a robber had entered her house. They asked her for permission to search. She did not object.[16] Several officers went through all three floors of the house. Bennie Hayden was found *feigning* sleep in an upstairs bedroom. When officers on the other two floors announced that no other man was in the house, Hayden was arrested. Another officer heard a toilet running. In the tank he found two weapons. A third officer found the described clothing in a washing machine. Another officer found a clip of ammunition for one of the weapons and a cap fitting the description the robber wore under the mattress of the bed Hayden was in. The ammo for the second weapon was found in the bureau drawer in that same room.

Seems like a pretty intrusive search. Do you think the court would require a warrant in this situation?

Neither *the entry* without warrant . . . nor *the search* for (the robber) without warrant was (illegal). Under the circumstances of this case, *the exigencies of the situation* (allowed it). . . . Speed here was essential, and only a thorough search of the house for persons and weapons could have insured that Hayden was the only man present and that the police had control of all weapons which could be used against them or to effect an escape.   *Hayden,* at 297–98.

(Remember, protection of the officers!!) They then added:

The seizures[17] occurred immediately contemporaneous with Hayden's arrest, as part of an effort to find a suspected felon, armed, within the house into which he had run only minutes before the police arrived. The permissible scope of the search, must be broad (enough) . . . (to prevent) the suspect in the house from resisting or escaping.[18]

Questions:

Couldn't the officers have put Hayden and his wife outside the house, and then applied for a search warrant?

_____

_____

_____

---

[16]Is that consent? Keep reading!

[17]The Fourth Amendment also prohibits unreasonable *seizures*, that is, taking what you found during the unreasonable searching!

[18]*Hayden,* at 297–98.

Was there an exigency that made that too dangerous to do?

_____

_____

_____

Did the officers' search exceed its scope? Did they go further than was necessary to protect themselves and any evidence, which might be lost?

_____

_____

_____

_____

_____

How does this case differ from _Chimel_ and why is the holding different?

_____

_____

_____

_____

Is the need to protect the police from danger recognized by the courts?

_____

_____

_____

Is that a reasonable concern?

_____

_____

_____

Does that make a search reasonable?

_____

_____

_____

_____

_____

Here's another emergency situation. Let's see how it is dealt with.

c. Search to prevent the imminent destruction of evidence:

Schmerber v. California, 384 U.S. 757 (1966)

Armando Schmerber, our next man made famous by the U.S. Supreme Court, was not a burglar or a robber. He was arrested for Driving Under the Influence (DUI). Because he was slightly injured in the resulting auto accident, and unable to go to the police station and *blow the balloon*, the police asked a doctor to draw some blood. The blood, and the corresponding percentage of alcohol in it, was admitted into evidence at his trial. He objected on the grounds that it "offends the sense of justice" to do that. He cited, as authority, an earlier case from the U.S. Supreme Court overturning a drug conviction, where an arrested person's stomach was pumped out to get the evidence.[19] "Not exactly the same," said the court's leading defender of civil liberties, Justice William Brennan, noting that the alcohol in a person's blood "Begins to diminish shortly after the drinking stops, as the body functions to eliminate it. . . ."

THE HOLDING:

Justice Brennan wrote for the court that "the test was performed in a reasonable manner. . . . We hold today that the Constitution does not forbid the states minor intrusions into an individual's body under stringently limited conditions and in no way permits more substantial intrusions."

So pumping the stomach is out, but a doctor taking blood is OK?

Questions:

What do you think about this?

_____

_____

_____

_____

_____

Do you think the distinction between DUI and possession of drugs made any difference?

_____

_____

_____

---

[19]*Rochin v. California*, 342 U.S. 165 (1952).

_____

_____

_____

d. The Plain View Doctrine:

Ker v. California, 374 U.S. 23 (1963) and *Coolidge v. New Hampshire*, 403 U.S. 443 (1971) (Not really a search exception, just a reason to seize evidence.)

George Ker was supplying marijuana to several dealers in Los Angeles. One of those dealers had sold a pound of marijuana to Sergeant Cook of the Sheriff's Office the day before. Surveillances were instituted and the investigators followed Ker to his apartment in the vicinity of Fairfax and Slauson Avenues. Upon entering the apartment to arrest him, the investigators saw, *in plain view*, a brick of marijuana on the kitchen counter.

Did seizing it violate the Fourth Amendment, or was it reasonable to take it at that time? The court held, initially, in *Ker*:

> While an arrest may not be used merely as the pretext for a search without warrant, . . . the officers entered the apartment for the purpose of arresting George Ker and they had probable cause to make that arrest prior to the entry. . . . The discovery of the brick of marijuana did not constitute a search, since the officer merely saw what was placed before him in full view.[20]

Then in *Coolidge*, they explained the rationale for search warrants.

First, the judge prevents searches not based upon probable cause. Second, those searches deemed necessary should be as limited as possible and particularly describe the item to be seized. Returning to our history, they reminded us of the fear the colonists had of the British use of *the general warrant* and the rummaging through a person's belongings. The general warrant was essentially an order signed by a nonjudicial British official authorizing lesser officials, or soldiers, to seize whatever they wanted. No reason, or *probable cause*, was required, nor was the particular item mentioned in the warrant.

Now, why the warrant is *not* required in this situation:

THE HOLDING:

The *plain view doctrine* is not in conflict with the first objective because plain view does not occur until a search is in progress. In each case, this initial (entry) is justified by a warrant, or by an exception such as *hot pursuit* or *search incident to a lawful arrest*, or by (another) valid reason for the officer's presence. And, given the initial lawful intrusion, the seizure of an object in plain view is consistent with the second objective, since it does not convert the search into a general or exploratory one. (The item has already been seen!) As against the minor peril to Fourth Amendment protections, there is a major gain in effective law enforcement. Where, once *an otherwise lawful*

_____

[20]*Ker*, at 42.

search is in progress, the police *inadvertently* come upon a piece of evidence, it would often be senseless, and sometimes dangerous—to the evidence or to the police themselves—to require them to ignore it until they have obtained a warrant particularly describing it.[21]

Therefore, if the police officer sees evidence in plain view after having the right to be where he is, the evidence may be lawfully taken into custody (seized).

Questions:

Is the court still working with us?

_____

_____

_____

_____

If they took Ker out of his house and secured it, how much more is he protected if the cops apply for a search warrant to seize what they already saw, as they were arresting him?

_____

_____

_____

_____

Why isn't a warrant needed in this circumstance?

_____

_____

_____

What if you know of the item's presence, its location, and its evidentiary value? Can you walk into the house and seize it, claiming when you entered the house, you saw it in plain view?

_____

_____

_____

_____

---

[21]*Coolidge,* at 467.

The exception says the discovery of the item in plain view *must be inadvertent*. Suppose you enter a person's apartment in response to a *Sick Baby* call. As you walk through looking for the baby's room, you observe in plain view some crack cocaine packages on the top of the dresser, or a sawed-off shotgun leaning against the wall. If these observations were inadvertent to your purpose for lawfully being in the apartment, you can seize them. But *puhleese*, check on the baby too!

Questions:

Suppose a neighbor calls you to report the crack and the illegal weapon. You know the neighbor to be reliable. Is that probable cause? Do you see any exceptions to the warrant requirement? Would your entry and subsequent viewing of the items be inadvertent?

_____

_____

_____

_____

_____

Suppose we throw in that there is a crack party going on in the baby's room and the baby is starting to cough?

_____

_____

_____

_____

Notes and Discussion:

_____

_____

_____

_____

_____

_____

_____

_____

_____

_____

_____

_____

_____

_____

_____

e. **The Automobile Exception:**

Carroll v. U.S., 267 U.S. 132 (1925) and *Chambers v. Maroney*, 399 U.S. 42 (1970)[22]

Cars have always been a great source of search litigation. Even bad guys need transportation. Way back in 1925, the court recognized a difference between cars and homes and offices. Do you see it?

_____

_____

_____

_____

In December 1921, after conducting an undercover investigation, federal agents learned that George Carroll and John Kiro used their vehicle to transport prohibited alcohol products. They pulled over the vehicle in rural Michigan, and sixty-eight bottles of Scotch whiskey and Gordon's Gin were found behind the rear seat. The Supreme Court had to decide if a warrant was required to search this vehicle.

What do you think?

_____

_____

_____

_____

---

[22]*Chambers* is a great case for putting bad guys in jail. If it looks like a getaway car, that is to say, if there is probable cause to believe the occupants are, or have just, committed a felony, applying for a search warrant would only let them get away. So you just pull 'em over, arrest them for the felony, and search the car—great case!!

The court, after discussing the necessity for warrants in most instances, held as follows:

> It is clear the officers here had justification for the search and seizure. This is to say that the facts and circumstances within their knowledge . . . were sufficient . . . to warrant a man of reasonable caution in the belief that intoxicating liquor was being transported in the automobile which they stopped and searched.

Now, why cars are different:

> The Fourth Amendment has been (interpreted), practically since the beginning of (our nation), as recognizing a necessary difference between a search of a store, dwelling house, or other structure for . . . which a proper official warrant may be obtained, and a search of a ship, motor boat, wagon, or automobile for contraband goods, *where it is not practicable to secure a warrant*, because *the vehicle can be quickly moved. . . .*[23]

The Supreme Court, in 1970, had another chance to revisit this exception to the rule of searching by warrant. Prohibition was over, and there were more tow trucks available to secure the stopped vehicles and await a search warrant.

The lucky players this time were Frank Chambers and the three friends he committed his robberies with. On May 20, 1963, two men robbed a gas station in North Braddock, Pennsylvania. Shortly before the robbery, two teenagers observed a small blue compact station wagon containing four men, one of whom had a green sweater, circling the area. Shortly after the robbery, they saw it speeding away.

The victim of the gas station robbery said he was told to place the coins into his right-hand glove as the robbers took the currency. One of the robbers was wearing a green sweater and the other a trench coat. A description of the car and the robbers was broadcast over the police radio. Within an hour, a similar vehicle containing four men was stopped about two miles away. Our friend Frank was wearing a green sweater and there was a trench coat in the car. All were arrested and the car was driven to the police station, where it was thoroughly searched. Found under the dashboard were two weapons, a right-hand glove containing small change, and some business cards from another gas station robbed a week before. Both gas station attendants identified Frank as the robber. One identified the glove and the other the business cards taken during the earlier robbery.

Frank was charged with both robberies. Needless to say, he was convicted and sent to prison. The parole board also revoked his parole on a previous sentence, and this caused Frank to institute some lengthy appeals. Naturally, he objected to the search of his car, *inter alia*.[24]

The Supreme Court discussed whether this was a *search incident to a lawful arrest*. Nope, it was done at the station after the arrest.

---

[23]*Carroll*, at 153.

[24]No, that is not what you put on your pasta!! It means, *among other things*.

Any other ideas?

_____

_____

_____

_____

THE HOLDING:

The right to search and the validity of the seizure are not (based upon the) arrest. They are (based) on the (probable) cause the officer has for believing that the contents of the automobile (violate) the law. Only in exigent circumstances will the judgment of the police as to probable cause serve as a sufficient authorization for a search. *Carroll* holds a search warrant unnecessary where there is probable cause to search an automobile stopped on the highway; the car is movable, the occupants are alerted, and the car's contents may never be found again if a warrant must be obtained. Hence an immediate search is constitutionally permissible.[25]

OK, so the exigency allows you to take and secure the car. Why not get the warrant once the exigency is over? The car is in the police lot, the defendants are in handcuffs, and there are no environmental factors to make an immediate search necessary and, therefore, reasonable.

The court continued:

Arguably, because of the preference for a magistrate's judgment, only the immobilization of the car should be permitted until a search warrant is obtained; arguably, only the 'lesser' intrusion is permissible until the magistrate authorizes the 'greater.' But which is the 'greater' and which is the 'lesser' intrusion is itself a debatable question and the answer may depend on a variety of circumstances. *For constitutional purposes, we see no difference* between on the one hand *seizing and holding a car* before presenting the probable cause issue to a magistrate and on the other hand *carrying out an immediate search without a warrant. Given probable cause to search, either course is reasonable under the Fourth Amendment.*

How's that for a powerful tool to assist you out in the street?

The phrase *exigent circumstances* (in connection with the automobile exception) has caused great confusion over the years. The Supreme Court has been backing off that term, first used in *Chambers*, ever since. Several years later,[26] they told us that the

---

[25]*Chambers*, at 51.
[26]*California v. Carney*, 471 U.S. 386 (1985).

ability "to be *quickly moved* was clearly the basis of the holding in *Carroll* and our cases have consistently recognized ready mobility as one of the (reasons) of the automobile exception."

They went on to say that "(in) *Chambers* . . . we noted that the opportunity to search is fleeting since a car is readily movable." An earlier, but post-*Chambers* case[27] explained, "An immediate (search) is necessary because of the nature of the automobile in transit." A historical analysis was done on ships evading customs officials (at the time the Fourth Amendment was being adopted) "in movable vessels where they readily could be put out of reach of a search warrant." A statute from the first Congress clearly authorized such searches without a search warrant.

Many answers to difficult questions come from our history. About 25 members of the convention that drafted the Bill of Rights in 1787 were later elected to the first Congress in 1789. If those folks enacted such statutes between 1789 and 1799, the courts naturally assume they were aware of the Fourth Amendment many of them recently wrote. It becomes apparent that the "intent of the Framers" of the amendment did not believe search warrants were necessary for "moving vehicles."

The *Ross* court ended their analysis with a different reason authorizing the search without a warrant. There is a much-lessened *reasonable expectation of privacy*[28] in "vehicles capable of traveling on the public highways. . . ."

> Automobiles, unlike homes, are subjected to . . . periodic inspections and licensing requirements. As an everyday occurrence, police stop and examine vehicles when license plates or inspection stickers have expired, or if other violations, such as exhaust fumes or excessive noise are noted, or if headlights or other safety equipment are not in proper working order. . . . The public is fully aware that it is accorded less privacy in its automobiles because of this compelling governmental need for regulation. In short, the pervasive schemes of regulation, which necessarily lead to reduced expectations of privacy, and the exigencies (*there goes that word again!!*) attendant to ready mobility justify searches without prior recourse to . . . a magistrate so long as the overriding standard of probable cause is met.

The final deathblow came almost thirty years after *Chambers*.

> As we recognized nearly 75 years ago in *Carroll*, there is an exception to this requirement for searches of vehicles. The 'automobile exception' has *no separate exigency requirement*. We made this clear in *Ross*, when we said that in cases where there was probable cause to search a vehicle 'a search is not unreasonable if based on facts that would justify the issuance of a warrant *even though a warrant has not been obtained.*'[29]

---

[27]*U.S. v. Ross*, 456 U.S. 798 (1982).

[28]This is the phrase made famous in *Katz v. U.S*. We will discuss it soon.

[29]*Maryland v. Dyson*, 527 U.S. 465 (1999).

It is now very clear that all you need to search a car is probable cause to believe its contents *offend the law*. The requirement of exigent circumstances is satisfied by the "ready mobility *inherent* in all automobiles that *reasonably appear* to be capable of functioning. . . . It is clear . . . that there are only two questions that must be answered in the affirmative before (you) may conduct a warrantless search of an automobile. The first is whether the automobile is readily mobile. All that is necessary to establish this element is that the automobile is operational. The second, probable cause, is determined under the facts of each case."[30]

Some commentators have renamed this the *movable container* exception. Anything capable of growing legs and not being around when you return with the search warrant may be searched without a warrant, so long as probable cause is present. Many times your search will be in the police pound, you will have the keys, and no one can drive the car away. The mere fact that the car has tires and an engine gives you the right to search it for the contraband you reasonably believe it contains.

A related question is *where* in the car may you search. There was prior case law prohibiting the opening of locked pieces of luggage in the trunks of car, when they were believed to contain narcotics. The locks on the luggage were held to be an indication of the owner's expectation of privacy in those items. After several inconsistent opinions, that issue, too, was resolved.

> The scope of a warrantless search of an automobile is *not* defined by the nature of the container in which the contraband is secreted. Rather, it is defined by the object of the search and the places in which there is probable cause to believe that (the contraband) may be found. . . . The scope of the warrantless search authorized by this exception is no broader and no narrower than a magistrate could legitimately authorize by warrant. *If probable cause justifies the search of a lawfully stopped vehicle, it justifies the search of every part of the vehicle and its contents (the luggage) that may conceal the object of the search.*   Ross, at 824, 825.

Translating that into everyday English means that, if your probable cause tells you the dope is somewhere in the car, search wherever it may be located. If the dope is in the suitcase the perp is carrying from the airport conveyer belt to a car, do not search the car, just take the luggage. That's what the judge would order you to do, anyway. Remember, the automobile exception merely removes the judge's permission; the parameters of the search remain the same.

Can you search *movable containers* found outside cars?

_____

_____

_____

_____

---

[30]*U.S. v. Watts*, 329 F.3 1282 (11th Cir. 2003).

The Court in *Ross* discussed that issue; however, the word *may* appears many times. I would follow the rule suggested by the sign on the wall in the Homicide Bureau:

No case will be solved before its time . . . and a half.

Take your time. If not sure what to do, just take everyone and everything to the stationhouse and start asking for help. If time permits, prepare a search warrant affidavit. It's like chicken soup; it couldn't hurt.

If you stop a car on the road, having probable cause to believe there is contraband inside, is there any constitutional difference between searching it on the street or towing it to a police garage or pound?

_____
_____
_____
_____
_____

If your PC indicates that you are looking for several kilos of cocaine, are you authorized to open any containers smaller than a football?

_____
_____
_____

What happens after you find the keys and arrest the occupants? Can you search the rest of the car?

_____
_____
_____

Discussion:

_____
_____
_____
_____
_____

Notes:

_____

_____

_____

_____

_____

_____

_____

_____

_____

_____

Here's another car-type search to consider:

f. Inventory search (of a vehicle taken into police custody for safekeeping):

South Dakota v. Opperman, 428 U.S. 364 (1976)

In a similar vein is the inventory search. In short, if the driver is arrested, or injured, or in some other way unable to take care of his property, or if the car is towed for some other reason, you must protect it. How is that done?

Make a list of everything in the car. Secure any valuables. This way there is a record should he ever make a claim for missing property. You can't leave the car on the side of the road. So impound it, inventory the contents, and charge him for storage! And if you see some drugs next to the spare, or an illegal gun in the glove box, that's *the plain view doctrine* we recently discussed.

_____

_____

_____

_____

Regardless of what many police officers may think, this next case shows you who your best friend really is. When you consider the various exceptions to the search warrant requirement we have studied so far, they all seem to deal with safety and emergencies. Where does this one fit in?

g. Stop and Frisk:

Terry v. Ohio, 392 U.S. 1 (1968) (Full opinion in appendix.)

In this case, we learn more about the arresting officer than the defendant. Why?

Detective Martin McFadden, of the Cleveland, Ohio, Police Department, was patrolling in plain clothes in downtown Cleveland. It was early afternoon on October 31, 1963. McFadden had been a policeman for thirty-nine years and a detective for thirty-five years. He had been working this beat for thirty years, watching for pickpockets and shoplifters. He had developed *routine habits of observation* and would later testify in court that he "would stand and watch people or walk and watch people at many intervals of the day." He then added, "Now in this case when I looked over they didn't look right to me at the time."

What was it that caught this experienced cop's attention? It was his actions that day that have saved many a cop's life since then.

According to John Terry and Richard Chilton, they were just taking a walk in the vicinity of Huron Road and Euclid Avenue when Det. McFadden's activities got them sentenced to the state penitentiary.

This is what McFadden saw and testified to in court:

His interest aroused, Officer McFadden took up a post of observation in the entrance to a store 300 to 400 feet away from the two men. 'I (began my observations) when I (saw) their movements,' he testified. He saw one of the men leave the other one and walk southwest on Huron Road, past some stores. The man paused for a moment and looked in a store window, then walked on a short distance, turned around and walked back toward the corner, pausing once again to look in the same store window. He rejoined his companion at the corner, and the two conferred briefly. Then the second man went through the same series of motions, strolling down Huron Road, looking in the same window, walking on a short distance, turning back, peering in the store window again, and returning to confer with the first man at the corner. The two men repeated this ritual alternately between five and six times apiece—in all, roughly a dozen trips. At one point, while the two were standing together on the corner, a third man approached them and engaged them briefly in conversation. This man then left the two others and walked west on Euclid Avenue. Chilton and Terry resumed their measured pacing, peering and conferring. After this had gone on for 10 to 12 minutes, the two men walked off together, heading west on Euclid Avenue, following the path taken earlier by the third man.

By this time Officer McFadden had become thoroughly suspicious. He testified that after observing their elaborately casual and oft-repeated reconnaissance of the store window on Huron Road, he suspected the two men of 'casing a job, a stick-up,' and that he considered it his duty as a police officer to investigate further.[31] He added that he feared 'they may have a gun.' Thus, Officer McFadden followed Chilton and Terry and saw them stop in front of Zucker's store to talk to the same man who had conferred with them earlier on the street corner. Deciding that the situation was ripe for direct action, Officer McFadden approached the three men, identified himself as a police officer and asked for their names. At this point his knowledge was confined to what he had observed. He was not acquainted with any of the three men by name or by sight, and he had received no information concerning them from any other source. When the men 'mumbled something' in response to his inquiries, Officer McFadden grabbed petitioner Terry, spun him around so that they were facing the other two, with Terry between McFadden and the others, and patted down the outside of his clothing. In the left breast pocket of Terry's overcoat, Officer McFadden felt a pistol. He reached inside the overcoat pocket, but was unable to remove the gun. At this point, keeping Terry between himself and the others, the officer ordered all three men to enter Zucker's store. As they went in, he removed Terry's overcoat completely, removed a .38-caliber revolver from the pocket and ordered all three men to face the wall with their hands raised. Officer McFadden proceeded to pat down the outer clothing of Chilton and the third man, Katz.

---

[31]Compare this unusual and suspicious behavior to that in *Florida v. J.L.*, 529 U.S. 266 (2000) where "an anonymous caller reported to the Miami-Dade Police that a young black male standing at a particular bus stop and wearing a plaid shirt was carrying a gun. So far as the record reveals, there is no audio recording of the tip, and nothing is known about the informant. Sometime after the police received the tip—the record does not say how long—two officers were instructed to respond. They arrived at the bus stop about six minutes later and saw three black males 'just hanging out [there].' One of the three, respondent J.L., was wearing a plaid shirt. Apart from the tip, the officers had no reason to suspect any of the three of illegal conduct. The officers did not see a firearm, and J.L. made no threatening or otherwise unusual movements. One of the officers approached J.L., told him to put his hands up on the bus stop, frisked him, and seized a gun from J.L.'s pocket. The second officer frisked the other two individuals, against whom no allegations had been made, and found nothing." *J.L.*, at 268.

Citing to *Terry*, the Supremes held:

"[W]here a police officer *observes unusual conduct* which leads him reasonably to conclude in light of his experience that criminal activity may be afoot and that the persons with whom he is dealing may be armed and presently dangerous, where in the course of investigating this behavior he identifies himself as a policeman and makes reasonable inquiries, and where nothing in the initial stages of the encounter serves to dispel his reasonable fear for his own or others' safety, he is entitled for the protection of himself and others in the area to conduct a carefully limited search of the outer clothing of such persons in an attempt to discover weapons which might be used to assault him." *Terry*, at 30.

In suppressing the gun, the court held, the requirement that an anonymous tip bears standard indicia of reliability in order to justify a stop in no way diminishes a police officer's prerogative, in accord with *Terry*, to conduct a protective search of a person *who has already been legitimately stopped. We speak in today's decision only of cases in which the officer's authority to make the initial stop is at issue.* In that context, we hold that an anonymous tip lacking indicia of reliability . . . does not justify a stop and frisk whenever it alleges the illegal possession of a firearm. *J.L.*, at 274.

He discovered another revolver in the outer pocket of Chilton's overcoat, but no weapons were found on Katz. The officer testified that he only patted the men down to see whether they had weapons, and that he did not put his hands beneath the outer garments of either Terry or Chilton until he felt their guns. So far as it appears from the record, he never placed his hands beneath Katz's outer garments. Officer McFadden seized Chilton's gun, asked the proprietor of the store to call a police wagon, and took all three men to the station, where Chilton and Terry were formally charged with carrying concealed weapons.   *Terry*, at 5–7.

They were searched before arrest, so this isn't a *search incident to a lawful arrest*. It's not *hot pursuit*. They were not in a car, nor were the guns in plain view.

How can this search be justified under the Fourth Amendment?

_____

_____

_____

_____

_____

In this case there can be no question, then, that Officer McFadden 'seized' petitioner and subjected him to a 'search' when he took hold of him and patted down the outer surfaces of his clothing. We must decide whether at that point it was reasonable for Officer McFadden to have interfered with petitioner's personal security as he did.

Consider the rest of the opinion and tell me you don't love them!!!

The crux of this case, however, is not (whether) Officer McFadden's (method of) investigating suspicious behavior (was proper), but rather, whether there was justification for McFadden's invasion of Terry's personal security by searching him for weapons in the course of that investigation. In addition, there is the more immediate (concern) of the police officer in taking steps to assure himself that the person with whom he is dealing is not armed with a weapon that could unexpectedly and fatally be used against him. Certainly it would be unreasonable to require that police officers take unnecessary risks in the performance of their duties. American criminals have a long tradition of armed violence, and every year in this country many law enforcement officers are killed in the line of duty, and thousands more are wounded. Virtually all of these deaths and a substantial portion of the injuries are inflicted with guns and knives. Fifty-seven law enforcement officers were killed in the line of duty in this

---

[32]The opinion was released in 1968.

country in 1966[32] bringing the total to 335 for the seven-year period beginning with 1960. Also in 1966, there were 23,851 assaults on police officers, 9,113 of which resulted in injuries to the policeman. Fifty-five of the 57 officers killed in 1966 died from gunshot wounds, 41 of them inflicted by handguns easily secreted about the person. The remaining two murders were perpetrated by knives.

Striking a balance between that risk to police officers and the rights of our citizens, they went on to hold:

> We must still consider, however, the (result to the citizen). Even a limited search of the outer clothing for weapons constitutes a severe, though brief, intrusion upon cherished personal security, and it must surely be an annoying, frightening, and perhaps humiliating experience. (Terry) contends that such an intrusion is permissible only incident to a lawful arrest, either for a crime involving the possession of weapons or for a crime the commission of which led the officer to investigate in the first place.

What's the answer?

_____

_____

_____

_____

_____

THE HOLDING:

Our evaluation of the proper balance that has to be struck in this type of case leads us to conclude that there must be a narrowly drawn authority to permit a reasonable search for weapons for the protection of the police officer, where he has reason to believe that he is dealing with an armed and dangerous individual, regardless of whether he has probable cause to arrest the individual for a crime. The officer need not be absolutely certain that the individual is armed; the issue is *whether a reasonably prudent man in the circumstances would be warranted in the belief that his safety or that of others was in danger*.

How do we determine if the *perp* is armed? Is it based upon *the policeman's hunch*? The court answered that question, as well:

In determining whether the officer acted reasonably in such circumstances, due weight must be given, not to his . . . suspicion or 'hunch,' but to *the specific reasonable inferences which he is entitled to draw from the facts in light of his experience.   Terry*, at 23–27.

Later cases would expand upon the phrase, *articulable suspicion*. The courts would have the officer testify to *exactly* what it was that made him suspicious, and why. Then the officer's reasons would be known and the court could determine if he was justified in his actions.

Questions:

Does anyone doubt that Det. McFadden knew a robbery *was going down*?

_____

_____

_____

_____

What if someone *just looks dirty*?

_____

_____

_____

Why is *Terry v. Ohio* known as the *Stop and Frisk* case?

_____

_____

_____

_____

What can you do if you have reason to believe *the perp* may be armed?

_____

_____

_____

_____

Remember, the two most important exceptions to the warrant requirement are (1) *safety of the officer* and (2) *to prevent the destruction of evidence*.

Due to the importance of this case, and the contributions of Det. McFadden to American law enforcement, this case will also be in the appendix, as is *State. v. Ramos*, a similar case that played out on the hot and sultry streets of Miami.

It's not what you think. It's *what you see and what you know*, based upon your training and experience that matters.

What happens when the person you see is just standing in a high-crime area holding a bag. Many of the *victims* of that high-crime area also live there. Can we be stopping and patting them all down? What happens when one of them looks in your direction and just takes off? Does that mean anything more than he just doesn't like cops and wants to leave the area?

That's what Officers Nolan and Harvey saw one September day in 1995 in Chicago. They were working in uniform on West Van Buren, an area known for high narcotics activity, when Sam Wardlow looked in their direction and took off. He was holding an opaque (not see through) bag. They chased him through a gangway and alley and finally caught him on the street. The officers patted Wardlow down, as their experience had taught them that where there were drugs, weapons were not far away. Officer Nolan squeezed the bag Wardlow was still holding and felt what his experience told him was a gun. Nolan was right. The bag contained a .38 caliber revolver with five live rounds. (There was no PC to look into the bag, thus, the squeeze.)[33]

> This case, involving a brief encounter between a citizen and a police officer on a public street, is governed by the analysis we first applied in *Terry v. Ohio*. In *Terry*, we held that an officer may, consistent with the Fourth Amendment, conduct a brief, investigatory stop when the officer has a reasonable, articulable suspicion that criminal activity is afoot. 392 U.S., at 30. While "reasonable suspicion" is a less demanding standard than probable cause and requires a showing considerably *less than preponderance of the evidence*, the Fourth Amendment requires at least a minimal level of objective justification for making the stop. . . . The officer must be able to articulate more than an "inchoate and unparticularized suspicion or 'hunch'" of criminal activity. Citing to *Terry*, at 27. *Illinois v. Wardlow*, 528 U.S. 119, 123 (2000).

Wardlow lost at trial, as the court ruled this was a valid *Terry* stop. His conviction for possessing a firearm by a felon was overturned in the appellate courts of Illinois, but the prosecutors convinced the U.S. Supreme Court to hear the case on the limited issue of whether "unprovoked flight is sufficient grounds to constitute reasonable suspicion." As you will remember from *Terry*, that's all you need to stop someone. So what is "reasonable suspicion?"

In civil trials, juries are instructed that a preponderance of the evidence is what tips the scales in one party's favor, that is, as little as 50.1 percent. Now we are told that reasonable suspicion is even less than that.

---

[33]Compare this instant recognition of the gun to what a Minneapolis police officer testified to in a case where it was conceded that the stop and frisk were authorized, based upon the subject leaving a "crack house" and changing direction after making eye contact with the officer. "[A]s I pat-searched the front of his body, I felt a lump, a small lump, in the front pocket. I examined it with my fingers and it slid and it felt to be a lump of crack cocaine in cellophane." The Supreme Court in *Minnesota v. Dickerson* held that the officer conducting the frisk determined that the lump in respondent's jacket was contraband *only after probing and investigating what he certainly knew was not a weapon.* 508 U.S. 366 (1993). Conviction reversed; a frisk was allowed, not a search.

Why can't Wardlow, or anyone else for that matter, just walk away? Has he done anything to suggest he is involved in criminal activity?

> In this case, moreover, it was not merely (Wardlow's) presence in an area of heavy narcotics trafficking that aroused the officers' suspicion, but his unprovoked flight upon noticing the police. Our cases have also recognized that nervous, evasive behavior is a pertinent factor in determining reasonable suspicion. (Citations omitted) Headlong flight – wherever it occurs – is the consummate act of evasion: It is not necessarily indicative of wrongdoing, but it is certainly suggestive of such. . . . Thus, the determination of reasonable suspicion must be based on common-sense judgments and inferences about human behavior. We conclude Officer Nolan was justified in suspecting that Wardlow was involved in criminal activity, and, therefore, in investigating further. *Wardlow*, at 124.

Citing to the bus cases we will read below, the court further explained:

> Such a holding is entirely consistent with our decision in *Florida v. Royer*, 460 U.S. 491 (1983) (an airport case), where we held that when an officer, without reasonable suspicion or probable cause, approaches an individual, the individual has a right to ignore the police and go about his business. And any "refusal to cooperate, without more, does not furnish the minimal level of objective justification needed for a detention or seizure." *Florida v. Bostick*, 501 U.S. 429, 437 (1991). But unprovoked flight is simply not a mere refusal to cooperate. Flight, by its very nature, is not "going about one's business;" in fact, it is just the opposite. Allowing officers confronted with such flight to stop the fugitive and investigate further is quite consistent with the individual's right to go about his business or to stay put and remain silent in the face of police questioning. *Wardlow*, at 125.

Now that we know when we can *pat down* a person, how about his car—or his house—or someone near him? If you follow the long established concerns of balancing protection of the officer, with the rights of the citizens, the answers become apparent.

In *Michigan v. Long*,[34] the court applied the principles of *Terry* in the context of a vehicular roadside encounter stating:

> The search of the passenger compartment of an automobile, limited to those areas in which a weapon may be placed or hidden, is permissible if the police officer possesses a reasonable belief based on 'specific and articulable facts which, taken together with the rational inferences to be drawn from those facts, reasonably warrant' the officer in believing that the suspect is dangerous and the suspect may gain immediate control of weapons.

---

[34]463 U.S. 1032 (1983).

The court, in *Long*, took that language right out of *Terry v. Ohio*, at 21.

Let's see what those facts were. Deputy Sheriffs Howell and Lewis were on patrol in rural Barry County, Michigan, when they observed a speeding and erratically driven car go into a ditch shortly after midnight. When the deputies approached the scene of the accident, they met David Long at the rear of the car. The driver's door was open. He was the only person present. Long had difficulty responding to repeated requests to produce his driver's license and registration and appeared to be "under the influence of something." As Long started walking toward the open car door, the deputies followed and observed a large hunting knife on the floorboard of the driver's side of the car. They shined their flashlights into the car and saw "something" protruding from under the armrest. Their intention was "to search for other weapons." At this point, Deputy Howell entered the vehicle to examine the armrest, and saw a pouch of marijuana on the front seat. After Long was convicted, he asked the U.S. Supreme Court to determine "the authority of a police officer to protect himself by conducting a *Terry*-type search of the passenger compartment of a motor vehicle during the lawful investigatory stop of the occupant of the vehicle."

The court held:

Our past cases indicate . . . that protection of police and others can justify protective searches when police have a reasonable belief that the suspect poses a danger, that roadside encounters between police and suspects are especially hazardous, and that danger may arise from the possible presence of weapons in the area surrounding a suspect. These principles compel our conclusion that the search of the passenger compartment of an automobile, limited to those areas in which a weapon may be placed or hidden, is permissible if the police officer possesses a reasonable belief based on 'specific and articulable facts which, taken together with the rational inferences from those facts, reasonably warrant' the officers in believing that the suspect is dangerous and the suspect may gain immediate control of weapons. *Terry*. [T]he issue is whether a reasonably prudent man in the circumstances would be warranted in the belief that his safety or that of others was in danger. If a suspect is 'dangerous,' he is no less dangerous simply because he is not arrested. If, while conducting a legitimate *Terry* search of the interior of the automobile, the officer should, as here, discover contraband other than weapons, he clearly cannot be required to ignore the contraband, and the Fourth Amendment does not require its suppression in such circumstances. *Coolidge v. New Hampshire, Michigan v. Tyler* [the arson case to be discussed in Chapter Four].   *Long*, at 1049.

Let's change the facts a bit. Let's say Long was already in handcuffs, having been placed under arrest. Could you still *pat down* the car? Is there still a danger? That's just what happened, rather recently, in Texas to Richard Wallen. Wallen was stopped for speeding. As the police officer was requesting his license and registration, he noticed several weapons in the vehicle. Wallen kept walking around the car and looking into it. Eventually, a records check revealed an outstanding traffic warrant, and Wallen was handcuffed and placed in the rear of the patrol car. Was there any need for a protective search of the car? Could Wallen get to those guns and hurt the officer? The U.S. Court of Appeals for the Fifth Circuit (Texas, Louisiana, and Mississippi) ruled that "suspects in handcuffs can remain a danger to the police, particularly when weapons are present . . . . The rule of *Long* and *Terry* applies here to legitimize this sweep, although Wallen was in handcuffs at the time."[35]

A few years after Deputy Howell *frisked* David Long's car for weapons, detectives in Prince George's County, Maryland, obtained arrest warrants for two men suspected of a recent armed robbery of a Godfather's Pizza restaurant in their jurisdiction. One of the robbers had been wearing a red running suit. The first to be arrested, two days later, was Jerome Edward Buie. A team of six or seven officers (even the court was not sure!) went to his home after calling first to make sure he was there. After gaining entry,[36] the officers fanned out through the first and second floor looking for him. A Corporal Rozar shouted into the basement, ordering anyone there to come out. When a male voice answered, Rozar announced, "This is the police, show me your hands." Finally Buie, and his hands, came up. He was arrested, searched, and handcuffed by Cpl. Rozar. So why did he have to *pat down* the house? *Chimel* says we can't search the house beyond the immediate areas of the arrest.

The second robber had not yet been apprehended. Who else was in the house that might attack the officers as they were taking Buie away? A Det. Frolich entered the basement (after Buie came up) to see if anyone else was down there. He noticed a red running suit lying in plain view and seized it. It was moved into evidence at Buie's trial and he was convicted. The first round of appeals went well for the prosecution and the conviction was upheld. The court found that Det. Frolich *did not go into the basement to search for evidence*, but *to look for the suspected accomplice* or anyone else who might pose a threat to the officers on the scene.

> Traditionally, the sanctity of a person's home—his castle—requires that the police may not invade it without a warrant except under the most exigent of circumstances. But once the police are lawfully in the home, their conduct is measured by a standard of reasonableness. . . . If there is reason to believe that the arrestee had accomplices who are still at large, something less than probable cause—reasonable suspicion—should be sufficient to justify a limited additional intrusion to investigate the possibility of their presence.[37]

---

[35]*U.S. v. Wallen*, 388 F.3d 161 (5th Cir. 2004).

[36]In 1980 the court ruled that probable cause aside, an arrest warrant was needed to enter a home to look for a person to be arrested. To put it bluntly, they told us that if you needed paper to enter and look for drugs or guns, why not the same for the homeowner (*Payton v. New York*, 445 U.S. 573 (1980)). I don't recall ever meeting Teddy Payton, who was convicted of murdering the manager of a gas station on Manhattan's upper East Side in January of 1970, but I did have many occasions to handle domestics in the building where his apartment was located, and entered without benefit of the now famous *Payton* arrest warrant: 682 East 141 St., in The Bronx. Teddy lived in apartment 5-C.

[37]*State v Buie*, 72 Md. App. 562, at 571 (1987).

But the highest court in Maryland disagreed and, with a 4–3 vote, found there were insufficient reasons to permit the entry into the basement after the arrest. The U.S. Supreme Court was then asked to determine the level of justification needed before the police could legally enter the basement to see if someone else, who might hurt them, was down there. If the police were lawfully in the basement, *the plain view doctrine* would allow them to seize the running suit. If not, the jury would never see it.

Justice White, who used to play touch football with the Kennedys on the White House lawn prior to his appointment to the court, first explained what a protective sweep is:

A 'protective sweep' is a quick and limited search of a premises, incident to an arrest and conducted to protect the safety of police officers or others. It is narrowly confined to a cursory visual inspection of those places in which a person might be hiding.

Then, speaking for the court, and building upon *Long* and *Terry*, he wrote:

We conclude that the Fourth Amendment would permit the protective sweep undertaken here *if* the searching officer possessed a reasonable belief based on specific and articulable facts which, taken together with the rational inferences to be drawn from those facts, reasonably warranted the officer in believing that the area swept harbored an individual posing a danger to the officer or others.[38]

What did he say?

Have a good reason, backed up with facts that you can point to, as Det. McFadden did, why you think it would be dangerous *not to look around* for someone who might hurt you. If your beliefs are reasonable, that is to say if they are *not unreasonable*, the courts will allow you to protect yourself. And if they disagree with you, and exclude anything you see in plain view, that's OK too. We would rather lose a case than a cop!

What facts can you articulate that would convince a court that other dangerous individuals might be in the house?

_____

_____

_____

_____

_____

---

[38]*Maryland v. Buie*, 494 U.S. 325 at 328 (1990).

Are those inferences you are drawing reasonable?

_____

_____

_____

What if there are no articulable facts to justify a protective sweep? What can you do?

_____

_____

_____

"As an _incident to the arrest_ the officers could, as a precautionary matter and _without_ probable cause or reasonable suspicion, look in closets and other spaces _immediately adjoining_ the place of arrest from which an attack could be immediately launched." Here, the court was relying upon _Chimel_, but once we go beyond those immediate areas, _additional_ reasonable articulable facts are required for _additional_ intrusions into the sanctity of the home. But they cautioned us:

> We should emphasize that such a protective sweep, aimed at protecting the arresting officers, _if_ justified by the circumstances, is nevertheless not a full search of the premises, but may extend only to _a cursory inspection_ of those spaces where a person may be found.   _Buie_, at 335.

Remember, they are allowing you to protect yourself—not search for evidence. If your articulable facts indicate that evidence will be found in the house, present those facts to the magistrate and get a search warrant.

When you conduct the protective sweep, what are you looking for?

_____

_____

_____

Let's extend this a bit. Suppose Buie was not in his home, but arrested in the neighborhood tavern. Who could you pat down there? An earlier case, _Ybarra v. Illinois_, 444 U.S. 85 (1980), gives us the answer.

In March 1976, a special agent of the Illinois Bureau of Investigation applied for and received a search warrant for the Aurora Tap Tavern, in Aurora, Illinois. The warrant authorized a search of the tavern and the bartender, one "Greg, a white male with blond hair, about 25 years of age," for tin foil packets of heroin that "Greg" was alleged to be selling in the tavern. To make this more interesting, Illinois had a statute authorizing the police to "reasonably detain and search any person in the place to be searched to protect himself from attack and to prevent the disposal of things described in the warrant."

On the date the warrant was issued, seven or eight officers (how come they never know?) entered the tavern and announced their purpose and that all present would have to submit to a "cursory search for weapons." One officer patted down 9–13 customers (there they go again) while the remaining officers conducted the search of the premises. Our friend, Ventura Ybarra, was found to have a "cigarette pack with . . . six tin foil packets of heroin in it."

Needless to say, Ybarra was indicted and convicted of possessing the heroin. His conviction was upheld in the Illinois state courts. However, the U.S. Supreme Court found that the search violated the Fourth Amendment.

> Upon entering the tavern, the police did not recognize Ybarra and had no reason to believe he was committing a crime. He made no gestures indicative of criminal conduct, and made no movements that might suggest an attempt to conceal contraband, and said nothing suspicious to the officers. His hands were empty and the police had no reason to believe he might assault them. All the police knew about Ybarra was that he was in a public tavern at a time when the police believed the bartender was selling heroin.   *Ybarra*, at 88–89 (Compare his actions to those of Terry and his associates.)

The court held that even though the police had a search warrant to search the tavern and Ybarra was in the tavern at that time, *neither a person's mere presence in that tavern, nor his closeness to the person to be searched (Greg) gives rise to probable cause to search that person*. There was no probable cause *particularized* to Ybarra. The court explained:

> Each patron who walked into the Aurora Tavern . . . was clothed with the constitutional protection against unreasonable search or . . . seizure. . . . Although the search warrant . . . gave the officers authority to search the premises and to search "Greg," it gave them no authority whatever to invade the constitutional protections possessed individually by the tavern's customers.   *Ybarra*, at 91.

What have we learned from the line of cases beginning with *Terry* and continued by *Long*, *Buie*, and *Ybarra*?

_____

_____

_____

_____

_____

_____

The final exception to the warrant requirement we will study is not really an exception. Remember, warrants are only needed to search when people object. What if there is no objection?

h. Consent searches:

Individuals in the street and in public transportation, joint occupiers, and apparent authority to consent.

It is well recognized that a search conducted pursuant to a valid consent is permissible under the Constitution and does not violate the Fourth and Fourteenth Amendments. One issue in consent searches is the *voluntariness* of the consent. How is consent determined? Just consider whether the person would consent, if you were *not wearing a badge and gun*. Another question is *who* may give the consent.

In the two World War II-era criminal cases, war profiteers were convicted under the War Powers Act, over their objections that the federal agents entered their places of business and removed certain physical evidence. In both cases, *Davis v. U.S.*, 328 U.S. 582 (1946) and *Zap v. U.S.* 328, 624 (1946), the soon-to-be indicted businessmen had previously agreed that the government could have access to their records. Furthermore, under the facts of both cases:

> the inspection was made during regular hours at the place of business. No force or threat of force was employed. Indeed, the inspection was made with the full cooperation of petitioner's staff.   *Zap*, at 628.

> The agents, therefore, were lawfully on the premises. They obtained by lawful means access to the documents. That much at least was granted by the contractual agreement for inspection. They were not trespassers. They did not obtain access by force, fraud, or trickery. Thus the knowledge they acquired concerning petitioner's conduct under the contract with the government was lawfully obtained (*plain view*?). Neither the Fourth nor Fifth Amendment[39] would preclude the agents from testifying at the trial concerning the (evidence they seized). The agents did not become trespassers when they took the (evidence). *Zap*, at 629.

There is a usual rule that when a person is asked to waive a constitutional right, there must be a showing that the person was fully aware of that right and knowingly

---

[39]"The law of searches and seizures as revealed in the decisions of this Court is the product of the interplay of these two constitutional provisions. *Boyd v. United States*, 116 U.S. 616 (1886). It reflects a dual purpose—protection of the privacy of the individual, his right to be let alone; (and) protection of the individual against compulsory production of evidence to be used against him. *Boyd*, supra, *Weeks v. United States*, 232 U.S. 383 (1914)," quoted in *Davis*, at 587. *Weeks* is the case that brought the exclusionary rule to the federal courts almost 50 years before becoming mandatory in the state courts.

relinquished it. We see this in criminal court every time a person pleads guilty. They are asked by the judge whether they understand that they are waiving their right to trial by jury, to cross examine witnesses, to testify or not. . . . This is also standard for waivers of the Fifth Amendment. Who hasn't heard of the advisements under *Miranda*?

Our next case, *Schneckloth v. Bustamonte*,[40] was taken up to resolve a conflict among the lower courts on the question of whether the defendant must know of his right to refuse to consent to the search.

> The precise question in this case, then, is what must the prosecution prove to demonstrate that a consent was 'voluntarily' given. And upon that question there is a square conflict of views between the state and federal courts that have reviewed the search involved in the case before us. The (federal) Court of Appeals for the Ninth Circuit concluded that it is an essential part of the State's initial burden to prove that a person knows he has a right to refuse consent. The California courts have followed the rule that voluntariness is a question of fact to be determined from the totality of all the circumstances, and that the state of a defendant's knowledge is only one factor to be taken into account in assessing the voluntariness of a consent. *Schneckloth*, at 220.

In *Schneckloth*, this questioned was answered.

It all started when Robert Bustamonte and his friends foolishly agreed to let three cops search the car they were riding in at 2:40 a.m. in Sunnyvale, California:

> When the subject of a search is *not* in custody and the State attempts to justify a search on the basis of his consent, the Fourth and Fourteenth Amendments require that it demonstrate that the consent was in fact *voluntarily* given, and not the result of duress or coercion, express or implied. Voluntariness is a question of fact to be determined from all the circumstances, and while the subject's knowledge of a right to refuse is a factor to be taken into account, *the prosecution is not required to demonstrate (that he knew he could say No)*.[41]

The facts of the case were rather routine, and more relevant to standard police work than selling gasoline without ration coupons, in violation of the War Powers Act of 1942:

> While on routine patrol Police Officer James Rand stopped an automobile when he observed that one headlight and its license plate light were burned out. Six men were in the vehicle. Joe Alcala and (the soon-to-be

---

[40]412 U.S. 218 (1973).

[41]Even though we don't have to prove the defendant knew he had a right to object to the search, I have put a *Consent To Be Searched* form into the appendix for you. If they will sign it, your job in court will be much easier.

defendant), Robert Bustamonte, were in the front seat with Joe Gonzales, the driver. Three older men were seated in the rear. When, in response to the policeman's question, Gonzales could not produce a driver's license, Officer Rand asked if any of the other five had any evidence of identification. Only Alcala produced a license, and he explained that the car was his brother's. After the six occupants had stepped out of the car at the officer's request and after two additional policemen had arrived, Officer Rand asked Alcala if he could search the car. Alcala replied, 'Sure, go ahead.' Prior to the search no one was threatened with arrest and, according to Officer Rand's uncontradicted testimony, it 'was all very congenial at this time.' Gonzales testified that Alcala actually helped in the search of the car, by opening the trunk and glove compartment. In Gonzales' words: '(T)he police officer asked Joe (Alcala), he goes, 'Does the trunk open?' And Joe said, 'Yes.' He went to the car and got the keys and opened up the trunk. Wadded up under the left rear seat, the police officers found three checks that had previously been stolen from a car wash. *Schneckloth*, at 220.

Does the fact that Alcala gratuitously opened the trunk and glove box, hoping no one would look under the rear seat, have any significance? The opinion does not discuss the proofs in the case, but apparently our soon-to-be famous friend owned up to the theft of the checks.

In determining what factors courts should look to in their inquiry, their review of the previous case law suggested that:

The significant fact about all of these decisions is that none of them turned on the presence or absence of a single controlling criterion (such as the subject's knowledge of his right to refuse to give consent); each reflected a careful scrutiny of all the surrounding circumstances. *Schneckloth*, at 226.

Now that it is clear that an individual may consent to have the police search his possessions and the government does not have to prove the defendant relinquished a known right, can *another* person give that consent? In *U.S. v. Matlock*,[42] the court held:

When the prosecution seeks to justify a warrantless search by proof of voluntary consent, it is not limited to proof that consent was given by the defendant, but may show that permission to search was obtained *from a third party* who possessed *common authority* over or other sufficient relationship to the premises or effects sought to be inspected.

The facts of the case indicated that Bill Matlock, who was suspected of robbing a bank in Wisconsin,

was arrested in the front yard of a house in which he lived along with a Mrs. Graff and others. (Three of the arresting officers went to the door

---

[42]415 U.S. 164, 171 (1974).

of the house and were admitted by Mrs. Graff, who was dressed in a robe and was holding her son in her arms. The officers told her they were looking for money and a gun and asked if they could search the house.) The arresting officers, who did not ask (Matlock) which room he occupied or whether he would consent to a search, were then admitted to the house by Mrs. Graff and, *with her consent* but without a warrant, searched the house, including a bedroom, which Mrs. Graff told them was jointly occupied by respondent and herself, and in a closet (therein) the officers found and seized money (in a diaper bag). Matlock was indicted for bank robbery, and moved to suppress the seized money as evidence.

The court upheld the search on the theory that any occupant of the house:

> *having joint access or control* . . . has the right to permit the (search) in his own right and that *the others have assumed the risk* that one of their number might permit the common area to be searched.   *Matluck,* at 172.

Is *Matlock* authority for you to get your suspect's mother's consent to search her juvenile son's bedroom?

First, ask yourself, a few questions. Does Junior know that his mother enters his room on a regular basis to clean it? To what areas does she have access? Does she open the dresser drawers to replace his clean clothes? Does she put fresh linen on his bed and look under it for his socks? Is it reasonable for him to assume no one is invading his privacy? What about that locked fishing box or toolbox in the closet? *The one with the lock on it?* What is the owner of that box telling us? Is there a reasonable expectation of privacy in that locked box? You know the answer!

What if Matlock, or your suspect, is in the house and objects to his girlfriend's, wife's, or roommate's giving of consent to search jointly occupied premises? That question was recently answered by the Supreme Court in *Georgia v. Randolph.*[43]

Randolph was another domestic, this time in Americus, Georgia. Wife Janet called the police when husband Scott took their child to a neighbor. Janet advised responding officers that her husband "was a cocaine user whose habit had caused (them) financial problems." As this was occurring, Scott returned to the home, denied drug use, and advised that Janet was the one who abused drugs and alcohol. With that, Sergeant Murray asked Scott for permission to search the house. Scott clearly refused. The sergeant then asked Janet for permission, which she readily gave. Janet led the officers to an upstairs bedroom that she indicated was Scott's. Sergeant Murray entered and saw the customary straw and white powder.

After Scott's indictment for cocaine possession, he moved to suppress the evidence on the grounds that he did not consent to the search and his refusal should overrule that of wife Janet's consent.

---

[43]547 U.S. 103 (2006).

Co-tenants or joint occupiers have equal standing in the home. Who wins here? Who controls the actions of the police? The Supreme Court accepted the case:

> to resolve a split of authority on whether one occupant may give law enforcement effective consent to search shared premises, as against a co-tenant *who is present and states a refusal to permit the search.*[44]

The court upheld the general rule of third party consent, by persons having joint access or control, as stated in *Matlock*; however, they went on to hold that:

> a *physically present* inhabitant's express refusal of consent to a police search *is dispositive as to him*, regardless of the consent of a fellow occupant. Scott Randolph's refusal is clear, and nothing in the record justifies the search on grounds independent of Janet Randolph's consent. (That means if he's the one going to jail, he can overrule her.)

They did drop a few hints of when that rule might not apply:

> The State does not argue that she gave any indication to the police of *a need for protection* inside the house that might have justified entry into the portion of the premises where the police found the powdery straw (which, if lawfully seized, could have been used when attempting to establish probable cause for the warrant issued later). Nor does the State claim that the entry and search should be upheld under the rubric of *exigent circumstances*, owing to some apprehension by the police officers that Scott Randolph would destroy evidence of drug use before any warrant could be obtained.   *Randolph*, at 123.

Since many of these cases originate as domestics, what happens when the potential defendant does not object as he is outside his home, sitting in the rear of the police car,[45] having been arrested for assaulting his beloved? Must you go outside and ask him too?

The *Randolph* court also spoke to that issue:

> So long as there is no evidence that the police have removed the potentially objecting tenant from the (home) for the sake of avoiding a possible objection, there is practical value in the simple clarity of complementary rules, one recognizing the co-tenant's permission when there is no fellow

---

[44]A footnote in the opinion states that the four U.S. Courts of Appeals to have considered this question have ruled that the consent of one is sufficient in the face of an objection by another, as have the majority of the state courts to address the question. Standing alone was the Supreme Court of the state of Washington, *State v. Leach*, 113 Wash.2d 735 (1989), which required the consent of all present occupants.
[45]It has been said that the heroes of America are not to be found in rock bands or on basketball courts. They ride in *the front* of police cars and hang on to the rear of fire trucks.

occupant on hand, the other . . . (allowing the other co-tenant who is present to object). (Any other rule) would needlessly limit the capacity of the police to respond to legitimate opportunities in the field if we were to require . . . the police to . . . find a potentially objecting co-tenant before acting on the permission they had already received. . . . Better to accept (this rule) than to impose a requirement, (that would be) time-consuming in the field and in the courtroom, with no apparent justification.   *Randolph*, at 121.

So what do we do when we get to those ever recurring domestics? If it is reasonable (the key question to all Fourth Amendment questions) to arrest the hubby/boyfriend and put him in the caged unit outside the house, as you continue to interview the battered spouse, do it. If your intent is merely to remove him so he cannot object if she gives consent to search, the rule of *Randolph* would apply to frustrate the search. Got it?

Lest we forget what is really important here, the *Randolph* court reminded us again of the main reason for the Fourth Amendment:

We have, after all, lived our whole national history with an understanding of "the ancient adage that a man's home is his castle to the point that the poorest man may in his cottage bid defiance to all the forces of the crown," quoting from *Miller v. United States*, 357 U.S. 301, 307 (1958). *Randolph*, at 115.

It appears his dope pales in comparison.

The issue of consent is a commonly recurring one. Many times police officers work the airports and the bus terminals in an effort to prevent the transportation of illegal drugs. The Supreme Court has had several opportunities to examine these issues over the years, subsequent to *Schneckloth*. In 1991, the court ruled:

The Fourth Amendment permits police officers to approach bus passengers at random to ask questions and to request their consent to searches, provided a reasonable person would understand that he or she is free to refuse.   *Florida v. Bostick*, 501 U.S. 429 (1991).

The issue of whether police officers must advise bus passengers of their right *not to cooperate* was still to be answered (*Schneckloth v. Bustamonte* was considered not binding, as the bus patrons, if they chose to leave the bus, would be stranded far from home and have to forfeit the balance of the ticket. Had Bustamonte wanted, he could have gotten back into the car and driven off). Eight years later, such a case came before the court.

These were the facts in question:

On February 4, 1999, respondents (after conviction, this is one way we refer to our subjects. If they are the ones bringing the petition for a Writ of Habeas Corpus to the Supreme Court after a loss below, we call them the petitioner) Christopher Drayton and Clifton Brown, Jr., were traveling on a Greyhound bus en route from Ft. Lauderdale, Florida, to Detroit, Michigan. The bus made a scheduled stop in Tallahassee, Florida. The passengers were required to disembark so the bus could be refueled and cleaned. As the passengers re-boarded, the driver checked their tickets and then left to complete paperwork inside the terminal. As he left, the driver allowed three members of the Tallahassee Police Department to board the bus as part of a routine drug and weapons interdiction effort. The officers were dressed in plain clothes and carried concealed weapons and visible badges. Once onboard Officer Hoover knelt on the driver's seat and faced the rear of the bus. He could observe the passengers and ensure the safety of the two other officers without blocking the aisle or otherwise obstructing the bus exit. Officers Lang and Blackburn went to the rear of the bus. Blackburn remained stationed there, facing forward. Lang worked his way toward the front of the bus, speaking with individual passengers as he went. He asked the passengers about their travel plans and sought to match passengers with luggage in the overhead racks. To avoid blocking the aisle, Lang stood next to or just behind each passenger with whom he spoke. According to Lang's testimony, passengers who declined to cooperate with him or who chose to exit the bus at any time would have been allowed to do so without argument. In Lang's experience, however, most people are willing to cooperate. Some passengers go so far as to commend the police for their efforts to ensure the safety of their travel. Lang could recall five to six instances in the previous year in which passengers had declined to have their luggage searched. It also was common for passengers to leave the bus for a cigarette or a snack while the officers were on board. Lang sometimes informed passengers of their right to refuse to cooperate. On the day in question, however, he did not. Respondents were seated next to each other on the bus. Drayton was in the aisle seat, Brown in the seat next to the window. Lang approached respondents from the rear and leaned over Drayton's shoulder. He held up his badge long enough for respondents to identify him as a police officer. With his face 12- to-18 inches away from Drayton's, Lang spoke in a voice just loud enough for respondents to hear: "I'm Investigator Lang with the Tallahassee Police Department. We're conducting bus interdiction [sic], attempting to deter drugs and illegal weapons being transported on the bus. Do you have any bags on the bus?" Both respondents pointed to a single green bag in the overhead luggage rack. Lang asked, "Do you mind if I check it?" and Brown responded, "Go ahead." Lang handed the bag to Officer Blackburn to check. The bag contained no contraband. Officer Lang noticed that both respondents were wearing heavy jackets and baggy pants despite the warm weather. In Lang's experience drug traffickers often use baggy clothing to conceal weapons or narcotics.[46] The officer asked Brown if he

---

[46]Has Investigator Lang articulated the reasons for his suspicions? However, due to the consent, PC is no longer an issue.

had any weapons or drugs in his possession. He also asked Brown: "Do you mind if I check your person?" Brown answered, "Sure," and cooperated by leaning up in his seat, pulling a cell phone out of his pocket, and opening up his jacket. Lang reached across Drayton and patted down Brown's jacket and pockets, including his waist area, sides, and upper thighs. In both thigh areas, Lang detected hard objects similar to drug packages detected on other occasions. Lang arrested and handcuffed Brown. Officer Hoover escorted Brown from the bus. Lang then asked Drayton, "Mind if I check you?" Drayton responded by lifting his hands about eight inches from his legs. Lang conducted a pat down of Drayton's thighs and detected hard objects similar to those found on Brown. He arrested Drayton and escorted him from the bus. A further search revealed that respondents had duct-taped plastic bundles of powder cocaine between several pairs of their boxer shorts. Brown possessed three bundles containing 483 grams of cocaine. Drayton possessed two bundles containing 295 grams of cocaine. *U.S. v. Drayton.*[47]

Going back to some earlier cases, the court reasoned:

Law enforcement officers do not violate the Fourth Amendment's prohibition of unreasonable seizures merely by approaching individuals on the street or in other public places and putting questions to them if they are willing to listen. See, *Florida v. Royer*, 460 U.S. 491, 497 (1983); *Florida v. Rodriguez*, 469 U.S. 1, 5–6 (1984) *(per curiam)* (holding that such interactions in airports are "the sort of consensual encounter[s] that implicat[e] no Fourth Amendment interest"). Even when law enforcement officers have no basis for suspecting a particular individual, they may pose questions, ask for identification, and request consent to search luggage—provided they do not induce cooperation by coercive means. See *Florida v. Bostick*, 501 U.S., at 434–435. If a reasonable person would feel free to terminate the encounter, then he or she has not been seized. *Drayton*, at 200–201.

There is no one factor that controls. The proper inquiry necessitates a consideration of "all the circumstances surrounding the encounter." Do you recognize this phrase? It tends to appear in many Fourth Amendment cases. The more facts you give the court, the better are your chances of prevailing at this "police-citizen encounter." Whether it's probable cause (to arrest or search), reasonable suspicion (to stop and frisk), or a consent search, lay all the facts on the table, including all of your training and experience. Then no one has to guess at what you "knew," especially all the judges that review the case as it works up the chain of appellate review.

---

[47]536 U.S. 194, 198 (2002).

There were ample grounds for the (federal) District Court to conclude that "everything that took place between Officer Lang and the respondents suggests that it was cooperative" and that there "was nothing coercive [or] confrontational" about the encounter. There was no application of force, no intimidating movement, no overwhelming show of force, no brandishing of weapons, no blocking of exits, no threat, no command, not even an authoritative tone of voice. It is beyond question that had this encounter occurred on the street, it would be constitutional. The fact that an encounter takes place on a bus does not on its own transform standard police questioning of citizens into an illegal seizure. See *Bostick*, 501 U.S., at 439–440. Indeed, because many fellow passengers are present to witness officers' conduct, a reasonable person may feel even more secure in his or her decision not to cooperate with police on a bus than in other circumstances. *Drayton*, at 204.

The rule here is very similar to the one we apply in the giving of the *Miranda* warnings. If the reasonable person would feel free to leave, then he has not been seized (is not in custody) and the familiar warnings are not required. If the facts of the encounter would indicate that a reasonable person was free to get up and go, and he agreed to let the police to search him, he has consented. As with all Fourth Amendment issues, it is the "totality of the circumstances" that control.

Now that we are starting to get a feel for the issue of consent, let's kick it up a notch. What happens if the person who gives the consent has no authority to give it? Must we ask everyone for a lease or a deed? Remember those domestics we all love so much? You know the drill. He throws her out; she calls you to help her get her clothes out.[48] The facts of *Illinois v. Rodriguez*[49] will seem familiar to many.

Gail Fischer called the police to her mother's apartment in Chicago. Her face showed signs of a recent severe beating. She reported that Edward Rodriguez, her boyfriend, had assaulted her and was now asleep in *our* apartment. She claimed her clothes and furniture were there. They drove her to the apartment where she unlocked the door and gave the officers permission to enter so they could arrest him for battery. They had neither arrest nor search warrants. Observed in plain view were the usual small packets containing white powder and the accompanying paraphernalia. If the entry were lawful, *the plain view doctrine* would apply. If the officers had no right to be there, the drugs would never see the inside of the courtroom.

As later shown at the preliminary hearing, Fischer, and her two children, had moved out of that apartment about a month earlier, but she went back on occasion. Her name was not on the lease, nor did she contribute to the rent. She did have a key, but it was not clear whether Rodriguez had given it to her or she had taken it. Based upon these facts, the lower courts determined that Fischer did not have *joint access or control* over the apartment and, therefore, had no right to invite the police in.

---

[48]In many of the domestics I responded to in The Bronx, half of her clothes were already in the stairwell and our job was to rescue the rest.

[49]497 U.S. 177 (1990).

Generally speaking, the Fourth Amendment prohibits warrantless entries of a person's home, whether to make an arrest or to search for objects. That prohibition does not apply when a voluntary consent has been obtained from the person, *Schneckloth*, or from a third person having joint control over the premises, *Matlock*.

Rodriguez asserted that the search and seizure were unreasonable. Neither he, nor another person having joint control over the premises, consented to the entry. The question is, was this entry into the apartment *reasonable*?

> In order to satisfy the 'reasonableness' requirement of the Fourth Amendment, what is generally demanded . . . of the magistrate, the officer executing the warrant or the officer searching or seizing under one of the exceptions to the warrant requirement, —is not that they always be correct, but that they always be reasonable. . . .
>
> Because many situations which confront officers in the course of executing their duties are more or less ambiguous, room must be allowed for some mistakes on their part. But the mistakes must be those of reasonable men, acting on facts leading (to reasonable conclusions). *Rodriguez*, at 185.

Even though Fischer did not have authority to consent to the officers' entry of Rodriguez's apartment, the warrantless entry was nonetheless valid if the officers *reasonably believed* that Fischer had authority to consent. Based upon the facts presented to the officers, it was reasonable to conclude that Fischer did have the authority to let them in.

What we learn from these exceptions is that not all searches are prohibited, just unreasonable ones. If there is no warrant, the search is presumed to be unreasonable and the government has to prove the reasonableness by one of the above exceptions. If there is a warrant, the search is presumed reasonable and the burden is upon the defendant to show some problem with the warrant or its execution.[50] If the exceptions are not there, warrants are generally required to search a person's home, his papers, his effects, and even his body. Wouldn't it be more efficient without warrants? Of course, but our history taught us the value of a man's home (the wind, the rain . . .). The Fourth Amendment reflects the view of those who wrote the Bill of Rights, and the citizens who ratified it, that the privacy of a person's home may not be sacrificed in the name of efficiency to enforce the criminal laws. Remember, the reason for the amendment was not to protect only the innocent. The British agents were seeking contraband and that too is protected. Another way to say it is that the Fourth Amendment, in addition to protecting (from the eyes of the government officials) untaxed rum, smuggled goods, narcotics, stolen goods, dope dealers, and yes, even dead bodies, also protects our privacy as a people, or *the right to be left alone*.

---

[50]Even that is getting harder to do. See Chapter Seven, for *The Good Faith Exception* (for faulty warrants) and Chapter Eight, for the consequences of violations in the execution of the warrant.

Questions:

What is the theory running through the cases in this chapter? What do they all have in common?

_____

_____

_____

_____

_____

Is it fair to have the citizen yield a little bit to ensure your safety?

_____

_____

_____

If your job is to enforce the law, and the law places limitations on your right to search, what should you do?

_____

_____

_____

_____

Should the criminal go free because the constable has blundered?[51]

_____

_____

_____

What is the alternative?

_____

_____

_____

---

[51]See Chapter Three—*Barry Headricks*.

We keep seeing the phrase *reasonable expectation of privacy*. It popped up in the car search cases and it seems to run through many of the search warrant exceptions. What does that mean and where did it come from? We owe it all to the arrest of a Los Angeles bookmaker named Charles Katz.

Katz, probably aware that federal agents were on to him and may have tapped the phone where he lived, used the public telephone booth outside his apartment to conduct his illegal business. It was constructed mostly of glass and his every movement was open to public scrutiny. I suppose lip readers could make out what he was saying into the mouthpiece. FBI agents had attached an electronic listening and recording device to the *outside* of the telephone booth. Earlier case law had prohibited trespasses upon a person's property by listening devises, ergo the attachment to *the outside* of the booth. The agents also refrained from listening to conversations that had no relationship to the gambling activities, something an eavesdrop warrant would order them to do.

Based upon Katz's overheard conversations, he was indicted for, and convicted of, transmitting wagering information from Los Angeles to Boston and New York, in violation of a federal statute prohibiting "the use of a wire facility for the transmission in interstate commerce of bets or wagers on any sporting event or contest," a felony punishable by two years in prison or a $10,000 fine, or both.

The *Olmstead* case, decided almost 40 years before, held that such intercepted telephone communications were not protected by the Fourth Amendment. Despite the strong and prophetic dissents of Justices Holmes and Brandeis, cited in the Introduction, the court held that "the taps from house lines were made in the streets near the houses." Olmstead was a major bootlegger working in Seattle, Washington. Many of his agents worked from their homes. Prohibition agents had inserted wires into the ordinary telephone wires leading from Olmstead's office and some of the residences. "The insertions were made without any trespass upon any property of the defendants." The majority opinion of the court distinguished the interception of phone conversations from the protections accorded mail as follows:

The United States takes no such care of telegraph or telephone messages as of mailed sealed letters. The (Fourth) amendment does not forbid what was done here. There was no searching. There was no seizure. The evidence was secured by the use of the sense of hearing and that only. There was no entry of the houses or offices of the defendants. By the invention of the telephone 50 years ago, and its application for the purpose of extending communications, one can talk with another at a far distant place. The language of the amendment cannot be extended and expanded to include telephone wires, reaching to the whole world from the defendant's house or office. The intervening wires are not part of his house or office, any more than are the highways along which they are stretched.[52]

---

[52]*Olmstead v. U.S.*, 277 U.S. 438, at 464 (1928).

Now, what does all this have to do with *the reasonable expectation of privacy?*

At Katz's trial, the government argued that there was no trespass *within* the telephone booth. Katz, on the other hand, argued that the booth, at least when he was in it and paying for his call, was a "constitutionally protected area." The Supreme Court rejected both arguments. They held that the *Fourth Amendment protects people, not places*. The court explained:

> The Government stresses the fact that the telephone booth from which the petitioner made his calls was constructed partly of glass, so that he was as visible after he entered it as he would have been if he had remained outside. But what he sought to exclude when he entered the booth was not the intruding eye—it was the uninvited ear. He did not shed his right to do so simply because he made his calls from a place where he might be seen. No less than an individual in a business office, in a friend's apartment, or in a taxicab, a person in a telephone booth may rely upon the protection of the Fourth Amendment. One who occupies it, shuts the door behind him, and pays the toll that permits him to place a call is surely entitled to assume that the words he utters into the mouthpiece will not be broadcast to the world. To read the Constitution more narrowly is to ignore the vital role that the public telephone has come to play in private communication.[53]

The court continued:

> The Government's activities in electronically listening to and recording the petitioner's words violated the privacy upon which he justifiably relied while using the telephone booth and thus constituted a 'search and seizure' within the meaning of the Fourth Amendment. The fact that the electronic device employed to achieve that end did not happen to penetrate the wall of the booth can have no constitutional significance.[54]

Now that we are starting to understand the concept of a *reasonable expectation of privacy* (sometimes called a REOP), suppose Katz was tape recorded, not in the phone booth, but in the jail after his arrest, or in the police car, talking to an associate on the way to the police station. Are his words always protected?

Back in 1957, a Harry Lanza went to visit his brother, who was confined as a prisoner in a jail in the state of New York. They met in the public visitors' room, set

---

[53]*Katz v. U.S.*, 389 U.S. 347, at 352 (1967).

[54]*Katz*, at 354. Even though *Katz* is well known as the case that established the concept of the *reasonable expectation of privacy*, that phrase is not found in the main opinion. Justice Harlan, in a concurring opinion, explained that "I join the opinion of the Court, which I read to hold only that an enclosed telephone booth is an area where, like a home . . . a person has a constitutionally protected *reasonable expectation of privacy.*" Six months later, in *Terry v. Ohio*, the court formally coined the phrase, citing to Justice Harlan's concurrence in *Katz*.

aside for such visits, and spoke to each other. Unbeknownst to them, the authorities had electronically recorded their conversation. When Lanza's words were to be used against him at a later trial, he objected. He contended that the surreptitious eavesdropping amounted to an unreasonable search and seizure.

In those pre-*Katz* days, the court was still using the phrase *constitutionally protected area*. Included in those protected areas were homes, businesses, hotel rooms, automobiles, and occupied taxicabs. However, the court drew the line at jails.

> Without attempting either to define or to predict the ultimate scope of Fourth Amendment protection, it is obvious that a jail shares none of the attributes of privacy of a home. . . . In prison, official surveillance has traditionally been the order of the day.[55]

In a post-*Katz* case, the court again had an opportunity to revisit this issue in another jail case. This time they discussed whether or not there was a REOP in jail. "The applicability of the Fourth Amendment turns on whether the person invoking its protection can claim a . . . reasonable . . . expectation of privacy . . . We must decide, in Justice Harlan's words, whether a prisoner's expectation of privacy in his prison cell is the kind of expectation that 'society is prepared to recognize as reasonable.'" *Katz*.[56]

They continued by explaining why prisoners should not expect any privacy in jail. If you know you are being watched, or may be listened to, there is no REOP. And if there isn't for you, how about the people visiting you?

> Prisons, by definition, are places of involuntary confinement of persons who have a demonstrated proclivity for antisocial criminal, and often violent, conduct. . . . During 1981 and the first half of 1982 (the case was decided in 1984), there were over 120 prisoners murdered by fellow inmates in state and federal prisons. A number of prison personnel were murdered by prisoners during this period. Over 29 riots or similar disturbances were reported in these facilities for the same time frame. And there were over 125 suicides in these institutions. . . . There were in the same system in 1981 and 1982 over 750 inmate assaults on other inmates and over 570 inmate assaults on prison personnel. . . . Within this volatile "community," prison administrators are to take all necessary steps to ensure the safety of not only the prison staffs and administrative personnel, but also visitors. . . .
>
> A prison "shares none of the attributes of privacy of a home, an automobile, an office, or a hotel room." *Lanza v. New York*. We strike the balance in favor of institutional security. We believe that it is accepted by our society that loss of freedom of choice and privacy are inherent incidents of confinement. *Hudson*, at 526.

[55]*Lanza v. New York*, 370 U.S. 139 (1962).
[56]*Hudson v. Palmer*, 468 U.S. 517 (1984).

So much for the lack of privacy in prison. How about in the police car? No one has been convicted yet, or even arrested.

Steve McKinnon and a friend of his were allowed to sit in the rear of a Florida state trooper's car. The friend, who had been the driver, voluntarily agreed to let the trooper search the trunk of his car. He had been stopped for unsafe lane changing but passed the sobriety tests and was not under arrest. Unbeknownst to the two, their conversations were recorded, and the trooper heard them discuss the location of drugs in the car. After McKinnon's arrest, and indictment in federal court, he moved to suppress his statements as he argued he was not in a jail and not even under arrest in the police car. The U.S. Court of Appeals for the Eleventh Circuit (covering all federal courts in Florida, Georgia, and Alabama) held that there was no reasonable expectation of privacy in a police car, even for those *not under arrest*.[57]

While the Supreme Court did not rule on this matter, the Court of Appeals relied upon numerous other state courts that came to the same conclusion. They determined that there is no distinction between pre-arrest and post-arrest situations. It is the location of the conversations that controls, not the status of the speakers. Harry Lanza could have told them that.

Why is there no reasonable expectation of privacy in the rear of a police car?

_____

_____

_____

Why is the person who hasn't been arrested treated the same as an arrested person in the police car?

_____

_____

Before we leave this area, and the Fourth Amendment, let's consider the case of Alex Oppenheimer of East 139 Street, another great collar I made while protecting life and property in The South Bronx. In 1969, shortly after Serpico became a household word, the NYPD was very interested in showing gambling arrests, particularly by the uniformed force. Consequently, the department, which routinely gave an officer a day off for a good arrest, typically a felony, offered up to three days off for a gambling arrest. I never understood why, but when the choice was between a few days in The Hamptons, on Long Island, or in Fort Apache, I didn't have to be told twice. Serpico's allegations of corruption in the enforcement of the gambling laws almost brought the department to its knees. By the time I hit The South Bronx, and started going to court in 1968 and 1969, Serpico was testifying against his former partners at their trials for bribery and perjury.

---

[57]*U.S. v. McKinnon*, 985 F.2d 525 (11th Cir. 1993).

But for Serpico, I probably never would have devoted any time to Alex Oppenheimer. We were far too busy but it did make for an interesting diversion. Alex was running a Three-Card Monte game in front of 536 East 139 Street. He had two red Kings and a black Ace, on an inverted checkerboard, atop some fruit crates. Passers-by would bet on finding the Ace, after our slight of hand con man moved the overturned cards around rather quickly. Each time I drove down the street, however fast, everybody scattered and there was never a sign of Alex or the gaming device. So the plan was developed. I had my partner drop me off around the corner, on Brook Avenue. (I'm told that many years before a brook flowed there; by the late 1960s the only things flowing there were heroin addicts.) I climbed six flights of stairs, side stepping the urine and stray dogs,[58] and then walked across the roof to the 139 Street side. While there were different addresses all along the block, the entire square block was a group of connected buildings, each one pressing up to the next one,[59] and every seven or eight windows another stoop came out, with its own entranceway and a different address. Looking down I saw Alex working the crowd. He was in rare form. I radioed my partner and the game began. He drove down the block very slowly. Alex had plenty of time to pocket the money, hide the gambling paraphernalia under a parked car, and slowly walk into the building's hallway. As our radio car slowly drove around the block, Alex resumed his illegal activities again, but now we were ready for the big bust. The car circled the block and came speeding to a stop in front of 536. My partner saw nothing but a few people sitting on the stoop (a New York term for the thing people drink beer on in the summer). By this time, I was down the six flights and waiting for Alex to enter the hallway. I grabbed him and walked out to the waiting car. He screamed, "You got nuttin' on me," which was the signal for the rocks and bottles to fly. Having about a year in The Bronx now and having been exposed to everything, I tucked my head under his armpit and hustled him to the waiting car, stopping for a second at the curb to scoop up the checkerboard and three cards from under the parked car, where Alex had hid them. My collar turned red and said, "That ain't fair."

Now, I suspect that his attorneys might argue that Alex had a reasonable expectation of privacy in the area under the car. That is where he hid the tools of his trade from the government's eyes, but I think that's a bit dubious.[60] However, that wasn't my main concern in those days. My job was to gather the evidence and let the lawyers fight over it in court. It took awhile for the pronouncements of the marble palace in Washington to reach us. Alex paid his $50 fine, my partner and I each got two days off, and Alex and I waived to each other whenever I passed Brook and 139. I like to think I went into police work to help the people who needed it most, to be like Robin Hood. How did I wind up being the Sheriff of Nottingham Forest instead?

---

[58]As dangerous as it may have been to police The South Bronx, your psyche always suppressed those thoughts. What I could never remove from my mind was my childhood fear of stray dogs and the possibility of slipping on the urine soaked tenement steps and cracking my skull as I tumbled back to the ground floor.

[59]In law school, that was called *the duty to support.*

[60]If the entire neighborhood saw where he hid it, how great was his expectation of privacy? Can he only hide it from us? These rules, besides being frustrating to deal with in the street, or when evaluating a prosecution, can be very interesting to think about, but not when the bottles are flying.

CHAPTER 3

Barry Headricks

THE SIXTH COMMANDMENT

Thou Shalt Not Kill

Should the criminal go free because the constable has blundered?

You're on patrol. The dispatcher gives you a job, *Shots Fired!* As you toss the coffee and head towards the address, you wonder why you took this job (police work, not the call) and run up to the front door. You step to the side[1] and announce your purpose and authority: *Police, Open up!*

Maybe they left and you are off the hook? Good try, but they pay you the big bucks to handle these calls. What can you do? Can you force the door and enter? Is there *probable cause*? Do you need a warrant? Is the person calling 911 reliable? Is this *an exijentzy*? If you go in, what can you do inside? Can you look for the shooter? How about possible victims? What if you see a DOA? Tough questions.

The tragic story of Police Officer Barry Headricks, Tucson, Arizona, Police Department, provides the answers. On October 28, 1974, Officer Headricks was working in an undercover capacity for the Metropolitan Area Narcotics Squad. He had just negotiated to buy a quantity of heroin from a Rufus Mincey. Having left the apartment, ostensibly to get his money, but really to get the rest of the team for the bust, Headricks returned with his *money man*, Det. Schwartz. Eight other members of the squad and the prosecutor (I like a guy who starts preparing his case early) waited nearby, ready to rush in and make the pinch. There was trouble at the door. Soon to be a defendant, Hodgman saw the crowd and tried to close the door. Officer Headricks got in before

---

[1] So the bullets coming through the door pass harmlessly by you. Not that that always helps. Pete Cainas, a Hialeah, Florida, police officer attended college and law school at night for many years. Upon passing the bar exam, he resigned from the department and became a prosecutor in Dade County. After 13 months in court, and wanting to get married, he decided he needed the higher pay of a police officer. He went back to Hialeah. Six weeks later, while standing off to the side at a *loud radio* call, a bullet came through the frame of the apartment's front door at a sharp angle, striking him in the head, killing him instantly.

the door closed behind him. He ran to a rear bedroom. Schwartz and the others forced open the door and put the cuffs on Hodgman, only to hear several shots from the room Headricks entered. Barry Headricks stepped out and fell to the floor, his .38 caliber revolver empty. Hit five times, our dear brother was removed to a nearby hospital but died shortly thereafter. His backup went to the bedroom and found Mincey lying on the floor, barely conscious. Doctors would later remove several .38 caliber projectiles from his body; apparently Barry got a piece of him. Under Mincey's hand were an empty Llama .380 semi-automatic pistol and seven spent casings.

His fellow officers searched the apartment for other victims. An injured woman was found in Mincey's bedroom closet. Three of Mincey's acquaintances were taken into custody in the living room; one had a bullet in his head. It had been fired by Mincey's automatic pistol. The narcotics officers summoned medical assistance for the injured but did no further investigating. Within ten minutes of the ill-fated raid, the Tucson Police Department's homicide detectives arrived and took over the scene. *After* the injured had been removed, the detectives proceeded to gather evidence. The facts, as related in the U.S. Supreme Court opinion in *Mincey v. Arizona*, 437 U.S. 385 (1978),[2] were:

> Their search lasted four days, during which period the entire apartment was searched, photographed, and diagrammed. The officers opened drawers, closets, and cupboards, and inspected their contents; they emptied clothing pockets; they dug bullet fragments out of the walls and floors; they pulled up sections of the carpet and removed them for examination. Every item in the apartment was closely examined and inventoried, and 200 to 300 objects were seized. In short, Mincey's apartment was subjected to an exhaustive and intrusive search. No warrant was ever obtained.

Remember your police academy training and what they teach lawyers in law school: Deal with the emergency—but once it's over, return to the regular rules.

Can the back-up narcotics officers force their way in as part of the emergency?

_____

_____

_____

_____

How about when they hear shooting?

_____

_____

_____

_____

---

[2]The case can be found in Appendix A.

It goes without saying that the backup narcotics officers had every right to go into the apartment to help their fellow officer, even before the shooting began; even more so afterward. Finding the wounded woman in the closet and assisting the man on the living room floor may have saved their lives. Searching other rooms for the three acquaintances possibly prevented more bloodshed. But *after* this occurred, and the emergency was over, shouldn't we return to the regular rules?

The Arizona courts, relying upon several previous decisions of the Arizona Supreme Court, held the extended search to be valid, as Mincey, having shot the officer had *forfeited* any reasonable expectation of privacy in his apartment. They also accepted the intrusion as an emergency situation demanding immediate action. It was held that investigating a homicide while it was fresh satisfied a *vital public interest*. It held that a warrantless search of a crime scene was an exception to the warrant requirement of the Fourth Amendment.

Questions:

Does that seem like a reasonable position to take?

_____

_____

_____

_____

Shouldn't the homicide investigation, especially of a police officer, start as soon as possible?

_____

_____

_____

On the other hand, is there any good reason why the crime scene technicians couldn't wait a few hours to take their photos and pick up the firearms evidence?

_____

_____

_____

_____

By the time the case reached the U.S. Supreme Court, known as *The Supremes* in some circles, the right of the police to respond to emergency situations was well settled. There is nothing new about police officers rushing into buildings to aid injured people. Can you imagine a fire truck stopping at the courthouse and waiting for a search warrant to be prepared before entering a house or apartment to put out a fire? The law also permitted police officers coming upon a homicide scene to make a prompt warrantless search of the area to see if there were other victims or if the killer was still on the premises. The need to protect or preserve life or avoid serious injury is justification for what would be otherwise illegal, absent an exigency or emergency. The police may seize any evidence that is in plain view during the course of their legitimate emergency activities. (This *was* the law, nothing new here.)

What they are telling us is that you *can* deal with the emergencies that cannot wait. What if Mincey was still holding his gun? Should we wait for him to shoot another cop? Headricks, and the other injured people, need medical treatment *now*, not hours later. That is what the Supremes are telling us. There was nothing wrong with what *the narcotics officers* did.

However, the Court disagreed with what *the homicide investigators* had done.

The Fourth Amendment proscribes all unreasonable searches and seizures, and it is a cardinal principle that 'searches conducted outside the judicial process, without prior approval by judge or magistrate, are *per se* unreasonable under the Fourth Amendment—subject only to a few specifically established and well-delineated exceptions.'   Citing to *Katz v. U.S.*

Then they went on to tell us what *was allowed* to be done without a search warrant.

A warrantless search must be 'strictly circumscribed by the exigencies which justify its initiation. . . .' (How's that for a mouthful. What they mean is that if your entry is only permitted due to the emergency; dealing with that emergency *defines and limits* your activities.) . . . and it simply cannot be contended that this search (by the homicide investigators) was justified by any emergency threatening life or limb. All the persons in Mincey's apartment had been located before the investigating homicide officers arrived there and began their search. And a four-day search that included opening dresser drawers and ripping up carpets can hardly be rationalized in terms of the legitimate concerns that justify an emergency search.

This is how the court dealt with the position of the State of Arizona:

The mere fact that law enforcement may be made more efficient can never by itself justify disregard of the Fourth Amendment. The investigation of crime would always be simplified if warrants were unnecessary. But the Fourth Amendment reflects the view of those who wrote the Bill of Rights that the privacy of a person's home and property may not be totally sacrificed in the name of maximum simplicity in enforcement of the criminal law. For this reason warrants are generally required to search a person's

home or his person unless *the exigencies of the situation* make the needs of
law enforcement so compelling that the warrantless search is objectively
reasonable under the Fourth Amendment. Except for the fact that the
offense under investigation was a homicide, there were no exigent
circumstances in this case. . . . There was no indication that evidence
would be lost, destroyed, or removed during the time required to obtain a
search warrant. Indeed, the police guard at the apartment minimized that
possibility. And there is no suggestion that a search warrant could not
easily and conveniently have been obtained. We decline to hold that the
seriousness of the offense under investigation itself creates exigent
circumstances of the kind that under the Fourth Amendment justify a
warrantless search.

What did they say? Once the injured are in the hospital, and the shooter is ren-
dered harmless, what's the rush? Why can't you wait and tell a judge why you want
to enter. Give *him* a good reason and he will permit it.

It must be remembered that the Fourth Amendment only prohibits *unreasonable*
searches and seizures, not all intrusions. The reasons here for entering Mincey's
apartment seem reasonable. So what's the problem?

The *Mincey* court did not say the homicide investigators didn't have a good reason for searching the house. What they said was that the search should have been
done under court supervision. In Chapter Two, "Roots," we learned that one of the
reasons for the American Revolution was British soldiers searching our homes upon
the order of some government official.

Question:

**If we didn't want the British officials to enter our homes, why should we
want American, or state, or city, or county officials to enter and search?**

_____

_____

_____

_____

We also learned in Chapter Two that there are many exceptions to the warrant
requirement; however, only when the officers may be in danger, or there is a chance
that any evidence on or near the person to be arrested may be lost or damaged, can
we conduct *immediate, limited* searches. If you are not in danger, and the evidence is
safe, take your time and follow the rules.

Having a judge, who is not part of the law enforcement team, review an officer's request makes it easier to swallow. The judge is impartial and has to presume
the people you arrest are innocent when brought before him for trial. If you have
probable cause, you should get a warrant. Remember, judges too have to follow the

law. If your "competitive enterprise of ferreting out crime" (to quote from another Supreme Court case) has clouded your judgment, and you do not have probable cause, the warrant will not be issued. Either way, you have nothing to lose. By the way, now that you are in the business, we call it *PC*. *PC* does not mean *politically correct*; all it does is get your bad guy into the rear of the police car. If you really want to slow down his criminal activities and have the DA file a winnable case, you need something known as *beyond and to the exclusion of every reasonable doubt*. Sometimes that doesn't even do it.

So, what's the bottom line? Where can you look for shooters and victims? Any place they can be. Where can't you look? Any place they can't. Webster's dictionary defines exigent as "requiring immediate aid or action." Now that we know what you can do—what can't you do at the crime scene? Anything that doesn't act to neutralize the emergency. Once the shooters and victims are located and dealt with—get out and apply the regular rules. Once it becomes clear that the Minceys of the world are unwilling or unable to give consent—pull back, secure the scene, and start preparing your search warrant affidavit. Can you mention the things you saw while on the premises? Only those observed during your emergency activities. Tell the judge about the overturned furniture, blood on the floor, injuries observed, and weapons seen. Give the magistrate[3] enough facts to allow him/her to find *probable cause* to believe that a crime occurred and that you have to do a full crime scene examination to investigate it and gather the evidence therein.

What do you do with the evidence that won't be there several hours later when the warrant arrives? Well, that too is an *exijentzy* and may be dealt with before you lose it. We had to deal with such a situation in Chapter Six. Have the medical examiner (ME) or some member of the team who isn't too squeamish check the victim for *body heat*, or its absence; *liver mortis* (the settling and darkening of blood still in the body), and the beginnings or absence of *rigor mortis* (stiffening of the muscles). Hours later, when that evidence is gone, determining time of death will be much more difficult.

WHAT HAVE WE LEARNED FROM BARRY HEADRICKS' TERRIBLE SACRIFICE?

a. His killer's Fourth Amendment rights against unreasonable searches and seizures were violated.
b. Once the emergency is over, there is no authority for the police to search in a protected area.
c. Get a search warrant.
d. The rule applying the Fourth Amendment to dope dealers' apartments where police officers have just been killed is known as *Mincey v. Arizona*; don't tell us you weren't familiar with that rule of law. The case *did* come down in 1978.

---

[3]In case you are confused, the terms *magistrate* and *judge*, are almost interchangeable. A magistrate is a judge, handling the preliminary steps of the criminal prosecution. They hear applications for arrest and search warrants, conduct *first appearance* and bond hearings, arraignments, and any other matters the trial judge wants to assign them. In earlier days, they were called justices of the peace and police justices. He's the guy you see in Night Court.

Because of the ruling, much of the evidence needed to prosecute Mincey was suppressed. That is to say the prosecution could not use it in court.

Why? To teach the police officers not to violate the Fourth Amendment of the Constitution. *That* is the supreme law of the land. All Mincey was charged with was violating a mere criminal statute!!!

Punishing police who violate the constitutional rights of defendants, or suing them, once thought to be sufficient to get them to comply with the law, failed to do the trick. The remedy of suppression, or exclusion, was then thought to be the sanction that would be understood best. Seize evidence illegally and it can't be used. Eventually, police officers will learn to follow the rules. Should a bad guy walk because the cops make a mistake?

Should the criminal go free because the constable has blundered?

Good question. Benjamin Cardozo, the great judge of the New York Court of Appeals, asked that very question in 1926. Later to be appointed to the U.S. Supreme Court, he was faced with that decision while still on the New York court. His view was that society suffers when a bad guy *walks* because a police officer made a mistake. He said punish the policeman, not the entire community.

What do you think? Are there any alternatives that might work?

_____

_____

_____

_____

Judge Cardozo refused to adopt the exclusionary rule for the courts of New York.[4] He felt that such a rule harmed society, and that if it should be the law, the legislature, the true representative of the people, should adopt it.

These were his words:

We are (convinced) when we (realize) how far-reaching in its effect upon society the new consequences would be. The pettiest peace officer would have it in his power through overzeal or indiscretion to confer immunity upon an offender for crimes the most flagitious. A room is searched against the law, and the body of a murdered man is found. . . . *The privacy of the home has been infringed, and the murderer goes free.*[5] Another search, once more against the law, discloses counterfeit money or the implements of forgery. The absence of a warrant means the freedom of the forger. Like instances can be multiplied. We may not subject society to these dangers until the Legislature has spoken with a clearer voice. . . . There (is) no blinking (at) the consequences. The criminal is to go free because the constable has blundered.[6]

---

[4]He agreed with the 31 other state courts that also declined to adopt it.

[5]How did he know *Mincey* would be with us 50 years later?

[6]*People v. Defore*, 242 N.Y. 13 (1926).

In 1961, the U.S. Supreme Court, in *Mapp v. Ohio*, disagreed and made the exclusionary rule the law of the land.

When next in Phoenix, Arizona, I suggest a visit to the state capitol grounds. Amidst the monuments to the 1,100 sailors who went down on the *USS Arizona*, and her honored war dead from Korea and Vietnam, sits Arizona's Peace Officers' Memorial. Listed there on a wall, among the approximate 200 fallen police officers, deputy sheriffs, town marshals, Bureau of Indian Affairs agents, border patrolmen, and other federal and state law enforcement officers, is the name of Barry Headricks. Above the wall kneels an old-time town marshal, grieving for his brother officers who fell in battle in the war against the forces of evil.

Attached at the end of this book is a *Mincey* search warrant, which I prepared for Det. Dean Surman of the Metro Dade Police Department Homicide Bureau. It was the only way to remove the body of the late Edward Singleton from his home for transport to the Dade County Medical Examiner's Department for his *post mortem examination*. As you can see from the affidavit, Mr. Singleton fell in love one evening at the local tavern and brought his beloved home for a few days. That short tenure may have given her Fourth Amendment standing in his apartment. As she was gone and he was unable to give consent (we asked!!), we had to ask the magistrate to let us in. Some may argue that she abandoned the love nest or Edward revoked his consent for her to remain as she was plunging the knife into his chest. You may be right, but remember the sign in the Homicide office that says:

No crime will be solved before its time . . . and a half.

Take your time and do it right, and don't take chances. Those who speak for the dead have a solemn obligation. That sign is right next to another one nobody pays much attention to. It's in Gothic lettering and says:

Thou Shalt Not Kill

Did Mincey walk? The saga took over ten years. On November 26, 1984, the same U.S. Supreme Court, which overturned his first conviction, chose not to review his *third* murder conviction. Mincey occasionally files post-trial motions, but he's had his moment of fame. Now he's just another cop killer doing life. In his second trial, at the Motion to Suppress ordered by the U.S. Supremes, everything was suppressed that was not in plain view during the suspect-victim search. However a Det. Reyna, who got there moments after the shooting, and stood guard over the fallen officer, was allowed to testify to everything he saw in the room. His actions were found to be a part of the exigencies of the day.

You will remember, the shooting occurred on October 28, 1974. Mincey's lease expired at *the end of October.* Guess who rented the apartment on November first? You're right; it was the Pima County DA's Office. Now that they lawfully had possession, measurements were taken. Based upon those and everything Det. Reyna saw, (in plain view, when he was lawfully present in the apartment) a model was built. From the bullet holes in the walls (remember, the projectiles were themselves suppressed) trajectories were laid out, and the entire scene was re-created. All of this physical evidence was admitted at trial and affirmed on appeal by the Supreme Court of Arizona. Problem was the trial judge gave an improper Homicide instruction to the jury, *that Mincey's lawyer never objected to,*[7] and the Arizona Supremes affirmed everything *but* the murder conviction! The attempted murder (remember the man shot in the head by the automatic?) and the narcotics charges were upheld. The third trial was in May of 1982 and Rufus was convicted again. The Public Defender must have had his whole staff on the case. The second appeal raised fifteen issues and the third one raised eleven. After the Arizona Supreme Court went through them one by one, for 40 pages, it held:

> In addition to examining the issues raised by the appellant, we have searched the entire record for additional error. We have found none. The judgment and sentence are affirmed.

That's when the U.S. Supremes decided Mincey had his day(s) in court. They denied his petition for review. Finally, Barry can rest in peace. Being supreme means you don't have to hear every case presented. They pick and choose their cases. Too bad you can't.

Questions:

Did the *narcotics* officers violate Mincey's rights when they forced their way into his apartment, without permission or a warrant?

_____

_____

_____

_____

_____

Confused? What authority was there for the subsequent police entry? There are several theories. One is the implied permission to return (to complete the dope deal).

> An officer who enters a defendant's premises lawfully and who temporarily leaves the premises solely for the purpose of obtaining the funds to consummate a transaction has an implied invitation to return without the necessity of knocking and announcing his identity and purpose. The fact that he enlists the aid of other officers does no injustice to

---

[7]There is a procedural rule of evidence that requires lawyers to object at the time something is done, to preserve it for appeal. There are two reasons for that rule. The court might *correct the condition* before moving on, and the objection prevents the lawyer from strategically using what has happened to his benefit, and then arguing against it on appeal.

the statute or the constitution. It neither adds to, nor detracts from, the reasonableness of the reentry. *State v. Steffani*, 398 So.2d 475 (Fla. 3rd DCA 1981), *approved*, 419 So.2d.2d 323 (Fla. 1982).

How about the *exigency* we have been talking about? In *U.S. v. Harris*,[8] the U.S. Court of Appeals held:

> We do not believe that either the knock and announce statute or the fourth amendment were violated by the warrantless re-entry, because exigent circumstances were present to justify the failure to announce the agents' official capacity and to secure a search warrant. The possibility that the cocaine would be destroyed was significant . . . . Although the bedroom did not have a private bath, there was a bathroom on the first floor of the townhouse that was easily accessible to the conspirators. The cocaine could have been destroyed before the agents re-entered the house.

We also find support in *U.S. v. Tolliver*,[9] in which the undercover agent who posed as *the banker* left to retrieve the purchase money and later re-entered with other agents to effect the arrests. The danger that the evidence would be destroyed excused both the noncompliance with the statute (knock and announce) and the failure to secure a warrant. This is also known as *the continuing ruse* rule.

Why were the homicide detectives criticized by the court? A police officer was killed, isn't that important enough?

_____

_____

What is the rule of *Mincey v. Arizona*?

_____

_____

_____

_____

Does it only apply to homicide cases? Where else might it apply?

_____

_____

_____

_____

---

[8]713 F.2d 623 (11th Cir. 1982).
[9]665 F.2d 1005 (11th Cir.). *cert denied*, 456 U.S. 935 (1982).

What if Mincey's girlfriend lived there with him. Could she give the officers permission to enter that apartment and search?

_____

_____

_____

_____

Could she give permission to the police to search his suitcase in the closet? What if it were locked?

_____

_____

_____

_____

What if she had some clothes in the suitcase?

_____

_____

_____

_____

What if she gave permission, but Mincey objected?

_____

_____

_____

_____

Notes:

_____

_____

_____

_____

_____

_____

Which is more important, presenting the evidence in court or protecting the rights of the criminal?

_____

_____

_____

_____

"We didn't need a search warrant because..."

We got a 911 call; the guy got killed here!

This was a fresh pursuit, so you can go in now.

We asked the manager to evict him.

We have to determine the "cause and origin" of the fire.

We only searched "her" side of the bed.

Discussion:

_____

_____

_____

_____

_____

_____

_____

_____

_____

_____

_____

_____

_____

_____

_____

_____

_____

_____

_____

_____

_____

_____

CHAPTER 4

Fire

THE BRAVEST

Most of the jurisdictions in the English-speaking world (except Louisiana)[1] use the common law system. That simply means judges rely upon previous cases as authority to decide current ones. This way similar fact cases get decided in the same way. Whatever the law was yesterday, we assume will be the law tomorrow. It is *common* throughout the realm.[2] Nevertheless, I have known some judges who could wipe out a thousand years of law with the stroke of a pen.

Mincey relied in part upon a case decided twenty-two days before, *Michigan v. Tyler*, 436 U.S. 499 (1978).[3] The facts in *Tyler* showed that two men, Loren Tyler and Robert Thompkins, ran a retail furniture store in Oakland County, Michigan. Apparently, the insurance value was much higher than future business prospects. A fire broke out shortly before midnight on January 21, 1970. The fire department responded and by 2 a.m., when the chief arrived (typical of the bosses, to get there late), was "just watering down smoldering embers." The chief who was there to determine *cause and origin* was met by a fire lieutenant, who informed him that two plastic containers with flammable liquids had been found in the building. The chief "concluded that the fire could possibly have been arson" (that's why he's a chief!) and called Det. Webb of the state police. Webb tried to take photos of the interior of the building, but "finally abandoned his efforts because of the smoke and steam." Chief See continued looking about for more evidence, but by 4 a.m. he and the others left as the "fire had been extinguished."

---

[1]Anyone know why? Their history is the French system, rather than English common law.

[2]According to *Black's Law Dictionary, the common law* is the system of laws originated and developed in England and based on court decisions, on the legal theories explaining those decisions and on usages and customs of immemorial antiquity, rather than on the codified statutes enacted by legislatures. The common law of England on July 4, 1776 became the law in the United States, except as modified by the Constitution of the United States, of any state, or later statutes or court decisions.

[3]This case too, is in Appendix A.

Hopefully the issue before us is apparent. Is the fire out? Is the emergency over? If so, let's get out. Well, it gets somewhat complicated now. At 8 a.m., Chief See, and Asst. Chief Somerville, who is charged with determining "the origin of all fires that occur within the Township," return. It is conceded that by this time the fire was out and all fire personnel had left the building.

By 9 a.m., Det. Webb joined the investigating party and discovered "burn marks in the carpet which he could not see earlier that morning, because of the 'heat, steam, and the darkness.'" They left the building *again*, this time to obtain tools, and re-entered and proceeded to remove sections of the carpet and stairs to use as evidence. As in Mincey's apartment, there was no consent or a search warrant.

Just to make the DA's job a bit more interesting, Webb's boss, a Sergeant Hoffman, of the Michigan State Police, Arson Section, entered *again*, without paper, on January 28th, 29th, and February 16th. He took photos, checked circuit breakers, inspected the furnace, and found remnants of a fire. All items seen or removed, or opinions formed from them, were used at trial, where our two furniture magnates were convicted of arson and insurance fraud.

Based upon what we learned from the yet-to-be-decided case of *Mincey v. Arizona*, once the emergency was over, Chief See and company had no legal right to remain or re-enter the building, right? Well, the DA's first argument was that Tyler had abandoned the building by setting it on fire. Sounds good, but how can we use illegally seized evidence to prove an arson and use the arson to prove abandonment? Nice try, though!

Those of us in this business for some time know that cops and firemen are cut from the same cloth and many times come from the same families. This common heritage was recognized by the court in holding that both cops and firemen (now called *firefighters*) must obey the Fourth Amendment. The uniform of the government official conducting the search for the cause of the fire, as opposed to evidence of a crime, is immaterial. Now the genesis of *Mincey*, found in *Tyler* at p. 510:

> Our decisions have recognized that a warrantless entry by criminal law enforcement officials may be legal when there is a *compelling need* for official action and *no time to secure a warrant* (citing cases allowing for *hot pursuit* and to *prevent the imminent destruction of evidence*).

As if there was any doubt, the court, speaking through Justice Stewart said: A burning building clearly presents an exigency of sufficient proportions to render a warrantless entry *reasonable*.

Ok, so the firefighters don't need a warrant to enter a burning building. And once in the building, they may seize evidence of arson in plain view—that covers the two containers—the initial holding of the court seems clear. How about the additional entries to search for and gather evidence? Can they be justified as coming within the scope of the emergency? Let's see—the court went on to say:

> a prompt determination of the fire's origin *may be necessary to* prevent its recurrence as through the detection of *continuing dangers* such as faulty wiring or a defective furnace.

Query: May these problems continue to place people at risk? Can they cause the fire to flare up again? Can smoldering embers under the floorboards cause a resurgence? Is the emergency clearly over just because the last flame was doused?

"*Immediate investigation may be necessary* to preserve evidence from intentional or accidental destruction." Medical examiners *and* firefighters take notice here! Since the Fourth Amendment deals with privacy interests, the court suggested that the sooner the fire officials complete their duties, the sooner Mr. Tyler gets back his burned out building.

What does *Tyler v. Michigan* teach us?

_____

_____

_____

_____

_____

_____

Fire officials need no warrant to *remain* in a building, for a reasonable time, to investigate the cause of a blaze *after* it has been extinguished. That's because the fire *might not be out*. Their presence is not permitted, though, merely to *search for evidence to be used at trial*.

Judges are not firefighters, and all fires are different. In determining what constitutes a reasonable time to investigate *appropriate recognition must be given to the exigencies that confront government officials* serving under these conditions, as well as to an individual's reasonable expectation of privacy. *What does that mean in English?* Let the experts do their job—just act reasonably and professionally—prevent further property damage and loss of life—and the court will back you up. Hold it! They left at 4 a.m. when the fire was out, why didn't they check the furnaces then? Why is their return four hours later part of the emergency? The court recalled that their "visibility was severely hindered by the darkness, steam and smoke." Remaining in the building four more hours to await daylight would only be a legal fiction to justify their continued presence.

"Not necessary," said Mr. Justice Stewart, "the morning entries were no more than an actual continuation of the first (entries), and the lack of a warrant did not invalidate the resulting seizure of evidence." That means the investigators could use the evidence. There was no illegal search.

Looks like a reasonable position to me. What about Sgt. Hoffman and his three subsequent entries (beginning *seven days* later)? Justice Stewart, found them to be unrelated to, and beyond the scope of, the emergency. The jury will never see what he found.[4]

---

[4]As helpful as this case is to the administration of justice, Justice Potter Stewart is best known for his definition of *hard-core pornography*. "I shall not today attempt to further define the kinds of material I understand to be embraced within that shorthand description; and perhaps I could never succeed in intelligibly doing so. *But I know it when I see it.*" *Jacobellis v. Ohio*, 378 U.S. 184 at page 197 (1964).

What allowed the subsequent re-entry without a warrant?

_____

_____

_____

_____

Tyler was re-visited six years later by the Supremes. In that later case, *Michigan v. Clifford*,[5] an arson investigator entered a fire-damaged home in Detroit, Michigan, six hours *after* the firefighters extinguished the fire and left the scene. There was no question of an exigency as there had been in *Tyler*. Needless to say, the investigators found ample evidence of arson. In the basement were empty fuel cans and a crock pot wired to a timer, set to go off shortly before the fire was discovered. Further evidence of criminal intent was found in other areas of the home:

> After determining that the fire had originated in the basement, Lieutenant Beyer and his partner searched the remainder of the house. The warrantless search that followed was extensive and thorough. The investigators called in a photographer to take pictures throughout the house. They searched through drawers and closets and found them full of old clothes. They inspected the rooms and noted that there were nails on the walls but no pictures. They found wiring and cassettes for a video tape machine but no machine.   *Clifford*, at p. 291.

The soon-to-be defendants, Raymond and Emma Jean Clifford, were out of town on a camping trip when the fire was discovered. They called their insurance company when a neighbor notified them of the fire and asked that the house be boarded up against intruders (sounds like the Cliffords *did not want anyone entering their home*). The fire was confined to the basement, and although the upper floors had smoke damage, they were not fire damaged. The court found that the defendants retained a reasonable expectation of privacy in those upper areas, as well as in the basement.

A divided court reaffirmed *Tyler* and required a search warrant when later entries are made to gather evidence for a criminal prosecution. The court applied the rule of *Katz* (see Chapter Two) to determine when a homeowner loses his privacy interests in the damaged house:

> We observed in *Tyler* that reasonable privacy expectations may remain in fire-damaged premises. "People may go on living in their homes or working in their offices after a fire. Even when that is impossible, private effects often remain on the fire-damaged premises." *Tyler*, 436 U.S., at 505. Privacy expectations will vary with the type of property, the amount of fire damage, the prior and continued use of the premises, and in some cases the owner's efforts to secure it against intruders. Some fires may be

---

[5]464 U.S. 287 (1984).

so devastating that no reasonable privacy interests remain in the ash and ruins, regardless of the owner's subjective expectations. The test essentially is an objective one: whether "the expectation [is] one that society is prepared to recognize as 'reasonable.' " *Katz v. United States*, 389 U.S. 347 (1967). See also *Smith v. Maryland*, 442 U.S. 735, 739–741 (1979). If reasonable privacy interests remain in the fire-damaged property, the (search) warrant requirement applies, and any official entry must be made pursuant to a warrant in the absence of consent or exigent circumstances.

Clifford, at pp. 292–93.

When the original firefighters were in the basement performing their lawful duties, they came across an empty fuel can. They later brought it up to the driveway and Lt. Beyer saw it when he arrived. Realizing the firefighters believed this fire to be arson, Beyer waited until the work crew finished pumping the water out of the basement and then:

> Beyer and his partner, without obtaining consent or a warrant, entered the Clifford residence and began their investigation into the cause of the fire. Their search began in the basement and they quickly confirmed that the fire had originated there beneath the basement stairway. They detected a strong odor of fuel throughout the basement, and found two more Coleman fuel cans beneath the stairway. As they dug through the debris, the investigators also found (the) crock pot with attached wires leading to an electrical timer. . . . All of this evidence was seized and marked. After determining that the fire had originated in the basement, Lieutenant Beyer and his partner searched the remainder of the house.

The ruling of *Tyler* remains. What we should take from these cases are the words of Justice Powell:

> A burning building of course creates an exigency that justifies a warrantless entry by fire officials to fight the blaze. Moreover, in *Tyler* we held that once in the building, officials need no warrant to *remain* for "a reasonable time to investigate the cause of the blaze after it has been extinguished." 436 U.S., at 510. Where, however, reasonable expectations of privacy remain in the fire-damaged property, additional investigations begun after the fire has been extinguished and fire and police officials have left the scene, generally must be made pursuant to a warrant or the identification of some new exigency.   *Clifford*, at 292.

There was a four-justice dissent. They felt there was no difference between the six hours in this case and the five-hour delay in *Tyler*, but we can see it. *Here the fire was out*. The scene in *Tyler* was too smoky and dark to tell. In any event, the first thing they teach you in law school is simple math: five is more than four!!

So when the fire investigators tell you they can enter to "determine the cause and origin of the fire," you remind them that you have to "protect life and property" but the constitution comes first. Then help them with a search warrant and put in everything the firefighters saw that made them suspicious.

Another fire, this one at 534 East 148 Street in The Bronx, wasn't as well known as Tyler's, but it almost pre-empted this book years before it was ever contemplated. Seems your author was walking a foot post on Brook Avenue again (having spent my first six months in the precinct there) and noticed smoke coming from some windows on the third floor of a tenement building. Being young, healthy, inexperienced, and rather foolish, he ran up to the roof (yes, they all had six floors), hopped over the side and went down the fire escape. Upon entering the smoke-filled apartment, he realized the error of his ways. Before his eyes closed-up, he checked the two bedrooms for sleeping occupants or children hiding under beds or in closets or bathrooms. Finally, not being able to breathe, he searched for the front door. Sliding along the walls finally brought him to your typical ghetto door; a fox lock going down to the floor and six Schlage locks above the doorknob. Not being able to open it, the young fool ran back to the window for a breath of air. Now ready to continue the search (without a warrant!) he again charged foolishly ahead. It didn't take long for this young policeman to try for the front door again. Opening the locks was impossible, mainly because two of them were deadbolts that had been locked with keys from the outside. (It's amazing how easy the junkies got into these places from the outside). By this time the apartment was so full of smoke, finding those open windows was impossible. Contemplating what his mother would say at the funeral, he worked his way back to the front door, one more time. A huge axe broke open the door and the two most beautiful firemen ever seen pulled him and a smoldering mattress into the hallway.

As he was gasping for air on the rear step of Ladder #29, a grizzly old battalion chief came up and started yelling at him. He had been in The South Bronx longer than the Ole Sarge. He said "Kid (seems everyone called me that), your job is down here keeping the dirtbags offa my apparatus" (it took me a while to learn that's what they called fire trucks). Many years later in the courtrooms of Dade County, our narcotics detectives would testify mysteriously of "aparatos" they had heard the Colombian dopers, known as the *Cocaine Cowboys*, offering for sale. The chief then added, "You stay outa dem buildins, you'll jes' get hurt." My mother also said that a lot.

From that day on, whenever I saw or heard of a fire, I dutifully called in the location, directed traffic as the "apparatus" arrived, kept everyone away from the trucks, and wondered how else I could get killed in The South Bronx.

I thought I learned my lesson, but some time later, when I was in a radio car doing a late tour,[6] My partner and I again saw smoke coming from some windows, this time on Willis Avenue. Having learned something from the previous experience, I gave CB the address, requested *Fire*, but ran in anyway. It was 5 a.m. and I feared most people would be asleep. I started banging on the apartment doors with my nightstick, yelling "Fire, leave the building." Most people came out, except the

---

[6]They're called late tours, because they start real late. They begin at 12 midnight and last till 8 a.m.

dopers; they thought it was the guys from Narco with a new trick. The firemen arrived moments later (I never saw a fire *lady* in The Bronx) and ran up the steps past me. Of course I didn't know why. Then I heard the crash of glass from above. Yes, this dummy looked up towards the sound and got a face full of broken glass from the recently smashed skylight. That's how the building was ventilated to get the heat and smoke out. The firemen near me all lowered their heads and the pieces of glass bounced harmlessly off their hard hats covering their heads and necks.

Once again the battalion chief's words came home to roost. "Get killed somewhere else Kid, not at my fire." I chose not to stick around to determine the *cause and origin* (probably some junkies keeping warm in a vacant apartment). It was only a quick ride to the all-night Greek diner on Bruckner Boulevard for some scrambled eggs and wheat toast. That's what I ate three times a day when doing *late ones*. I then called in a *10–18* to CB.

Engine Company #82 was known as the busiest firehouse in the world. It was located around the corner from the 41 Precinct, affectionately called *Fort Apache* by the shell-shocked cops who worked there. The firehouse would get about thirty calls during the 6 p.m. to 9 a.m. shift. The breakdown was about equal amounts of mattresses/abandoned cars on fire, false alarms, and *All Hands*. As the name implies, all hands remained to handle the job with usually four pieces of apparatus (apparati?) and the battalion chief in his little red car. In between jobs, they cleaned the trucks, watched TV, played basketball in the rear yard, or slept, although not for long. In the two years I walked foot posts, I usually invited myself in for dinner on the 4x12s. For a buck and a half, I got some sort of stew with veggies or spaghetti; great winter meals.

The food was good but most times I ate alone. The fire bells always seemed to ring as we sat down to eat. So long as the fire wasn't on my post, or close enough where I could help, I continued eating; they had to go. I had great respect for these guys. No matter what trouble I got myself into with a bad guy, I could always try to talk my way out. There was no talking to a fire.

A few months before I joined the department, an *All Hands* was sounded for a fire in a drug store on East 23rd Street, near City College in Manhattan. The building had been renovated many times over the years and had been connected to adjoining buildings. The fire companies were unaware of a hidden cellar, which was totally engulfed by fire. As the first floor landing caved in, twelve firefighters fell into the inferno below. They never had a chance. Then, just after I joined the State Attorney's Office, six firefighters trying to ventilate the roof of a burning Waldbaum's Supermarket in Brooklyn fell into the heart of the fire as the heated roof collapsed beneath them. Boston had a similar tragedy in 1972. There is a beautiful monument on Commonwealth Avenue honoring the nine firefighters, including two lieutenants, who died when the Hotel Vendome collapsed on them. The cops may be called *The Finest*, but we knew the firefighters were *The Bravest*. Give me a bad guy any day.

On September 11, 2001, the second *Day of Infamy* in America's history, the horrific attacks upon the World Trade Center buildings and the Pentagon occurred. In New York City, 343 firefighters were either missing and presumed dead, or their battered bodies were pulled from beneath the rubble; some were never found. Their deaths occurred in every rank up to the chief of the department, including the department chaplain. He was killed while administering last rites to a firefighter struck by a terrified person jumping from the upper floors. The bagpipers played at countless funerals for days on end. Within a week, the commissioner had to make over 170 promotions to keep the department functioning. The new *Twin Towers* of New York City became the cops and firemen who searched for victims around the clock. Stories abounded from survivors who told how these heroes ran up the steps while everyone else ran down, and how they refused to leave when the buildings began trembling, insisting on helping the elderly and infirm down scores of flights until the final collapse. Many of them had just gotten off-duty, after working all night. With no room for them on the *apparatus*, they jumped into their private vehicles and drove to their deaths. They went from being *The Bravest* to instant American gods. If everyone loved a fireman before this day, then how should we describe our emotions now?

Nor can we forget the sixty cops, twenty-three NYPD, and thirty-seven Port Authority, who also died that day. Who else runs into buildings when everyone else runs out?

God Bless Them All.

CHAPTER 5

The Rest of It

WHO'S BEHIND THE STEREO?

In order to fully understand *Mincey*, we must read two other cases that went before the Supremes, in which they told us exactly what they meant in *Mincey*.

The violation of Mincey's rights[1] spanned four days, a sufficient distinction for some sheriff's deputies in Jefferson Parish, Louisiana. They had responded to an emergency situation at the home of a Lillian Thompson, on May 18, 1982. Seems Mrs. Thompson had dispatched Mr. Thompson to the great hereafter with the family semi-automatic, and then, not wanting to face the music, took all of her sleeping pills. However, before she went under, she changed her mind (that's still allowed in America) and called her daughter asking for help. The daughter called the police and that's how we got involved in this *Domestic*.

The deputies rushed over and the daughter admitted them. Thirty-five minutes *after* an unconscious Lillian was taken to the hospital, two homicide detectives arrived with everything except the knowledge of *Mincey*.

Now by this time it was conceded that Mr. T was beyond help and Mrs. T *was* being helped at the hospital. There was nothing these detectives could do for either one to neutralize the emergency, or was there?

Possibly aware of the four-day search condemned in *Mincey*, the detectives only spent *two hours* searching for evidence. Found was the .25 caliber pistol, that ended the marriage. It was *inside* a chest of drawers in the husband's bedroom. Also recovered was a torn-up note found in a wastebasket in an adjacent bathroom and a letter (alleged to be a suicide note) folded up *inside* a Christmas card on top of a chest of drawers in *the (separate) bedroom from which defendant had been removed.*[2] The detectives entered that room, as a red Christmas card in May, lying in the open, was just too much temptation. They *opened it* and saw a four-page suicide note inside. Similar

---

[1]Do cop-killing dope dealers have rights? *The right of the people to be secure in their . . . houses . . . against unreasonable searches and seizures, shall not be violated. . . .* The Fourth Amendment to the U.S. Constitution apparently includes them as well.

[2]A good sign that there is trouble in Paradise.

to the search of Mincey's apartment, no one consented to the search nor was a warrant ever obtained.

The Supreme Court of Louisiana, in reviewing Mrs. Thompson's conviction for second degree murder noted that

> The homicide investigators entered the residence and began *a general exploratory search for evidence of a crime.*   State v. Thompson (1984)

Even though the defendant convinced the trial judge that the gun and the suicide note were illegally seized, and should be kept out of evidence, the other *torn up note . . . found in the wastepaper basket* was admitted.

Despite the good faith of the detectives, their search could be justified with a little common sense. Remember, Mrs. T took a drug overdose. Wouldn't it be within the scope of that exigency to determine *what* pills she took and get that information to the emergency room? Wouldn't it be within the purview of saving her life to open all drawers, envelopes, and closets to look for empty pill containers or evidence of who her doctor was or *what* he had prescribed for her? We are only looking for *reasonable* conduct here; we are not building rocket ships!

What daughter wouldn't allow the police to search for the empty pillbox to save Mom's life? And what detective, worth his salt, wouldn't ask? Remember, the scope of a search is only limited by the exigencies presented and your imagination in dealing with them.

What did the Supreme Court of Louisiana have to say about this? Despite what we now believe the law to be, the state won the appeal. Three of its five justices determined that a two-hour, same-day search conducted at the Thompson residence was far less aggravated than the four-day intensive investigation that was the subject of the *Mincey* opinion.

Not only did they uphold her conviction; they reversed the trial judge, holding *he should have* admitted the gun and the other note! They found *Mincey* not to apply.

> There is a clear basis for distinguishing the relatively brief search of *the murder victim's own home* from an extended four-day search of premises occupied by someone other than the murder victim.   *Justice Lemmon, concurring.*[3]

Then they found that Mr. Thompson *would have consented if he could!*

The *Mincey* case, however, involved a victim killed on another's property. The policeman killed had no privacy interest in the apartment that was searched. In the case before us, the victim was killed in his own home. While the policeman shot in *Mincey* could not have consented to the search of the apartment he was shot in, as he had no authority over that

---

[3]Their distinction being this wasn't the officer who was killed in Mincey's apartment, but Mr. T, who did live where he was killed. What they overlooked was that Mrs. T also lived there.

apartment, Mr. Thompson had authority over the premises wherein he was killed and, *had he survived* until the police arrived, *could have consented* to their search even over the protests of the defendant. [See *Georgia v. Randolph*, in Chapter Two, on consent searches for joint premises, for the current state of the law.]

The Attorney General of Louisiana argued, in a fall back position, that the daughter's granting of permission for the detectives to enter her parents' home somehow justified the search as a consensual one. Nice try, but our honest (but somewhat behind in their reading) detectives testified that they received no consent.

The ruling of the Louisiana court was slam dunked by a unanimous U.S. Supreme Court.

Although we agree that the scope of the intrusion (*that's the search*) was greater in *Mincey* than here, nothing in *Mincey* turned on the length of time taken in the search or the date on which it was conducted. A 2-hour general search remains a significant intrusion on (defendant's) privacy and therefore may only be conducted subject to the constraints—including the warrant requirement—of the Fourth Amendment.   *Thompson v. Louisiana* (1985)[4]

In *Mincey v. Arizona*, we unanimously rejected the contention that one of the exceptions to the Warrant Clause (of the Fourth Amendment) is a 'murder scene exception.' Although we noted that police may make warrantless entries on premises where *they reasonably believe that a person within is in need of immediate aid . . . and that they may make a prompt warrantless search of the area to see if there are other victims or if a killer is still on the premises, . . .* we held that *the murder scene exception . . .* is inconsistent with the Fourth and Fourteenth Amendments[5]—that the warrantless search of Mincey's apartment was not constitutionally permissible simply because a homicide had recently occurred there.

As Chief Justice Dixon noted in his brief dissent to the ruling of the Louisiana Supreme Court, "All it would take to make this search legal is a warrant."

Remember folks, this job isn't hard—it just takes some thinking to do it well. There's a third case to round out the *Mincey* trilogy. It involves another bad guy named James Thomas Hicks.

On April 18, 1984, a man was shot, while sitting *in* his apartment in North Phoenix, Arizona (for those keeping count, that's six years *after* the rule of *Mincey* was announced). The bullet had come through the ceiling from the apartment above.

---

[4]This case is also in Appendix A.

[5]The Fourth Amendment you already know about. The Fourteenth requires the states to treat its citizens with *Due Process*—sometimes called fundamental fairness. The Bill of Rights, adopted in 1791, was intended as a limitation upon the new (distant and unknown) national government, not the states, where everyone knew and trusted their elected leaders. The Fourteenth Amendment, adopted after the Civil War, required the states follow most of the first ten amendments.

The police were called and pursuant to the *exigencies of the situation* were admitted to the apartment above by the building complex manager *to search for the shooter, for other victims, and for weapons*. They found three weapons, including a sawed-off rifle, the usual drug paraphernalia, and a stocking mask, but no occupants.

So far, no problem.

One of the policemen, an Officer Nelson, noticed two sets of "expensive stereo components, which seemed out of place in the *squalid and otherwise ill-appointed four room apartment*." (How would you like your place described like that in the official volumes of the U.S. Supreme Court Reports?)

Officer Nelson, being rather astute, suspected that they might be stolen, and being aware of *Mincey v. Arizona*, looked only for serial numbers that were open to plain view. However, one item, a Bang and Olufsen turntable was against the wall and its serial numbers were not visible. Nelson, not taking four days, or even two hours, moved the turntable just enough to see the numbers (two inches?) and then called them into NCIC and got a hit. As his experience had told him, it was stolen in a robbery by a perp with a sawed-off rifle wearing a stocking mask. The Bang and Olufsen was immediately seized, and a search warrant was obtained for the other components. All then registered hits at NCIC. The search warrant affidavit contained the information obtained by moving the stereo.[6]

Eventually the tenant, Jerome Hicks, was located and indicted for the armed robbery. He filed every defendant's favorite, the motion to suppress. Conceding that the initial entry by the officers was justified by the shooting of his downstairs neighbor, Hicks nevertheless complained that no *shooter, victim, or weapon* could reasonably be found between the turntable and the wall.

The trial judge agreed with him and suppressed everything found. The state took an appeal and lost again. Having been reversed once by the U.S. Supremes on this very point, the appellate judges of Arizona quoted *Mincey* at length in their opinion. After discussing the legality of the *search for the shooter, weapons, and other possible victims*, the court went on to hold that *Mincey* also teaches, however, that a "warrantless search must be 'strictly circumscribed by the exigencies which justify its initiation.'" The right to enter for one purpose may not be enlarged to allow a general rummaging through a person's effects however suspicious they may appear to the entering officer. The recording of the serial numbers was unrelated to the exigency justifying entry and involved an additional search not necessitated by the exigency. It was plainly unlawful.

Both the trial and appellate court explicitly rejected the State's arguments that Officer Nelson's actions were justified under the *plain view* doctrine. The Arizona Supreme Court, seeing the writing on the wall, denied review. Not accepting the three strikes thrown by them, the prosecution took the issue to the Supremes.

Speaking for a 6-3 majority, Justice Antonin Scalia approved the initial entry but wrote, "Taking action *unrelated* to the objectives of the authorized intrusion, . . . did produce a new invasion of (Hicks') privacy *unjustified* by the exigent

---

[6]Instead of calling this *the fruit of the poisonous tree*, Division 1 of the Court of Appeals of Arizona, rephrased it to *police officers cannot launder their prior unconstitutional behavior by presenting the fruits of it to a magistrate. State v. Hicks* (1985).

circumstances that validated the entry." (That's a mouthful for *who's hiding behind the stereo?* You were supposed to be looking for a shooter, remember!!!) *Arizona v. Hicks* (1987)[7]

A strong dissent argued that the intrusion into Hicks' privacy was not a search. The item was already in plain view (but even we realize its *numbers* were not), the intrusion was so minimal it wasn't worthy of Fourth Amendment considerations, and after seeing the item lawfully, what's the added harm of looking behind it?

One dissenter, Justice O'Connor, questioned what the answer would be if the numbers were not visible due to darkness. Would the officer's opening a window shade to illuminate the area violate the constitution?

Another dissenter, Justice Powell, noted:

'With all respect, this distinction between *looking* at a suspicious object in plain view and *moving* it even a few inches trivializes the Fourth Amendment.'[8]

No less of an authority than Chief Justice Rehnquist also dissented from the majority opinion.[9]

Justice Scalia countered by reminding us *the Constitution sometimes insulates the criminality of a few in order to protect the privacy of us all.* Sounds a lot like Justice Holmes in *Olmstead* (see the Introduction).

Questions:

Did Officer Nelson have probable cause to believe Hicks' apartment contained stolen property?

_____

_____

_____

---

[7]This case, reported at 480 U.S. 321 (1987), is also in Appendix A.

[8]Three justices asked: Under the Court's decision, if one watch is lying face up and the other lying face down, reading the serial number on one of the watches would not be a search, but turning over the other watch to read its serial number would be a search. Moreover, the officer's ability to read a serial number may depend on its location in a room and light conditions at a particular time. Would there be a constitutional difference if an officer, on the basis of reasonable suspicion, *used a pocket flashlight? Question*: If they don't know three years later, what are we to do when we are there?

[9]Is it only a coincidence that two of the dissenters are from Arizona? The late chief justice practiced law there before President Reagan brought him to the Justice Department, prior to his appointment, and Justice O'Connor served on the state Court of Appeals and in the state legislature.

_____

What did his training and experience tell him when he saw, in plain view, *a .45-caliber automatic pistol, a .22-caliber sawed-off rifle, and a stocking mask* (remember this is Arizona, not ski country!)?

_____

_____

_____

How about *the expensive stereo components . . . in the squalid and otherwise ill-appointed four-room apartment?*

Of course he did. But *Mincey* teaches us that *that* determination must be made by *a neutral and detached magistrate* and not by *the officer engaged in the often-competitive enterprise of ferreting out crime.*

Questions:

If you were the detectives in Louisiana, how could you *legally* look through all the dresser drawers, bathroom wastebaskets, and anyplace else small items might be secreted?

_____

_____

_____

How would trying to save Mrs. Thompson's life allowed you to completely search her home before awaiting the search warrant?

_____

_____

_____

What could have been in her dresser drawers, or the note card, that would have allowed you to look for it as part of the exigent circumstances that allowed the first entry?

_____

_____

_____

_____

What should Officer Nelson have done as soon as he learned that the person who fired the weapon was no longer in the apartment?

_____

_____

_____

_____

Did he have probable cause (*PC*) to believe that the apartment *probably* contained stolen property and evidence of a crime?

_____

_____

_____

_____

What would have been the safest thing to do once his safety, and that of the neighbors, was assured?

_____

_____

_____

_____

According to the dissenters, in *Arizona v. Hicks*, the stolen property was already in plain view. Why couldn't Nelson take it?

_____

_____

_____

_____

Had Nelson told a judge of his beliefs, do you think he would have gotten a search warrant?

_____

_____

_____

_____

Would using a flashlight, and opening window shades, violate anyone's constitutional rights?

_____

_____

_____

That young cop we keep hearing about in The South Bronx _never_ went into a nighttime burglary _without_ turning on all the lights. Maybe that's why he is still with us. And I couldn't even pronounce _exijentzy_ in those days!!!

Is your safety part of the exigency?

_____

_____

_____

_____

Generally, the Supremes just tell us once what they expect us to do. On occasion, they review the rule some years later and may tweak it a bit. They must really mean what they said in _Mincey_, as not only did they re-affirm it in 1984 and 1987 (not to mention the two arson cases discussed in Chapter Four) but as late as 1999 in _Flippo v. West Virginia_[10] they overturned a homicide conviction, stating once again:

> A warrantless search by the police is invalid unless it falls within one of the narrow and well-delineated exceptions to the warrant requirement, _Katz v. United States_, 389 U.S. 347, 357 (1967), none of which the trial court invoked here. It simply found that after the homicide crime scene was secured for investigation, a search of 'anything and everything found within the crime scene area was within the law.' . . . This position squarely conflicts with _Mincey v. Arizona_, where we rejected the contention that there is a 'murder scene exception' to the Warrant Clause of the Fourth Amendment.[11]

_____

[10]528 U.S. 11, 13–14 (1999).

[11]At pages 13–14.

For whatever it's worth, I would strongly suggest you follow the rule of *Mincey* if you want your homicide cases to stand up. Take your time and do it right. The overtime doesn't hurt either!

Discussion:

_____

_____

_____

_____

_____

_____

_____

_____

_____

_____

_____

_____

_____

_____

_____

_____

_____

_____

_____

_____

_____

_____

_____

_____

_____

_____

_____

_____

_____

_____

_____

CHAPTER 6

Joyce and Stanley Cohen

THE FOURTH AMENDMENT LIVES

Having now fully digested the leading cases brings us to *what should we have done* in Miami when Mrs. Joyce Cohen told us to leave her home, as her husband Stan's cold body was going through his post-mortem changes on the bedroom floor?

Joyce, 35, was on the phone with friends in Steamboat Springs, Colorado, at 5:30 a.m. The date, March 7, 1986, will prove significant for both the Cohens and the Waksmans, as it was also my daughter Danielle's fourth birthday. She claimed that's when she heard (*Joyce—not my daughter*) several shots in her 52-year-old husband's bedroom. Similar to the Thompsons of Jefferson Parish, that's a good indication of trouble in Paradise, both the separate bedrooms—and the shooting. Joyce *hung* up the phone, assumed her alibi was intact, and went to investigate. (People are *hanged*; pictures and phones, etc., are *hung*). There's another sign I saw on the wall of the detective squad room in the 40th Precinct:

Men are not hanged for stealing horses but that horses should not be stolen.[1]

Stanley couldn't help us as he had taken four shots to the head. Joyce said she saw two shadowy figures running down the steps and heard something in a Spanish accent, as they left the house. With Dade County's and Miami's large Hispanic population, it's typical to blame it on *two Latin males*.

The Cohens lived in upscale Coconut Grove, just off Biscayne Bay and south of downtown Miami. Their home sat upon a large limestone rock, in a quiet neighborhood known as *Silver Bluff*. Stan was in the construction business and had married Joyce, his secretary, twelve years earlier. They belonged to the Miami Ski Club and often went to Colorado. It was still ski season and hence the late call. They were also caught up in the speed of high living and big city thrills.

---

[1] In addition to deterrence, the scholars tell us there are three other recognized reasons for incarceration. Punishment, vengeance (for the victim as well as the community) and the one I favor most—warehousing violent criminals to postpone their next attack for as long as possible.

Joyce tripped the burglar alarm and several of Miami's finest arrived, among them Miami Police Officer Catherine Carter, later to become a homicide detective, and then a lawyer. While Carter's backup called Fire Rescue, Joyce was screaming, "Is he dead?" The paramedics moved Stanley to the floor and made a supreme effort, but the CPR that will neutralize multiple gunshot wounds to the brain hasn't been developed yet. As usual, they did their best and left us the debris.

Was this entry legal? Of course—Joyce called and announced the emergency. She was not formally asked, but the crime scene techs and detectives began their daily routine of dusting for prints, *shooting 360s* (photographing the entire room from the center) and examining the body. Joyce was then taken to the Homicide office, but wait. . . .

Question: Joyce let the police in without formally waiving her Fourth Amendment rights. She also did not object as they went about their duties. Can her silence be considered a consent? Usually, failure to object is considered approval. That's the general rule, except when constitutional rights are involved. However, our courts have ruled that mere silence and acquiescence to authority *do not* presume a waiver of constitutional rights. We must still prove a knowing and intelligent waiver of a person's constitutional rights by a preponderance of the evidence. A preponderance is only 51 percent, much less than *beyond a reasonable doubt*. That higher burden is only for proving guilt at trial. Therefore, whenever the widow, or the significant other, calms down, we get a signed waiver, and put it in the file. (I put one in the appendix for you.)

At the Homicide office, Joyce met, and was interviewed by, a skeptical Jon Spear, one of Miami's most senior and respected detectives. It was not a good time for a new case for him. Two weeks before, he picked up two floaters, off the Julia Tuttle Causeway. That's one of the several bridges that connect Miami Beach to the mainland. *The Tuttle* goes from N.E. 36 Street in Miami to 41st Street on the Beach. They might have been illegal aliens, who drowned swimming ashore. But the next day, the ME found some bullets in their heads. It would be tough to call them accidental deaths. The previous week, he was assigned two more *Who Dunits* and now a fifth one, all in two weeks. Even the legendary Jon Spear said, *"Too much!"*

Jon finally got around to the sleeping arrangements and asked when they last had sex. Joyce blew up and ended the interview:[2]

> I want to go home. Get everybody out of my house.

Thus began our *Mincey* problem.

There's no question we needed a warrant to search, but what can we do while awaiting the warrant? First we preserve and secure the scene. (*Hey, did someone look for the shooter and other victims yet? Puhleese don't forget that. That is the only reason we are allowed in, remember!!*) It may be her house and she can eject us—but it's *our* crime scene and we can eject her. Why? We have the right to maintain the status quo and preserve the crime scene. Allowing people to mill about before our evidence technicians examine the scene in great detail would permit tampering with and question

---

[2]It's never an interrogation; always use friendly words in court.

the reliability of any evidence collected. We want to find it just as the killer left it. Allowing the prime suspect to remain and destroy evidence is insane! On the other hand, it is her house. Until we have a warrant she can throw us out. Who wins here?—We do, to secure the scene. She puts us out and we put her out. We all then wait for the search warrant. What if she won't leave? Arrest her for interfering, obstructing, tampering, or the one I like best—Trespass! This way our crime scene remains secure.

Where is an appropriate place to write the warrant? When all the cops are at the scene and each has something to contribute—how about right there? *Mincey* says we can't *search*, it doesn't say I can't *write* in the house. Many times due to rain, heat, humidity, darkness, convenience, or the same rocks and bottles I attracted in The Bronx, I've written the warrant at the kitchen table.[3] Keep the A/C on, bring in some Diet Cokes and pizza (*No, not in the room with the bod(ies)*), and interview your affiant. He's the detective who gathers all the facts and swears to the affidavit that is presented to the judge. When the lead detective hands out assignments, the junior member is sent to the Seven-Eleven for the sodas and ice. A Styrofoam box in the trunk is standard equipment.

Levity aside, you can only include in the affidavit those items legitimately seen during the authorized *victim, shooter, weapons* search. Doesn't matter what was in the freezer, when you opened it to get some cubes for the Cokes. That information was illegally obtained—and neither you nor the judge can consider it.

By this time it was about 10 a.m. and I was in my office at the Metro Justice Building, less than a mile from police headquarters and maybe three miles from the Cohen residence. I was contemplating where to have lunch when Spear's boss, Sgt. Tom Waterson, called.

"David, we need a warrant, *woujabelevit*, the widow threw us out."

Averaging over 500 homicides a year in the mid-1980s, and having only one so far that day, I wasn't surprised to hear the phone (we needed over *1.37* a day to maintain our average!).

My first of the day was two crack heads fighting over the pipe in an abandoned building; one went to jail, the other, to the ME—no *Mincey* problem, as no one had any standing, or legal right, to object to the search. It wasn't their premises and they had no right to be there. To use the legal words, there was no *reasonable expectation of privacy*. That, and only that, is what the Fourth Amendment to the Constitution protects, as interpreted in *Katz v. U.S.* (1967). We read about Charley in Chapter Two.

When the homeless of America moved to sunny Florida and took over the downtown parks, the city fathers had their mini tent-city removed and all were arrested for sleeping in the park. A federal judge said they had a reasonable expectation of privacy *under* the blankets and newspapers they used for lean-to sleeping

---

[3]In *Segura v. U.S.*, 468 U.S. 796 (1984), the Supremes upheld the authority of two DEA agents to enter and remain in an apartment—19 hours—while awaiting a search warrant. "Securing a dwelling, on the basis of probable cause, to prevent the destruction or removal of evidence while a search warrant is being sought is not itself an unreasonable seizure of either the dwelling or its contents."

areas. Someone suggested they all move to the judge's front yard and challenge whether the Constitution went that far.

Handling murders in Miami is not exactly like being the Maytag repairman. The phone rang often and you never knew what it would bring. If we had a few quiet days, early on in the week, we didn't make any plans for the weekend. Even without the multiples that often showed up, you could expect seven to ten per week. We've had scenes with four, five, and even six DOA's.[4]

Waterson, having had eight years to digest the *Mincey* opinion—and plenty of opportunities to practice its holding in the Miami of the 1980s—came over with a rough draft of his search warrant affidavit. It was fine. However, to justify my existence, I added some Latin phrases and words with more than three syllables. I always teased Tom and Jon that, before they met me, the largest word they knew was *delicatessen*. After sending Waterson to the typing pool, I ran over to the scene for a quick walk-through (nothing the cops hadn't already seen). I was careful not to get any blood on my shoes or damage the scene at the Cohen house, as I considered lunch spots in The Grove.

Questions:

What did Sergeant Waterson put into his affidavit?

_____

_____

_____

_____

Was there an *exijentzy* to allow Officer Carter to enter the house?

_____

_____

_____

Where could she look?

_____

_____

_____

_____

---

[4]One killer of six (plus two more in an unrelated case), John Errol Ferguson, convicted in 1978, is prosecuting his umpteenth petition for a Writ of Habeas Corpus in federal court as we go to print. I have stopped trying to explain it to the victims' families. Now he alleges he is *incompetent to be executed*.

What did she see?

_____

_____

_____

_____

Could she stand by the paramedics and watch them work?

_____

_____

_____

_____

If all the above were lawful things she was doing, we can put _all_ her observations into the affidavit?

_____

_____

_____

_____

Now, what goes into the affidavit?

Everything Carter and the paramedics saw.

How about the things Joyce said to Spear?

_____

_____

_____

_____

Was she under arrest when being questioned?

_____

_____

_____

_____

If not, we can use her words.

_____

_____

_____

_____

Can Sergeant Waterson, who may not have seen or heard it all, repeat it in a sworn affidavit?

_____

_____

_____

_____

By the time the warrant was typed and presented to Chief Judge Ed Cowart, it was 3 p.m. and the *On Call* ME was summoned. Judge Cowart had an old photo in his chambers, of himself in uniform, on his Miami Police Department motorcycle. Detectives usually went to friendly prosecutors and judges with their warrant applications, and Cowart was a favorite. Although Sergeant Waterson naturally felt more comfortable with me and Judge Cowart, he still had to touch all the bases as another judge would have to rule on the validity of the warrant at a motion to suppress. That's the hearing where the defendant attempts to exclude any physical evidence found pursuant to a search. His job is harder if the detectives have a warrant, but if the affidavit in support of the warrant does not spell out *probable cause*, any evidence found may be suppressed.[5] Waterson would be cross-examined on what he put in the affidavit. Would it satisfy the requirement of *probable cause*?

Questions:

What does probable cause mean?

_____

_____

_____

How certain does the affiant have to be of his facts?

_____

_____

_____

When Dr. Charles Wetli, the Deputy Chief ME, arrived at 3 p.m. and was presented with the scenario given by the grieving widow (grieving, because we wouldn't

---

[5]See Chapter Seven for the *good-faith* exception.

let her into her house) his opinion was that Stan's *rigor mortis* and *livor mortis* were *consistent* with someone dead nine-and-one-half hours.

Rigor is the condition in which the muscles of the body become hardened as a result of chemical changes that occur after death. We are interested in when it begins to set in. That can help us determine the approximate time of death. It generally begins about two to four hours after death and continues, becoming more firm until it *fixes*—ten to twelve hours later. Fully developed rigor mortis remains in the body for upwards of twenty-four hours and then slowly disappears, with the softening of the muscles occurring once again.

Livor mortis is the purple discoloration of the skin on the lowest part of the victim's body. Usually that's the chest or the back and front or rear of the legs. If you die sitting *on the pot*, it's your buttocks and below the knees that will be purple. One of the problems homicide victims encounter is that their heart stops pumping their blood around the body. Gravity then takes over. After two to four hours (give or take a few) the blood *fixes* in the dilated capillaries of the skin and gives off the dark color because of the absence of oxygen in the blood.

Back to the *Mincey* problem—What problem you say? Original entry OK and re-entry by warrant—what's wrong?

The case took a strange twist about two months later.

A robbery detective had arrested one member of a home-invasion-robbery gang. During the debriefing, the *former* robber told of a murder-for-hire he participated in, in Coconut Grove, a few months before. I say former, as once he was offered the alternative of being a witness against his former gang members, or getting *a Buck Rogers* sentence (release date in the twenty-fifth century!), he decided to seek another type of work. His story was that Joyce hired his former associates and the *hit* was done shortly after 2 a.m., not 5:30 a.m., as Joyce had first told Carter. Naturally, my new best friend just stood there and did nothing!

My problem was to either corroborate or, more importantly, eliminate this as a credible story. The best way is with physical evidence. I've told juries for years: "Fingerprints don't lie. Serology and DNA have no motive. You can rely upon them."

What did we have to use to test this guy's story? The *rigor mortis* and *livor mortis* would give us the true time of death. There was the answer.

We went back to Dr. Wetli and gave him the new scenario. Assume the death was thirteen hours, not nine and a half, before you saw the body.

"Consistent with both," was the answer.

Post-mortem changes were the evidence we lost waiting for the ME. *Time* was the exigency that caused the *imminent destruction of physical evidence*. That is another thing you can look for, in addition to the shooter, weapons, and victims. See *Mincey*, at p. 394. Ever since then, the ME goes in, as we prepare the warrant. He's told, "Doc, do whatever you have to do (remember the Arson case in Michigan?) to determine time of death. You can dig out the bullets tomorrow." We flap wrists, feel armpits, and photo the *livor* (No, not the liver!), checking to see if rigor mortis and livor mortis have become *fixed*.

I once saw a woman who *apparently* shot herself in the head. She was lying on her back and the gun was still in her right hand, *palm up*. Problem was the palm was dark purple and the rear of her right hand, the side closest to the floor, was very white. That crime scene defied the laws of gravity. It proved that the victim's body was moved, at least her hand was moved, several hours *after* her hand rested on the floor, palm down.[6]

Getting a good look, and feel, of the body before rigor and livor fix makes it easier for the ME to determine the time of death. I've never photographed a liver but have seen the ME cut down to it and place a thermometer into it to get a reliable body temp—another way to determine time of death. The dead human body loses its body heat according to a certain schedule, so many degrees an hour.[7]

Imagine if the ME went in and examined Stan at 7 a.m. It would be really easy to see the difference between a DOA 90 minutes gone (still warm and floppy) and one dead five hours.

Naturally, at trial, the defense attacked the witness (or as they called him, *the man who got away with murder and a whole bunch of robberies!*). He did pass a lie-detector test; however, his version of a 2 a.m. shooting could not be verified!

According to the medical experts called by both sides, the time of death could have been between 5:30 a.m. and anytime back to midnight.

Thankfully there was other physical evidence that won the day. Found with the search warrant, in Joyce's bathroom wastebasket, was a tissue containing Joyce's DNA and gunshot residue. A very strange mixture; stuff from a fired gun and stuff from her nose! The tissue also had a few unexplained tears in it. Unexplained until Stanley's fired pistol was found in the bushes in front of their home. You know those little screws on the side of the gun? They had pieces of tissue around them, as if someone (guess who?) wiped the fingerprints off the gun before tossing it out the bedroom window.

That, when added to our witness, *who got away with murder*, sealed Joyce Cohen's fate. The trial judge upheld the search warrant, and the court of appeal upheld the jury verdict—guilty of first degree murder. Imagine if we kept searching after Joyce told us to leave. Joyce, like Rufus Mincey before her, is just another killer doing life in prison. I have placed Sergeant Waterson's warrant for the Cohen home at the end of this chapter. Do what lawyers do: if it worked before, why change it?

Questions:

Where could Officer Carter have looked upon arriving at the Cohen house?

_____

_____

_____

---

[6]When the suicide victim is still holding the gun, the scene should be examined extra carefully. Remember how that handgun jerked the last time you fired it? How does a dead person hold on to it so well?

[7]Before you think we can determine time of death with any certainty, none of these methods gives us anything but some very rough guidelines.

Did Officer Carter have to ask permission to enter the home?

_____

_____

_____

_____

How about the paramedics?

_____

_____

_____

_____

What allows Sergeant Waterson to repeat what everyone has told him and place it into the search warrant affidavit?

_____

_____

_____

_____

Does the person swearing to the affidavit have to convince the judge who committed the murder?

_____

_____

_____

_____

What does probable cause mean?

_____

_____

_____

_____

We have been talking of _probable cause_ for some time now.

As early as 1813, Chief Justice John Marshall observed that probable cause "means less than evidence which would justify condemnation. . . . It (allows) a seizure made under circumstances which warrant suspicion."[8] If we look to _Black's_

---

[8]_Locke v. U.S.,_ 7 Cranch 339 (1813).

Law Dictionary, a good place to start, the definitions go on for a page and a half. They tell us that probable cause is reasonable cause; that helps! Other definitions are "a set of probabilities grounded in the factual and practical considerations which govern the decisions of reasonable and prudent persons and is more than mere suspicion but less than the quantum of evidence required for conviction" (sounds like what Marshall said). Probable cause to arrest is defined as "where facts and circumstances within officers' knowledge and of which they had reasonably trustworthy information are sufficient in themselves to warrant a person of reasonable caution in the belief that an offense has been or is being committed; it is not necessary that the officer possess knowledge of facts sufficient to establish guilt, but more than mere suspicion is required." Another way of saying it is "where officer has more evidence favoring suspicion that person is guilty of crime than evidence against such suspicion, but there is room for some doubt."

In *Ybarra* (the Aurora Tavern pat-down case), we learned that probable cause is "a reasonable ground for belief of guilt, and that the belief of guilt must be particularized with respect to the person to be searched or seized." Just in case you think you are getting a handle on this, the U.S. Supreme Court suggested, "the probable cause standard is incapable of precise definition or quantification into percentages[9] because it deals with probabilities and depends on the totality of circumstances."[10] They went on to say, "The quanta of proof appropriate in ordinary judicial proceedings are inapplicable to the decision to issue a warrant." Another case offered, "Finely tuned standards such as proof beyond a reasonable doubt or by a preponderance of the evidence, useful in formal trials, have no place in the probable cause decision. . . . To determine whether an officer had probable cause to arrest an individual, we must examine the events leading up to the arrest, and then decide whether those facts, viewed from the standpoint of an objectively[11] reasonable police officer, amount to probable cause."

The best way to learn the law is to apply it to the facts of a case and see where the court goes. That's why we have been reading all these cases.

Probable cause is needed to search. It is also a requirement to support a lawful seizure or arrest. Should the arrest not be supported by probable cause, the reading and waiving of *Miranda*[12] rights will not cure the error, and the fruits of that constitutional error, the defendant's statement, will be suppressed.[13] In the next case we discuss, the issue was whether there was sufficient probable cause (PC) to arrest Joseph Pringle and therefore to support the legality of his later confession.

If there was no PC, the *Mirandized* confession would fall.

In the early morning hours of August 7, 1999, Pringle and two of his friends were driving through Baltimore County, Maryland. The car, driven by one Dante Partlow, was stopped for speeding. As Partlow looked in his glove box for the registration, the police officer noticed a large roll of bills. Partlow had no wants and he

---

[9]Some commentators have suggested it is 51%.

[10]*Brinegar v. U.S.,* 338 U.S. 160 (1949).

[11]The objective standard means that not you, but how would other reasonable officers view the facts.

[12]384 U.S. 436 (1966).

[13]*Dunaway v. N.Y.,* 442 U.S. 200 (1979).

was issued an oral warning. That should have been the end of it, but another officer asked Partlow if there were any guns or drugs in the car. Partlow said he had none but foolishly allowed the officer to search the car. Found were the rolled up bills, amounting to $763, and behind the rear armrest, five glassine baggies containing cocaine. The armrest had been upright and flat against the back seat when the officer pulled it down. The baggies were between the armrest and the back seat of the car. All three men in the car denied knowledge of the drugs and all three were arrested and transported to the police station. Pringle was the right front passenger and the third man was in the rear (closest to the drugs).

Now as a prosecutor, I realize I cannot file charges against any of them as I have to prove *beyond a reasonable doubt* that *someone* had possession and control (and knowledge of the contents) of the baggies. But remember Chief Justice Marshall: "Less than evidence which would justify condemnation." Well later that morning, Pringle, after waiving his *Miranda* rights, owned up to the baggies and said "he and his friends were going to a party where he intended to sell the drugs or use it for sex." After being indicted for possession with the intent to sell, he moved to suppress his confession on the grounds that there was no probable cause for his arrest. If he were not illegally arrested, he would not have been taken to the police station and read, and waived, *Miranda*. He wanted the whole house of cards to crumble.

A *unanimous* Supreme Court, speaking through Chief Justice Rehnquist, held:

> It is uncontested in the present case that the officer, upon recovering the five plastic glassine baggies containing suspected cocaine, had probable cause to believe a felony had been committed. The sole question is whether the officer had probable cause to believe that Pringle committed that crime. . . .
>
> Probable cause is a fluid concept—turning on the assessment of probabilities in particular factual contexts—not readily, or even usefully, reduced to a neat set of legal rules. . . .
>
> In this case, Pringle was one of three men riding in a Nissan Maxima at 3:16 a.m. There was $763 of rolled-up cash in the glove compartment directly in front of Pringle. Five plastic glassine baggies of cocaine were behind the back-seat armrest and accessible to all three men. Upon questioning, the three men failed to offer any information with respect to the ownership of the cocaine or the money. . . .
>
> *We think it an entirely reasonable inference from these facts that any or all three of the occupants had knowledge of, and exercised dominion and control over, the cocaine.* Thus a reasonable officer could conclude that there was probable cause to believe Pringle committed the crime of possession of cocaine, either solely or jointly.
>
> Pringle's attempt to characterize this case as a guilt-by-association case is unavailing. His reliance on *Ybarra v. Illinois* is misplaced.
>
> This case is quite different from *Ybarra*. Pringle and his two companions were in a relatively small automobile, not a public tavern. A car passenger—unlike the unwitting tavern patron in *Ybarra*—will often be engaged in a common enterprise with the driver, and have the same interest in concealing the fruits or the evidence of their wrongdoing. Here we

think it was reasonable for the officer to infer a common enterprise among the three men. The quantity of drugs and cash in the car indicated the likelihood of drug dealing, an enterprise to which a dealer would be unlikely to admit an innocent person with the potential to furnish evidence against him.[14]

So what happened?

The court found there was probable cause to arrest Pringle, even though there was not enough evidence (without the confession) to charge or convict him. Why is that important? Because the arrest was lawful, there was no fruit of a poisonous tree to suppress. Once Pringle waived *Miranda*, both his Fourth and Fifth Amendment rights had been protected, and he went off to the slammer for ten years, *without parole*.

So what is probable cause? Without adding to the reams of paper already written upon to describe this *fluid concept—turning on particular facts*, let us say that it is not what is needed to convict. If the facts before you tend to suggest that the subject may be involved, you may be authorized to make an arrest and then see if the evidence continues to rise to the level needed for court. Make reasonable inferences, act in good faith, use your common sense and experiences, and maybe you will *make a nice collar*. Remember the most important part though—*Be careful out there!*

Notes and Discussion:

_____

_____

_____

_____

_____

_____

_____

_____

_____

_____

_____

_____

_____

_____

[14]*Maryland v. Pringle*, 540 U.S. 366 (2003).

IN THE CIRCUIT COURT OF THE
ELEVENTH JUDICIAL CIRCUIT
OF FLORIDA

STATE OF FLORIDA)
)
COUNTY OF DADE   )

AFFIDAVIT FOR SEACH WARRANT

Before me, _Sidney B. Shapiro_ ,
a Judge of the Circuit Court of the Eleventh Judicial Circuit of Florida,
personally appeared Sgt. Tom Watterson, Homicide Investigator, City of
Miami Police Department, who being by me first duly sworn, deposes and
says that he has probable cause to believe and does believe that at the
premises described as.

The address of said premises being 1665 South Bayshore Drive,
City of Miami, Dade County, Florida. The premises is a two story single
family home. "The Premises" is a Coral Rock structure and is the first
structure East of 17th Avenue on the North side of Bayshore Drive.

"The Premises" being in the City of Miami, Dade County,
Florida, hereinafter referred to as "The Premises", a weapon,
instrumentality or means by which a felony to- wit: Murder, in
violation of 782.04 Florida Statutes, has been committed, or evidence
relevant to proving said felony has been committed, is contained
therein, to- wit: Fingerprints, human blood, projectiles, casings,
firearms, personal papers and any other miscellaneous evidence relevant
to the murder committed at 1665 South Bayshore Drive at approximately
5:30 a.m. on March 7, 1986.

Affiant's reasons for the belief that "The Premises" are
being used as stated above and that "The Property" above-mentioned is
being concealed and stored at "The Premises" above-described and the
facts establishing the grounds for this affidavit and the probable
cause for believing that such facts exist, are as follows.

Your affiant Sergeant Thomas Watterson a City of Miami Police
Officer with more than fifteen years experience as a Police Officer and
four years as a Investigator. Your affiant is currently assigned to
assist with the investigation of the murder of ▆▆▆▆▆▆▆▆▆▆▆
Miami Case ▆▆▆▆▆▆

Judge's Initials _____

Page 1

On March 7, 1986 at approximately 0530 hours, Miami Police and Fire Rescue Units were dispatched to 1665 South Bayshore Drive. Reference a man shot. At 0540 hours Fire Rescue advised that the victim was dead.

The victim's wife, Mrs. ████████, was present in the house during the murder. She stated that she heard a loud bang and then she observed two shapes run down the stairs and out the door.

The victim's wife was asked to come to the Miami Police Department to give a statement as to the facts involved in this case. At the station Mrs. ████ became very upset and requested to leave.

Mrs. ████ was asked to sign a Consent to Search Form and after discussing the form with a friend over the phone she refused to sign the form.

Homicide Investigators presently have the Premises secured outside but they are unable to process the scene or even examine the
** body.

WHEREFORE, affiant prays that a Search Warrant be issued commanding the Director of the Metro-Dade Police Department, Dade County, Florida, who is also known as the Sheriff of Metropolitan Dade County, Florida, or his Deputies, and the Commissioner of the Florida Department of Law Enforcement, or any of his duly constituted Agents, and all Investigators of the State Attorney of the Eleventh Judicial Circuit of Florida, and all police officers of the City of Miami Police Department, with the proper and necessary assistance, to search "The Premises" above-described, and all spaces therein, and the curtilage thereof, and any persons found inside "The Premises" for "The Property" above-described, amking the search in the Daytime or the Night-Time, as the exigencies may demand or require, or on Sunday, and if the same be found at "The Premises" to seize the same as evidence and to arrest any person in the unlawful possession thereof.

_____
Affiant

SWORN TO AND SUBSCRIBED before me this the
day of _____, 1986.   7th

_____
JUDGE OF THE CIRCUIT COURT OF THE
ELEVENTH JUDICIAL CIRCUIT OF FLORIDA

Judge's Initials_____

** See attachment   Page 2

Addendum page II

Your affiant was present when fire rescue was in the house. Your affiant saw the victim in an upstairs bedroom with an apparent gun shot wound to the head. The victim's wife was downstairs preparing for a yard sale, at the time of the loud bang she claims she heard.

Your affiant observed a kitchen door with a broken glass window pane and a coral rock lying outside. She claims not to have heard this window break. There is broken glass inside the kitchen door. The victim's wife claims her dog did not bark or respond to anything prior to the loud bang.

Your affiant saw an empty holster for a pistol next to the victim's bed.

Your affiant has been advised by a uniform officer who was securing the house during the initial police responds that he saw a shiny object under thick follige on the property near the front of the house.

Judge's Initials _____

Addendum Page 2

IN THE CIRCUIT COURT OF THE
ELEVENTH JUDICIAL CIRCUIT
OF FLORIDA

STATE OF FLORIDA)
)   SS
)
COUNTY OF DADE)

SEARCH WARRANT

IN THE NAME OF THE STATE OF FLORIDA, TO ALL AND SINGULAR:

The Director of the Metro-Dade Police Department, Dade
County, Florida, who is also known as the Sheriff of Metropolitan Dade
County, Florida, or his Deputies, and the Commissioner of the Florida
Department of Law Enforcement, or any of his duly constituted Agents,
and all Investigators of the State Attorney of the Eleventh Judicial
Circuit of Florida, and all police officers of the City of Miami Police
Department of Dade County, Florida.

Affidavit having been made before me by Sgt. Tom Watterson
Homicide Investigator, City of Miami Police Department, that he has
probable cause to believe and does believe that at the premises
described as:

The address of said premises being 1665 South Bayshore Drive,
City of Miami, Dade County, Florida. The premises is a two story
single family home. "The Premises" is a Coral Rock structure and is
the first structure East of 17th Avenue on the North side of Bayshore
Drive.

"The Premises" being in the City of Miami, Dade County,
Florida, hereinafter referred to as "The Premises", a weapon,
instrumentality or means by which a felony to- wit: Murder, in
violation of 782.04 Florida Statutes, has been committed, or evidence
relevant to proving said felony has been committed, is contained
therein, to- wit: Fingerprints, human blood, projectiles, casings,
firearms, personal papers and any other miscellaneous evidence relevant
to the murder committed at 1665 South Bayshore Drive at approximately
5:30 a.m. on March 7, 1986.

Judge's Initials_____

Page 1

And as I am satisfied that there is probable cause to believe that "The Premises" are being used as aforesaid and "The Property" above described is being concealed and stored at "The Premises" above described, I expressly find probable cause for the issuance of this Search Warrant.

YOU ARE HEREBY COMMANDED to enter and search forthwith "The Premises" above-described, and the curtilage thereof, and any persons found inside "The Premises" for "The Property" above-described, serving this warrant and making the search in the Daytime or Nighttime, as the exigencies may demand or require, or on Sunday, with the proper and necessary assistance, and if "The Property" above-described be found there, to seize it and to arrest all persons in the unlawful possession thereof, leaving a copy of this warrant and a receipt for the property taken and prepare a written Inventory of the property seized and return this warrant and bring the property and all persons arrested before a court having competent jurisdiction of the offense within ten (10) days from the date of issuance as required by law.

WITNESS MY HAND and seal this the _____ 7th _____, day of _____ March _____, 1986.

JUDGE OF THE CIRCUIT COURT OF THE ELEVENTH JUDICIAL CIRCUIT OF FLORIDA

Judge's Initials _____

Page 2

STATE OF FLORIDA }
                         ss
COUNTY OF DADE }

RETURN AND INVENTORY

I, _Sgt. Thomas A. Whitterson_, received the within
Search Warrant on _March 7_, 1986 and duly executed
it as follows:

On _March 7_, 1986, at _2:05_ o'clock
_P_.M., I searched (the person) (the premises) described in
the Search Warrant and left a copy of the Search Warrant with:
Left in house, together with an
inventory of property taken pursuant to the Search Warrant:

1-5 shot. smith & wesson Blue steel revolver
(From Front yard)

Two Pillows one containing a projectile
Two pillow cases.
1-SW 357 magnum From Dresser Drawer (in case)
Drug paraphenalia in Dresser Drawer
One empty revolver holster
Numerous. Fingerprints.
One pair of open toed slippers.
One ring and chain from body.
One gate Lock
Glass found by back door
One Rock
1 pair Rubber gloves

(USE REVERSE SIDE FOR CONTINUATION)

I, _Sgt T.A. Whitterson_, the officer by whom
the warrant was executed, do swear that the above Inventory
contains a true and detailed account of all the property taken
by me on said Warrant.

STATE OF FLORIDA   )
)   SS
COUNTY OF DADE   )

RETURN AND INVENTORY

I, _JON K. SPEAR_, received
the within Search Warrant on _11 MAR._, 19_86_.
and duly executed it as follows:

On _11 MAR._, 198_6_, at _1920_ o'clock
_P_.M., I searched (the person) (the premises) described in
the Search Warrant and left a copy of the Search Warrant
with: _IN KITCHEN_, together
with an inventory of the property taken.

The following is an inventory of property taken
pursuant to the Search Warrant:

1 BACK DOOR
1 People-w/Maroon Jogging Suit

(USE REVERSE SIDE FOR CONTINUATION)

I, _JON K. Spear_, the officer by whom
the warrant was executed, do swear that the above Inventory
contains a true and detailed account of all the property
taken by me on said Warrant.

Jon K. Spear

CHAPTER 7

Warrants: The Good, the Bad, and the Ugly

THE GOOD-FAITH EXCEPTION

We have discussed the various exceptions to the search warrant requirement of the Fourth Amendment. We also now know when we *do* need a search warrant and have seen some examples of properly prepared search warrant affidavits and the search warrants themselves. There are two main parts of the search warrant. One is the sworn affidavit requesting the search warrant and the other is the warrant itself. The search warrant is an order from the court telling you what to do: where to search, what to look for, and what to do with any such property found. The affidavit, as described in the Fourth Amendment, is your recitation of the facts explaining to the court why you want to search, where you want to search, and what you expect to find. You must swear, under oath, that you have a good-faith basis that your facts are reasonably true. To swear to facts you know are not true is *perjury*. Doing that will end your law enforcement career rather prematurely.

Let's take another look at the Fourth Amendment's warrant requirement:

> *No warrants shall issue, but upon probable cause, supported by oath or affirmation, and particularly describing the place to be searched, and the persons or things to be seized.*

That is what you must put into your affidavit. The facts spelling out the *probability that the place has the things*[1] *you believe are evidence or contraband.* Then you must swear to those facts, particularly describing the place to be searched and the person or things to be searched. It's as simple as that! Some states even allow this to be done by phone.

If your affidavit satisfies the court of those things, the judge will then order you to search *that* place for *those* things. To put it in legalese, if the court (the magistrate,

---

[1]Warrants can be for *persons* or things. A warrant can order a person to stand in a line-up, speak certain phrases, give handwriting or voice samples, allow his body to be examined for signs of injuries, and to allow fingerprints or samples of hair, blood, or other body fluids to be taken.

the judge) finds probable cause to believe that a particular place contains particular things and those things are either evidence to either prove a crime was committed (like bloodstains, spent projectiles and casings, fingerprints, or strands of hair), or evidence in and of themselves (like drugs or other things unlawful to possess), it will order you to look for them and seize them, if found.

OK, you have conducted your preliminary investigation, seen certain things while walking through the crime scene when looking for *victims, the shooter, or weapons* or otherwise while lawfully on the premises doing something else (like answering a *sick baby* call or a *domestic*). You have placed your observations and what people told you into a written affidavit, gone to the judge and swore that those facts were true and correct. That is what you are supposed to do. If you don't: if you search without doing that and the various warrant exceptions do not apply, you have conducted a search which violates the Fourth Amendment and according the U.S. Supreme Court case of *Mapp. v. Ohio*,[2] the trial judge will not allow what you found to be used as evidence in the trial. Those items will be excluded from the trial at the pre-trial motion, called a motion to suppress. Why is it that important evidence may not be used? To encourage you to respect the defendant's constitutional rights. It has been thought (over very strong opinions to the contrary) that by not letting you use evidence obtained illegally, you will learn to respect the law and the rights of those you search. That philosophy has been debated for years and was eloquently discussed by Judge Cardozo in *State v. Defore*.

> *Should the criminal go free because the constable has blundered?*

But what happens if you do what is required of you, you go to the judge, swear to whatever facts you have, tell him/her exactly what you are looking for and where you believe it is, and what facts lead you to those beliefs and the judge orders you to search, but the *trial* judge[3] later determines that your affidavit was insufficient. That is to say, either your facts did not spell out probable cause or the items or the place were not particularly described. In effect, he tells you the first judge you went to made a mistake and should not have signed the warrant. *What happens when the judge ordering the search made the mistake, not you?*

Do we punish him in an effort to make him a better judge? Does he care whether you win your case? Isn't he supposed to be neutral and detached?

Let's take it a step further. Let's say your affidavit is fine, but the warrant has a problem. In the judge's order to search (that you prepared!!!) it does not tell you exactly what it should. You are told to search for the wrong thing or at the wrong place.[4] Once again, whom do we punish? What did *you* do that was wrong?

---

[2]367 U.S. 643 (1961).

[3]It's not that judges come to different conclusions based upon the same facts, although they may. At the motion to suppress, witnesses are cross-examined and more facts may develop, or inconsistencies may appear, that cause the judge hearing the motion to decide that the information given to the magistrate was wrong, speculative, or insufficient.

[4]One Miami judge suppressed a search warrant for a car because one digit of the 17-digit VIN number was wrong. The tag, year, make, model, and color were fine. He claimed the officers did not know *which* car to search. Long before the *good-faith* exception was announced, he was quickly reversed by the appellate court!

Let's discuss a few more cases and see what happens.

In August of 1981, a confidential informant of *unproven reliability* informed a police officer of the Burbank, California, Police Department that *Armando* and *Patsy* were selling large amounts of cocaine and methaqualone from their residence at 620 Price Drive in Burbank. Officer Cyril Rombach, *an experienced and well-trained narcotics investigator*,[5] followed up on this information and found that the two soon-to-be defendants kept the main stash at another residence they had, that methaqualone was stored at a third house used by an Alberto Antonio Leon, and that all three used their cars as they went about their illegal activities.

Officer Rombach prepared an application for a search warrant to search the three residences and the three vehicles. It contained an extensive list of items believed to be related to the suspects' drug trafficking activities. He then showed it to several deputy district attorneys and received their approval to apply for the warrant. The court issued a valid warrant and it was executed. After large quantities of drugs were found in the homes and two of the vehicles, the suspects were indicted in federal court in California.

At the pre-trial motion to suppress (the seized evidence), the trial court disagreed with the judge who signed the warrant and found *the affidavit was insufficient to establish probable cause.* However, he did find that Officer Rombach had acted in good faith but was bound to follow existing law that did not allow for a good-faith exception. The motion to suppress was granted and the seized evidence was excluded from the trial. On appeal, a divided panel of the Court of Appeals upheld the suppression (thereby excluding the evidence from trial) and also refused to recognize a good-faith exception to the exclusionary rule, established to protect, and put teeth into, the Fourth Amendment. These courts acted properly as only the U.S. Supreme Court could modify its exclusionary rule. The federal prosecutors took an appeal to the Supreme Court in an effort to do just that.

At the same time that the Supremes were considering *Leon*, a similar case came up from the state court in Massachusetts. In *Leon*, the affidavit was found to be bad (by *some* of the judges reviewing it). In the state case, *Sheppard*,[6] *it was the warrant that failed.*

Our heart has to go out to Detective Peter O'Malley. He tried his best to comply with the law. Assigned to investigate the death of Sandra Boulware, whose badly burned and beaten body was found in the Roxbury section of Boston in May of 1979, he gathered evidence suggesting that a former boyfriend, Osborne Sheppard, had beaten her to death in his residence. Det. O'Malley first went to his sergeant for help. Then he sought out the advice of the district attorney, and the DA's first assistant, all of whom told him he had probable cause to believe incriminating evidence would be found at Sheppard's residence. The affidavit was fine. It was conceded that *he did* have probable cause and that the affidavit *particularized* what was to be searched for, and where. So what's the problem?

Because it was now Sunday, the courthouse was closed as was much of the police station. O'Malley did find some search warrant forms in the *narcotics* office of

---

[5]From p. 903 of the opinion. *United States v. Leon*, 468 U.S. 897 (1984).

[6]*Massachusetts v. Sheppard*, 468 U.S. 981 (1984).

the Dorchester District. Do you see where we are going? The warrant was titled "Search Warrant—*Controlled Substance*." O'Malley realized he needed some help in altering the form document. He attempted to remove all the references to narcotics and replaced Dorchester with Roxbury. He then presented his affidavit to the judge, who found it adequate and told him he would authorize the search. The judge also made some changes to the narcotics warrant, but because we are talking about it now, you know he didn't do a good job. The bottom line here is that the search warrant authorized a search for *narcotics* and not the wire and rope matching that on the victim's body, or the blunt instrument that might have been used on the victim, or any women's clothing with blood, gasoline, or burns marks on them, or other items containing her fingerprints, all particularly described in the affidavit.

At the pretrial motion to suppress, the trial court found that the search warrant did not particularly describe the items to be seized. Of course not. O'Malley was ordered to *search for drugs!!* However, differing from the California judge, this judge found that despite the defect in the warrant, the police acted in good faith upon what *they reasonably thought was a good warrant*.

Nice try, but the Supreme Judicial Court of Massachusetts reminded all that a good-faith exception had not yet been established and they reversed the trial judge, even though a majority of justices found the officer acted in good faith.

There was one dissenting opinion. One bold justice declared that since exclusion of the evidence *would not serve to deter any police misconduct*, the evidence should be admitted. In this case, the State of Massachusetts appealed to the Supremes.

Before we even get to how the U.S. Supreme Court dealt with this issue, what could Officer Rombach and Det. O'Malley have done differently?

_____

_____

_____

_____

As a fingerprint comparison technician told me many years ago, four eyes are better than two. *Before* going to the judge, ask a prosecutor to look at your affidavit *and* warrant. If you are going to lose a search warrant in court, better make sure a prosecutor approved it first. It also takes the pressure off you. In this complicated business, where the decisions you make on the spot are reviewed in the sanctity of an appellate court's quiet library many months or years later, and many times by a 5–4, 4–3, or 3–2 vote, you should get all the help you can.

Then on July 5, 1984, the good-faith exception was established by the U.S. Supreme Court. Reminding us again of the purpose of the exclusionary rule, the court held that it is designed to deter *police* misconduct. What else could Det. O'Malley have done? He presented the court with the results of his investigation and swore to it. The affidavit spelled out probable cause and specified with great particularity what was to be searched for and where it was supposed to be found. He showed the judge the warrant and asked for help in making it valid. The judge made some corrections and told O'Malley he was authorizing the search. *Why punish*

O'Malley, and the community, by letting the guilty murderer go free? How about Sandra Boulware and her family. Aren't they entitled to some justice?

How about the judge? Shouldn't he be punished? The Supremes reminded us that judges are not part of the law enforcement team. They have no stake in the outcome of a particular criminal prosecution. Suppressing evidence of searches they erroneously authorized would have no deterrent effect on the issuing judge. Exclusion of evidence is *intended to alter the behavior of individual police officers and their departments*, not to punish the errors of judges and magistrates. So, even though one affidavit was faulty (*Leon*) and another warrant was terrible (*Sheppard*), the evidence was allowed to be admitted. Why?

What is the logic of *Leon*?

_____

_____

_____

_____

The *Leon* doctrine also applies to situations where a police officer arrests a person based upon an erroneous computer indication of an outstanding arrest warrant, due to a court clerk's failure to advise that the arrest warrant was no longer active. Eleven years after *Leon/Sheppard*, the Supreme Court[7] upheld such an arrest as lawful, and therefore the subsequent search as *incident to a lawful arrest*. The good faith is assumed, so long as the police officer is not advised of the error prior to searching the arrested person. The reasoning of *Leon* continues. The police officer:

1. acted reasonably in relying upon a computer record, and excluding the evidence will not change his future behavior, and
2. excluding such evidence would not deter such errors by court clerks. Like the judge in *Sheppard*, they have no stake in the outcome of a particular criminal case.

In a very similar vein is an arrest based upon a statute later determined to be unconstitutional by the courts. Once again, a police officer acts properly in making an arrest, pursuant to a particular statute, and the search pursuant to *that arrest* is valid, even though the appellate courts later determine that statute to be unconstitutional. Just as in the court clerk/computer error case, the Supreme Court has ruled that if "an officer acts in objectively reasonable reliance on a statute,"[8] suppressing evidence resulting from that arrest will have no deterrent effect on his future conduct. "Unless a statute is clearly unconstitutional, an officer should not be expected to question the judgment of the legislature that passed the law." The officer need not question the law, unless a reasonable man would believe the law is not valid. Such a law might be something left over from our darker past prohibiting specified persons from congregating at certain locations.

---

[7] *Arizona v. Evans*, 514 U.S. 1 (1995).

[8] *Illinois v. Krull*, 480 U.S. 340 (1987).

What might be an example of a blatantly unconstitutional statute? One that a reasonable police officer should know he should not enforce?

_____

_____

_____

_____

Exclusion of evidence is not required by the Fourth Amendment, unless there is a greater good to society to be gained from the exclusion. The court created that remedy to safeguard Fourth Amendment rights through a deterrent effect. If police officers who follow the rules and actually do what a judge tells them to do (or reasonably rely upon a statute or a computer check) have acted properly, "application of the exclusionary rule . . . would have little deterrent effect on future police misconduct, which is the basic purpose of the rule." _Krull_, at 347.

There has been much disagreement over the value of the exclusionary rule. Suspects clearly guilty go free. That breeds disrespect for the law and the administration of justice. Even though the rule has a value in deterring improper police practices and ensuring that the constitutional rights of all are respected, the rule must be applied only to those areas where it will serve the best purpose. This rule, as are most, must balance the benefit against the societal cost. Is it worth letting the criminal off? How severe was the police misconduct? _Should the criminal go free because the constable has blundered?_

Does this good-faith exception mean you no longer have to take care with your work? Can you put anything into an affidavit and hope the judge doesn't read too well? Can we go to judges who may be considered friendly to the police?

Several years before Leon and Sheppard found justice, a suspected rapist named Jerome Franks[9] argued that certain allegations in the search warrant affidavit for his apartment were false. He claimed that the affidavit attributed statements to him that he had not made and the insertion of those facts was done in "bad faith." He wanted the knife and clothing found in his apartment, that matched those of the rapist, suppressed. The affidavit supposedly containing those misstatements was submitted to a magistrate and a search warrant was issued. He requested, by pretrial motion, a hearing to attempt to show that the allegations were false. His motion was denied and he was convicted in Dover, Delaware. He then took his case to the Supremes. They said he was entitled _to attempt_ to prove that the affidavit contained deliberate falsehoods or the affiant had a reckless disregard for the truth. Any such falsehoods are to be removed from the affidavit, and probable cause is then determined by what remains. If insufficient evidence is left, the warrant fails. However, if probable cause remains, after the removal of the false facts, the evidence will not be suppressed.[10]

---

[9]_Franks v. Delaware_, 438 U.S. 154 (1978).

[10]Whether he will prevail at that hearing is, of course, another issue. _Franks_, at 172.

Allegations of neglect or innocent mistake will not meet the requirement. There must be proof of an intent on the part of the police to deceive the magistrate, clearly a very high burden. The fact that the police were misled by others is also insufficient.

In addition to *misstatements*, the issue of *omissions* can arise. What if the affiant omits placing information into the affidavit *that if included* would have defeated probable cause? While there is some disagreement among the federal circuits, the leading case of *U.S. v. Colkley*[11] holds that the omitted material "must be such that its inclusion in the affidavit would defeat probable cause." The issue of intentional misstatements by the affiant is easier for the courts to deal with than the reason for certain omissions. Many times an officer will not include certain investigative leads, fragments of information, or other minor pieces of information that might be of benefit to a defendant, or facts that he feels may not be relevant. Before the warrant will fall, the defendant must show there was an intent to deceive the magistrate. In the *Colkley* case, the court held:

> The most that the record here reveals about (the officer's) failure to include the (missing) information is that he did not believe it to be relevant to the probable cause determination. At the very worst, he was merely negligent in disclosing all relevant considerations to the magistrate. His acts fell far short of the level of flagrant police action *Franks* is designed to prevent, and a hearing under that decision was not required. . . .
>   Omitted information that is potentially relevant but not dispositive is not enough to warrant a *Franks* hearing.[12]

Some commentators have recognized that some may disagree with the relevance of the large amount of information that will necessarily be omitted in preparing search warrant affidavits, "since the police routinely collect far more information than goes into the affidavit." Some omissions may be intentional, but reasonable to conclude, in good faith, that the information is marginal, extraneous, or cumulative. This is a valid part of the warrant process. Other items are simply overlooked in the exigencies of the moment without any intent to deceive or recklessness with respect to the truth.[13]

What do we learn from these cases? Oft times during the hurried investigation of serious crimes, the information that comes to the investigator may not be accurate, the witnesses may be speculating as opposed to relating facts, the affidavit he/she prepares may not be perfect, and the judge may sign a defective search warrant. In order to ensure your search holds up in court, you must still act in good faith, not have a reckless disregard for the truth, follow all the rules, and not knowingly mislead the issuing judge. Prepare a search warrant and affidavit that is as specific and accurate as possible. Include in your affidavit any evidence that the magistrate may find relevant to *not finding probable cause*. Remember, we are conducting a search for the truth. Then, maybe your search will survive despite any errors.

---

[11]899 F.2d 297 (4th Cir. 1990), followed by *U.S. v. Shorter*, 328 F.3d 167 (4th Cir. 2003).

[12]*Colkley*, at 301.

[13]See Wayne R. LaFave, *Search and Seizure: A Treatise on the Fourth Amendment*, sec. 4.4(b) 1987.

Questions:

Because of the *Franks* case, is it advisable to place as many facts into the affidavit as possible? Why?

_____

_____

_____

_____

If some of the facts alleged are removed as being not true, what happens to the rest of your affidavit?

_____

_____

_____

_____

What happens if you just put in everything witnesses tell you without making some reasonable effort to verify them as truthful and accurate?

_____

_____

_____

_____

When preparing an affidavit and the accompanying search warrant, it may be advisable to do the following:

1. Discuss the case with a superior officer.
2. Talk to an officer who was part of the underlying investigation (he may realize your error and tell you the house he bought the dope from was *the red one* on the corner, not *the yellow one* next door to it, or the address was 482 Main St., not *428*).
3. Call the local State Attorney's (or DA's) Office, or the attorney your department uses for police legal advice.
4. Never assume your search warrant and affidavit are perfect. Find one that survived a motion to suppress and use it as a basis. (If yours holds up in court, share it with your colleagues.)
5. Compare your observations (being sworn to) to those of other officers on the scene. You may be cross-examined on those facts and impeached[14] by another officer's testimony.

---

[14]Impeachment is being presented with facts that contradict the testimony you are giving. Besides being embarrassing, the judge and jury may not believe you if others disagree with you.

6. If possible, have another officer with you when you apply to the judge for the search warrant. If the actions of the judge or you are questioned, it is helpful to have another witness available to testify to what occurred.

In conclusion:

The requirements of swearing to your affidavit and obtaining a search warrant from a judge encompass two central concepts, which you must always remember.

1. You are involved in the finding, arresting, prosecuting, and preventing of criminal behavior. You are viewed as a nondetached agent of the machine that believes the person to be guilty. You have a "stake in the outcome" of the search. Your opinions are not important. You must present only those facts to the judge that will cause *him to have an opinion* that the particular search will be fruitful. That is why you must sign under oath a complete factual statement that will allow the judge to form that opinion.
2. The involvement of a judge satisfies the constitutional requirement that the judicial branch stand between the citizen to be searched (assuming none of the exceptions to the search warrant requirement apply) and the police. The judge has no "stake in the outcome" of the case. You present the facts, he or she makes the conclusions. As one judge told me once, "You tell me it is a small furry animal with four feet and a tail, and I will decide if it is a cat or a dog."

Why can't we let police officers make these conclusions?

The point of the Fourth Amendment, which often is not grasped by zealous officers, is not that it denies law enforcement the support of the usual inferences which reasonable men draw from evidence. Its protection consists in requiring that those inferences be drawn by a neutral and detached magistrate instead of being judged by the officer engaged in the often competitive enterprise of ferreting out crime.[15]

Let's take this a step further now. Your affidavit and warrant are fine, as is your method of entry (see Chapter Eight, *Hudson v. Michigan*), or they are not, but the exceptions apply. Now when you enter the home to execute the warrant, you learn that the original fraud and identity theft suspects who lived there, one of which was the registered owner of a 9-mm Glock, had moved out three months earlier. That is just what happened in Lancaster, California, in December of 2001.

Upon entry, seven deputy sheriffs find the current homeowner, and his live-in girlfriend, in bed, under the sheets. Her 17-year-old son had opened the door pursuant to the knock and announce of the police. The opinion of the U.S. Supreme Court tells us that:

The deputies' announcement awoke Rettele and Sadler. The deputies entered their bedroom with guns drawn and ordered them to get out of their bed and to show their hands. They protested that they were not wearing

---

[15]*Johnson v. U.S.*, 333 U.S. 10 (1948).

clothes. Rettele stood up and attempted to put on a pair of sweatpants, but deputies told him not to move. Sadler also stood up and attempted, without success, to cover herself with a sheet. Rettele and Sadler were held at gunpoint for one to two minutes before Rettele was allowed to retrieve a robe for Sadler. He was then permitted to dress. Rettele and Sadler left the bedroom within three to four minutes to sit on the couch in the living room.

By that time the deputies realized they had made a mistake. They apologized to Rettele and Sadler, thanked them for not becoming upset, and left within five minutes. They proceeded to the other house the warrant authorized them to search, where they found three suspects. Those suspects were arrested and convicted.   See *Los Angeles County, California et al. v. Max Rettele*, 550 U.S. 609, 127 S.Ct. 1989 (2007).

How did the deputies learn of their mistake? It was easy. The original suspects were four African Americans; Max and his girlfriend were not! They did not move to suppress any contraband found in their home as none was there, nor were they arrested. They filed a lawsuit in federal court instead, under section 1983 of the U.S. Code, alleging their constitutional right to be free from unreasonable searches and seizures was violated. They conceded the warrant was valid, but that the deputies executed it in an unreasonable manner. The lawsuit was dismissed in the trial court as the deputies had a warrant.

The Court of Appeals for the Ninth Circuit reversed, concluding both that the deputies violated the Fourth Amendment and that they were not entitled to qualified immunity because a reasonable deputy would have stopped the search upon discovering that respondents were of a different race than the suspects and because a reasonable deputy would not have ordered respondents from their bed.   *Rettele.*

One judge dissented. In his view, the deputies had authority to detain the plaintiffs (soon to be called respondents when Los Angeles County took an appeal to the Supreme Court) for the duration of the search and were justified in ordering respondents from their bed because weapons could have been concealed under the bedcovers. What did the Supremes do?

Because respondents were of a different race than the suspects the deputies were seeking, *the Court of Appeals* held that "[a]fter taking one look at [respondents], the deputies should have realized that [respondents] were not the subjects of the search warrant and did not pose a threat to the deputies' safety." *We need not pause long in rejecting this unsound proposition*. When the deputies ordered respondents from their bed, they had no way of knowing whether the African-American suspects were elsewhere in the house. The presence of some Caucasians in the residence did not eliminate the possibility that the suspects lived there as well. As the deputies stated in their affidavits, it is not uncommon in our society for people of different races to live together. Just as people of different races live and work together, so too might they engage in joint criminal activity. The deputies, who were searching a house where they believed a suspect might be armed, possessed authority to secure the premises before deciding whether to continue with the search. *Rettele*, at S.Ct. 1992. (even though we have the official US cite, the pages are not in the computer yet)

Then they cited to earlier cases in which the:

Court held that officers executing a search warrant for contraband may "detain the occupants of the premises while a proper search is conducted." *Michigan* v. *Summers*, 452 U.S. 692 (1981). In weighing whether the search in *Summers* was reasonable the Court first found that "detention represents only an incremental intrusion on personal liberty when the search of a home has been authorized by a valid warrant." Against that interest, it balanced "preventing flight in the event that incriminating evidence is found"; "minimizing the risk of harm to the officers"; and facilitating "the orderly completion of the search." See also *Muehler* v. *Mena*, 544 U.S. 93 (2005).

In executing a search warrant, officers may take reasonable action to secure the premises and to ensure their own safety and the efficacy of the search. *Muehler*, at 98–100; see also at 103 (KENNEDY, J., concurring); *Summers*, *supra*, at 704–705. The test of reasonableness under the Fourth Amendment is an objective one. *Graham* v. *Connor*, 490 U.S. 386, 397 (1989) (addressing the reasonableness of a seizure of the person). {Discussed in Chapter 9} Unreasonable actions include the use of excessive force or restraints that cause unnecessary pain or are imposed for a prolonged and unnecessary period of time.

The orders by the police to the occupants, in the context of this lawful search, were permissible, and perhaps necessary, to protect the safety of the deputies. Blankets and bedding can conceal a weapon, and one of the suspects was known to own a firearm, factors which underscore this point. The Constitution does not require an officer to ignore the possibility that an armed suspect may sleep with a weapon within reach. (The case law is) replete with accounts of suspects sleeping close to weapons.

See *United States* v. *Enslin*, 327 F. 3d 788, 791 (CA9 2003) ("When [the suspect] put his hands in the air and began to sit up, his movement shifted the covers and the marshals could see a gun in the bed next to him"); see also *United States* v. *Jones*, 336 F. 3d 245, 248 (CA3 2003) (suspect kept a 9-millimeter Luger under his pillow while he slept); *United States* v. *Hightower*, 96 F. 3d 211 (CA7 1996) (suspect kept a loaded five-shot handgun under his pillow); *State* v. *Willis*, 36,759–KA, p. 3 (La. App. 4/9/03), 843 So. 2d 592, 595 (officers "pulled back the bed covers and found a .38 caliber Model 10 Smith and Wesson revolver located near where defendant's left hand had been"); *State* v. *Kypreos*, 115 Wash. App. 207, 61 P. 3d 352 (2002) (suspect kept a handgun in the bed).

The deputies needed a moment to secure the room and ensure that other persons were not close by or did not present a danger. Deputies were not required to turn their backs to allow Rettele and Sadler to retrieve clothing or to cover themselves with the sheets. Rather, "[t]he risk of harm to both the police and the occupants is minimized if the officers routinely exercise unquestioned command of the situation." *Summers*, 452 U.S., at 702–703.

This is not to say, of course, that the deputies were free to force Rettele and Sadler to remain motionless and standing for any longer than necessary. We have recognized that "special circumstances, or possibly a prolonged detention" might render a search unreasonable. There is no accusation that the detention here was prolonged. The deputies left the home less than 15 minutes after arriving. The detention was shorter and less restrictive than the 2- to 3-hour handcuff detention upheld in *Mena*. See 544 U.S., at 100. And there is no allegation that the deputies prevented Sadler and Rettele from dressing longer than necessary to protect their safety. Sadler was unclothed for no more than two minutes, and Rettele for only slightly more time than that. Sadler testified that once the police were satisfied that no immediate threat was presented, "they wanted us to get dressed and they were pressing us really fast to hurry up and get some clothes on." Deposition of Judy Lorraine Sadler (June 10, 2003), Doc. 26, Exh. 4, p. 55.

The Fourth Amendment allows warrants to issue on probable cause, a standard well short of absolute certainty. Valid warrants will issue to search the innocent, and people like Rettele and Sadler unfortunately bear the cost. Officers executing search warrants on occasion enter a house when residents are engaged in private activity; and the resulting frustration, embarrassment, and humiliation may be real, as was true here.

When officers execute a valid warrant and act in a reasonable manner to protect themselves from harm, however, the Fourth Amendment is not violated.

As respondents' constitutional rights were not violated, "there is no necessity for further inquiries concerning qualified immunity." *Saucier* v. *Katz*, 533 U.S. 194, 201 (2001). The judgment of the Court of Appeals is reversed.

It is so ordered.   *Los Angeles v. Rettele.*

No Fourth Amendment violation, no damages. Lawsuit dismissal upheld. Who else protects you like that?

Was the Amendment, and the cases decided under it, intended to protect criminals. Is this a built-in technicality for bad guys to get off, or is there another reason behind it?

What does our history tell us?

The fallacy in maintaining that the Fourth Amendment was designed to protect criminals only was emphasized by Judge Prettyman in *District of Columbia v. Little*, 85 U.S.App.D.C. 242, (1950), 'The argument is wholly without merit, preposterous in fact. The basic premise of the prohibition against searches was not protection against self-incrimination; it was the common-law right of a man to privacy in his home, a right which is one of the indispensable ultimate essentials of our concept of civilization. It was firmly established in the common law as one of the bright features of the

Anglo-Saxon contributions to human progress. It was not related to crime or to suspicion of crime. It belonged to all men, not merely to criminals, real or suspected. So much is clear from any examination of history, whether slight or exhaustive. The argument made to us has not the slightest basis in history. It has no greater justification in reason. To say that a man suspected of crime has a right to protection against search of his home without a warrant, but that a man not suspected of crime has no such protection, is a fantastic absurdity.'   *Frank v. Maryland*, 359 U.S. 360, at 377–78 (1959).

The court went on to explain:

The philosophy of the Fourth Amendment was well expressed by Mr. Justice Butler speaking for the Court in *Agnello v. United States*, 269 U.S. 20, 32 (1925) 'The search of a private dwelling without a warrant is in itself unreasonable and abhorrent to our laws.' We have emphasized over and again that a search without a warrant can be made only in exceptional circumstances. If a house is on fire or if the police see a fugitive enter a building, entry without a search warrant can of course be made. Yet absent such extraordinary situations (an *exijentzy*), the right of privacy must yield only when a judicial officer issues a warrant for a search on a showing of probable cause. . . .

   The presence of a search warrant serves a high function. Absent some grave emergency, the Fourth Amendment has interposed a magistrate between the citizen and the police. This was done not to shield criminals nor to make the home a safe haven for illegal activities. It was done so that an objective mind might weigh the need to invade that privacy in order to enforce the law. The right of privacy was deemed too precious to entrust to the discretion of those whose job is the detection of crime and the arrest of criminals. Power is a heady thing. . . . And so the Constitution requires a magistrate to pass on the desires of the police before they violate the privacy of the home. We cannot be true to that constitutional requirement and excuse the absence of a search warrant without a showing by those who seek exemption from the constitutional mandate that the exigencies of the situation (require it).   *Frank, at* 380–81.

Notes:

_____

_____

_____

_____

_____

_____

CHAPTER 8

The No-Knock Warrant and the Exclusionary Rule

Hudson v. Michigan

The Knock and Announce Violation

THE BEGINNING OF THE END FOR THE EXCLUSIONARY RULE?

In the last chapter we saw how the good-faith exception for defective search warrants and affidavits evolved. In those cases, affidavits with less than PC and warrants directing the searching officers to look for the wrong property were nonetheless upheld as the officers tried to follow the law, despite the errors. We also saw other examples of officers attempting to follow the law but getting bad information from computers or witnesses. Their searches were also upheld, despite the technical illegality of the arrest.

Now let's take this a step further. We are now at the execution stage of the search warrant.

Police officers in Detroit, Michigan, obtained a warrant authorizing a search for drugs and firearms at the home of petitioner Booker Hudson. They discovered both. Large quantities of drugs were found, including cocaine rocks in Hudson's pocket. A loaded gun was lodged between the cushion and armrest of the chair *in which he was sitting*. Hudson was charged under Michigan law with unlawful drug and firearm possession.

This case (was accepted by the U.S. Supreme Court) only because of the method of entry into the house. When the police arrived to execute the warrant, they announced their presence, but waited only a short time— perhaps 'three to five seconds,'—before turning the knob of the unlocked front door and entering Hudson's home. Hudson moved to suppress all the inculpatory evidence, arguing that the premature entry violated his Fourth Amendment rights.[1]

As the prosecutors in Michigan had already conceded that the knock-and-announce rule was violated, Hudson wanted all the drugs and his nearby and handy gun excluded from his trial. Wouldn't be much of a trial without them, as that's what he was charged with possessing.[2] First, let's talk about the knock-and-announce rule. What is it?

The rule is found in the early common law.[3] Why is that important, or relevant? Most of the states that had ratified the U.S. Constitution, and the Fourth Amendment, two years later, had previously enacted state statutes or state constitutional provisions incorporating the English common law into their own jurisprudence. One example is the constitution of the new state of New Jersey, which in 1776 said, "The common law of England . . . shall remain in force, until it shall be altered by a future law of the legislature." Similarly, the constitution of New York, adopted in 1777, had a similar provision. "Such parts of the common law of England. . . which was the law of New York shall be and continue (to be) the law of the State, subject to such alterations and provisions as the legislature of the State shall, from time to time, make."[4]

Now that we know why we refer to old English law, let's see what it said about the knock-and-announce rule.

Most of the case law discussing that rule cites an English case decided in 1603. *Semayne's Case*, 77 Eng. Rep. 194 (Kings Bench, 1603). The case held that despite the older rule that "'a man's house is his castle of defense and asylum,' when the King is a party, the sheriff (if the doors be not open) may break the party's house, either to arrest him, or to do other execution of the King's process, if otherwise he cannot enter." Serving a search warrant is executing *process*.

To this rule, the courts though, attached an important qualification:

> But before he breaks it, he ought to signify the cause of his coming, and to make request to open doors . . . , for the law without a (cause by) the owner abhors the destruction or breaking of any house (which is intended for his habitation and safety) by which great damage and inconvenience might (come) to the party (who may not have known of the) process, of which, if he had known, it is to be presumed that he would obey it. *Semayne's Case*, at 195–196.

Shall we continue to presume that today's dopers, armed with assault weapons, will also open the door merely because you're knocking!

---

[1] *Hudson v. Michigan*, 547 U.S. 586, 126 S.Ct. 2159, 2162 (2006).

[2] By reading between the lines, we see how this courtroom drama played out. The defendant originally won his motion to suppress by convincing the trial judge that the knock-and-announce violation required suppression. The state of Michigan appealed to their Court of Appeals and won a reversal. Now back for trial, the defendant waived his right to a jury trial and the trial judge found him guilty of possessing a lesser amount of drugs. There is no mention of the gun. The defendant was sentenced to eighteen months' probation. Was there a message here? *People v. Hudson*, an unpublished opinion only found at 2004 WL 1366947 (Mich.App.).

[3] Remember that? That's all about case law from England from long ago.

[4] See footnote 2, in Chapter Four, for the long definition of the common law.

Despite the age of that case, Justice Thomas, writing for a unanimous court in *Wilson v. Arkansas*,[5] a case that led to *Hudson*, found a statute from 1275 (what, you say, does that have to do with selling dope in Arkansas in 1992? Wait, it gets worse.) that said (referring to 1 Edw., ch. 17, in 1 Statutes at Large from Magna Carta to Henry 6 (cited in O. Ruffhead ed. 1769)) providing that if any person takes the beasts of another and causes them "to be driven into a Castle or Fortress," if the sheriff makes "solem[n] deman[d]" for deliverance of the beasts, and if the person "did not cause the Beasts to be delivered," the King "shall cause the said Castle or Fortress to be beaten down without Recovery."

Based upon that statute, and the *later* case of *Semayne*, an English court in 1774 held:

> As to the outer door, the law is now clearly taken that it is protected, but the door may be broken when the due notification and demand have been made and refused.   *Lee v. Gansell*, 98 Eng. Rep. 700 (K.B.1774).

Several legal commentators writing when our country was founded agreed that this was the law at the time. The legendary William Blackstone said it best, that the sheriff may "justify breaking open doors, if the possession be not quietly delivered" (3 Blackstone 412). Others were a bit wordier. According to Sir Matthew Hale, the "constant practice" at common law was that "the officer may break open the door, if he be sure the offender is there, *if after acquainting them of the business, and demanding the prisoner, he refuses to open the door*." (See 1 M. Hale, Pleas of the Crown 582.)

The Supreme Court finally announced that this rule was firmly a part of our jurisprudence in *Miller v. United States*, 357 U.S. 301, 313 (1958). Congress codified the rule in 1917, now known as 18 U.S.C. § 3109. More recently, the *Wilson* case decided that the rule was subject to the Fourth Amendment; that is to say, it had to be applied, or dispensed with, reasonably.

Would ya believe this was also true in colonial America? "Even the legislation creating the dreaded and oft-denounced writs of assistance [see Chapter Two] required that notice be given before entry was made. Commencing as early as 1813, with *Bell v. Clapp*, 10 Johns. R. 263 (N.Y.Sup.Ct., 1813), American courts began speaking of the necessity of giving notice in the execution of a search warrant. This became the generally accepted common law rule in this country, subject to only limited exceptions" (*LaFave*, below).

> Given the longstanding common-law endorsement of the practice of announcement, we have little doubt that the Framers of the Fourth Amendment thought that the method of an officer's entry into a dwelling was among the factors to be considered in assessing the reasonableness of a search or seizure. . . . We hold that in some circumstances an officer's unannounced entry into a home might be unreasonable under the Fourth Amendment.[6]

---

[5]514 U.S. 927 (1995).
[6]*Wilson*, at 934.

Because the rule is subject to the reasonableness standard of the Fourth Amendment, the courts have held there are "many situations in which it is not necessary to knock and announce." It is not necessary when "circumstances presen[t] a threat of physical violence," or if there is "reason to believe that evidence would likely be destroyed if advance notice were given," or if knocking and announcing would be "futile." *Richards v. Wisconsin*, 520 U.S. 385, 394 (1997).

Typical of state statutes requiring the announcement is Florida Statute 933.09:

> The officer may break open any outer door, inner door or window of a house, or any part of a house or anything therein, to execute the warrant, if *after due notice* of the officer's authority and purpose he or she is refused admittance to said house or access to anything therein (enacted in 1923).

Cases around the country have held that police officers acted reasonably when:

> Entering without knocking in a "raid in execution of search warrant . . . as officers had reasonable grounds to fear destruction of cocaine if they had knocked and announced their authority and purpose; contraband sought was maintained by defendant in quantities readily disposable in residential sink or toilet."[7]

Other exceptions to the knock-and-announce requirement are permitted where persons within already know of officers' authority and purpose; where officers are justified in belief that persons within are in imminent peril of bodily harm; where officers' peril would have been increased by announcement; or where officers are justified in belief that escape or destruction of evidence is being attempted. See the excellent discussion by Justice Thomas in *Wilson*, citing to cases from 1619, 1819, 1838 and an early police manual written in 1884 (indicating that there is nothing new here).[8]

---

[7]They can be found annotated at 17 A.L.R.4th 301. For cases reporting violations, *see, e.g.*, 34 Geo. L.J. Ann. Rev.Crim. Proc. 31–35 (2005) (collecting court of appeals cases); Annot., 85 A.L.R. 5th 1 (2001) (collecting state-court cases).

[8]This is not to say, of course, that every entry must be preceded by an announcement. The Fourth Amendment's flexible requirement of reasonableness should not be read to mandate a rigid rule of announcement that ignores countervailing law enforcement interests. As even petitioner concedes, the common-law principle of announcement was never stated as an inflexible rule requiring announcement under all circumstances. *See Ker v. California*, 374 U.S. 23 (1963) (plurality opinion) ("[I]t has been recognized from the early common law that . . . breaking is permissible in executing an arrest under certain circumstances") (this is the plain view case discussed in Chapter Two); *see also, White & Wiltsheire*, 81 Eng.Rep. 709, 710 (K.B.1619) (upholding the sheriff's breaking of the door of the plaintiff's dwelling after the sheriff's bailiffs had been imprisoned in the plaintiff's dwelling while they attempted an earlier execution of the seizure); *Pugh v. Griffith*, 112 Eng.Rep. 681, 686 (K.B.1838) (holding that "the necessity of a demand . . . is obviated, because there was nobody on whom a demand could be made" and noting that *White & Wiltsheire* leaves open the possibility that there may be "other occasions where the outer door may be broken" without prior demand). Indeed, at the time of the framing (of our Constitution), the common-law admonition that an officer "ought to signify the cause of his coming" (*Semayne's Case*, 77 Eng.Rep., at 195) had not been extended conclusively to the context of felony arrests. ("The full scope of the application of the rule in criminal cases . . . was never judicially settled"); *Launock v. Brown*, 106 Eng.Rep. 482, 483 (K.B.1819) ("It is not at present necessary for us to decide how far, in the case of a person charged with felony, it would be necessary to make a previous demand of admittance before you could justify breaking open the outer door of his house"); W. Murfree, Law of Sheriffs and Other Ministerial Officers § 1163, p. 631 (1st ed. 1884) ("[A]lthough there has been some doubt on the question, the better opinion seems to be that, in cases of felony, no demand of admittance is necessary, especially as, in many cases, the delay incident to it would enable the prisoner to escape"). The common-law principle gradually was applied to cases involving felonies, but at the same time the courts continued to recognize that under certain circumstances the presumption in favor of announcement necessarily would give way to contrary considerations (*Wilson*, at pp. 934–935).

Now that it is clear the law allows, in certain circumstances, forgoing the knock and announce prior to executing the search warrant, what is the burden, the degree of proof needed, to justify that action? In *Richards*, Justice Stevens, speaking again for a unanimous court, held:

> In order to justify a "no-knock" entry, the police must have a *reasonable suspicion* that knocking and announcing their presence, under the particular circumstances, would be dangerous or futile, or that it would inhibit the effective investigation of the crime by, for example, allowing the destruction of evidence. This standard—*as opposed to a probable-cause requirement*—strikes the appropriate balance between the legitimate law enforcement concerns at issue in the execution of search warrants and the individual privacy interests affected by no-knock entries. (For an example see *Maryland v. Buie*, 494 U.S. 325, 337 (1990), allowing a protective sweep of a house during an arrest where the officers have "a reasonable belief based on specific and articulable facts that the area to be swept harbors an individual posing a danger to those on the arrest scene"); *Terry v. Ohio*, 392 U.S. 1, 30 (1968) (requiring a reasonable and articulable suspicion of danger to justify a patdown search). This showing is not high, but the police should be required to make it whenever the reasonableness of a no-knock entry is challenged.[9]

The *Hudson* case built upon that and added:

> [I]n *Wilson*, (we held) that the knock-and-announce requirement could give way 'under circumstances presenting a threat of physical violence,' or 'where police officers have reason to believe that evidence would likely be destroyed if advance notice were given. . . .' This Court has encountered before the links between drugs and violence, . . . and the likelihood that drug dealers will attempt to dispose of drugs before police seize them, see, *Ker v. California*, 374 U.S. 23, 28, n.3 (1963) [the plain view doctrine discussed in Chapter Two].   *Hudson*, at 589.

What about those "no-knock" warrants we often hear about? Cases from around the country have held that:

> No-knock warrants are disfavored under the law and limited largely to those states that have enacted statutory provisions authorizing their issuance.[10] In fact, "[t]he prevailing . . . view is that a magistrate may not issue a so-called no-knock search warrant in the absence of such a statute or provision. . . ."

---

[9]*Richards*, at 394.

[10]A number of states give magistrate judges the authority to issue "no-knock" warrants if the officers demonstrate ahead of time a reasonable suspicion that entry without prior announcement will be appropriate in a particular context. *See, e.g.*, 725 Ill.Comp.Stat., ch. 725, § 5/108–8 (1992); Neb.Rev.Stat. § 29–411 (1995); Okla.Stat., Tit. 22, § 1228 (Supp.1997); S.D. Codified Laws § 23A-35–9 (1988); Utah Code Ann. § 77–23–210 (1995). *Richards*, at 395.

The reasoning against no-knock warrants is convincing. Circumstances that may seemingly justify issuance of a no-knock search warrant may change drastically after issuance but before execution of the warrant. Conditions must be assessed at the scene at the time of entry: While a search warrant must necessarily rest upon previously obtained information, . . . facts existing at the time of obtaining a warrant may no longer exist at the time of entry. Such an emergency, therefore, can be judged only in light of circumstances of which the officer is aware at the latter moment. *Parsley v. Superior Court*, 9 Cal.3d 934 (1973). As a matter of policy, no-knock warrants are disfavored because of their staggering potential for violence to both occupants and police, ... We conclude that in the absence of express statutory authorization no-knock search warrants are without legal effect in Florida. *State of Florida v. Bamber*, 630 So.2d 1048 (Fla. 1994). 2 Wayne R. LaFave, *Search and Seizure* § 4.8(g) (1987).

Once again, it appears the cop on the scene has more authority than the judge reviewing the facts in his chambers; just use it wisely.

Returning to *Hudson*, the court re-affirmed that the reasonableness of "when to knock" is a difficult call to make (like most we are called upon to make out in the field).

When the knock-and-announce rule does apply, it is not easy to determine precisely what officers must do. How many seconds' wait are too few? Our "reasonable wait time" standard, (announced in) *United States v. Banks*, 540 U.S. 31, 41, (2003), is necessarily vague. *Banks* (a drug case, like this one) held that the proper measure was not how long it would take the resident to reach the door, but how long it would take to dispose of the suspected drugs—but that such a time (15 to 20 seconds in that case) would necessarily be extended when, for instance, the suspected contraband was not easily concealed. [That means wait a little longer if the warrant is for stolen VCRs; they are bit harder to flush down the toilet.] If our *ex post* evaluation (after the fact) is subject to such calculations, it is unsurprising that, *ex ante* (before the fact), police officers about to encounter someone who may try to harm them will be uncertain how long to wait. Happily, these issues do not confront us here. From the trial level onward, Michigan has conceded that the entry was a knock-and-announce violation. The issue here is remedy. *Wilson* specifically declined to decide whether the exclusionary rule is appropriate for violation of the knock-and-announce requirement. That question is squarely before us now.[11]

This is a great example of the court first finding the law and then refining it to deal with new questions and new facts. First, Justice Scalia explains how the *Wilson* case imposed a requirement of reasonableness upon the decision of whether to knock, or if knocking, how long to wait before entering. A few years later, in *Richards*,

---

[11]*Hudson*, at S.Ct. 590.

the court said that generally certain exigencies might be deemed good reasons to forgo the rule altogether. Then he cites *Banks*, in which the rule of *Richards* is further developed by a specific example.[12] Back in 1275, we were concerned with saving the door and the homeowner's dignity. While still a concern in modern America, that must now be balanced by how quickly the doper can get to the toilet or grab his gun. In *Banks*, the police came at 2 p.m., when it was not likely that Banks was still in bed (could an argument be made that after selling or packaging dope all night, he might still be asleep in the afternoon?). Another critical factor was that it was "imminent disposal, not travel time to the entrance, that governs when police may reasonably enter. . . ." As we discussed earlier, it is the totality of the circumstances that governs Fourth Amendment law. Look to all the facts—bring them all to the court's attention at the pre-trial motion to suppress—to justify why it was *reasonable* to act as you did. Then argue, as we learned in Chapter Two—"we had to protect the police—and the evidence."

Because the state of Michigan conceded the violation of Hudson's Fourth Amendment rights, the court then reviewed the reasons for the exclusionary rule to determine whether it should apply to this type of violation.

Why is it that the courts won't let the police use certain evidence in trial? Why do we even consider not using reliable evidence to help the prosecution prove its case?

It was found that other methods of deterring violations of the Constitution did not work.

> In *Mapp (v. Ohio)*, the Court found that experience showed that alternative methods of enforcing the Fourth Amendment's requirements had failed. See 367 U.S. 643, at 651–653; (1961) see, *People v. Cahan*, 44 Cal.2d 434, 447 (1955) (Traynor, C.J.) ("Experience [in California] has demonstrated, how-ever, that neither administrative, criminal nor civil remedies are effective in suppressing lawless searches and seizures"). The Court consequently held that "all evidence obtained by searches and seizures in violation of the Constitution is, by that same authority, inadmissible in a state court." *Mapp*, 367 U.S., at 655. "To hold otherwise," the Court added, would be "to grant the right but in reality to withhold its privilege and enjoyment." *Hudson*, at 608 (Breyer, dissenting).

---

[12]Several Courts of Appeals have explicitly taken into account the risk of disposal of drug evidence as a factor in evaluating the reasonableness of waiting time. *See, e.g., United States v. Goodson*, 165 F.3d 610, 612, 614 (CA8 1999) (holding a 20-second wait after a loud announcement at a one-story ranch reasonable); *United States v. Spikes*, 158 F.3d 913, 925–927 (CA6 1998) (holding a 15-to-30-second wait in midmorning after a loud announcement reasonable); *United States* v. *Spriggs*, 996 F.2d 320, 322–323 (CADC 1993) (hold-ing a 15-second wait after a reasonably audible announcement at 7:45 a.m. on a weekday reasonable); *United States v. Garcia*, 983 F.2d 1160, 1168 (CA1 1993) (holding a 10-second wait after a loud announcement reasonable); *United States v. Jones*, 133 F.3d 358, 361–362 (CA5 1998) (relying specifically on the concept of exigency, holding a 15-to-20-second wait reasonable). *See also, United States v. Chavez-Miranda*, 306 F.3d 973, 981–982, n.7 (CA9 2002) ("*Banks* appears to be a departure from our prior decisions . . . . [W]e have found a 10 to 20 second wait to be reasonable in similar circumstances, albeit when the police heard sounds after the knock and announcement"); *United States v. Jenkins*, 175 F.3d 1208, 1215 (CA10 1999) (holding a 14-to-20-second wait at 10 a.m. reasonable); *United States v. Markling*, 7 F.3d 1309, 1318–1319 (CA7 1993) (holding a 7-second wait at a small motel room reasonable when officers acted on a specific tip that the suspect was likely to dispose of the drugs).

(Therefore, first) (i)n *Weeks v. United States*, 232 U.S. 383 (1914), we adopted the federal exclusionary rule for evidence that was unlawfully seized from a home without a warrant in violation of the Fourth Amendment.[13] We (then) began applying the same rule to the States, through the Fourteenth Amendment, in *Mapp*. *Hudson*, at 590.

If . . . private documents can thus be seized and held and used in evidence against a citizen accused of an offense, the protection of the 4th Amendment, declaring his right to be secure against such searches and seizures, is of no value, and, . . . might as well be stricken from the Constitution. *Weeks*, 232 U.S., *Hudson*, at 591.

This ruling, like many, has been relaxed over the years. Since *Mapp*:

Subsequent case law has rejected this (strict) application of the exclusionary rule. We had said as much in (*Arizona v. Evans*, (1995) (the clerk's error allowing the arrest warrant to remain in the computer) and *Leon*, (See Chapter Seven—the good faith exception) a decade earlier, when we explained that "[w]hether the exclusionary sanction is appropriately imposed in a particular case, . . . is 'an issue separate from the question whether the Fourth Amendment rights of the party . . . were violated by police conduct.'" *Leon*, 468 U.S., at 906. Both cited in *Hudson*, at 591.

Now, courts use the word *attenuation*. Did the violation directly result in the seizure? Would the evidence have lawfully been observed, even without the violation? Or is the result of the search *attenuated* from the violation? In the *Hudson* case, the reasons for the knock-and-announce rule are given:

One of those interests is the protection of human life and limb, because an unannounced entry may provoke violence in supposed self-defense by the surprised resident. Another interest is the protection of property. Breaking a house (as the old cases typically put it) absent an announcement would penalize someone who 'did not know of the process, of which, if he had notice, it is to be presumed that he would obey it. . . .' The knock-and-announce rule gives individuals 'the opportunity to comply with the law and to avoid the destruction of property occasioned by a forcible entry.' And thirdly, the knock-and-announce rule protects those elements of privacy and dignity that can be destroyed by a sudden entrance. It gives residents the 'opportunity to prepare themselves for' the entry of the police. 'The brief interlude between announcement and entry with a warrant may be the opportunity that an individual has to pull on clothes or get out of bed.' In other words, it assures the opportunity to collect oneself before answering the door.

---

[13]Fremont Weeks' home, at 1834 Penn Street, in Kansas City, Missouri, was entered and searched by local police officers when he was not present. He was arrested at work at Union Station at the time. The search was clearly not incident to the arrest! The police then invited the U.S. Marshal to join in the search. Over Weeks' objection, he was convicted in federal court of using the U.S. mails to transport shares in a lottery enterprise. This appeal followed.

What the knock-and-announce rule has never protected, however, is one's interest in preventing the government from seeing or taking evidence described in a warrant. *Hudson*, at 594.

Attenuation can occur, of course, when the causal connection is remote. *See, e.g., Nardone v. United States*, 308 U.S. 338, 341 (1939). Attenuation also occurs when, even given a direct causal connection, the interest protected by the constitutional guarantee that has been violated would not be served by suppression of the evidence obtained. "The penalties visited upon the Government, and in turn upon the public, because its officers have violated the law must bear some relation to the purposes which the law is to serve."[14]

We have not . . . mechanically applied the [exclusionary] rule to every item of evidence that has a causal connection with police misconduct. [As] causation in the logical sense alone [citing earlier cases] can be too attenuated to justify exclusion.

Even in the early days of the exclusionary rule, we declined to "hold that all evidence is 'fruit of the poisonous tree' simply because it would not have come to light *but for* the illegal actions of the police. Rather, the more apt question in such a case is 'whether, granting establishment of the primary illegality, the evidence to which instant objection is made has been come at by exploitation of that illegality or instead by means sufficiently distinguishable to be purged of the primary taint.' "   *Wong Sun v. United States*, 371 U.S. 471, 487–88 (1963).

That quote from *Wong Sun*, memorized by legions of law students, is still, nonetheless, a bit of a mouthful. By reading the facts of the case, it becomes more easily understandable. At about 2 a.m., on the morning of June 4, 1959, federal narcotics agents in San Francisco arrested a Hom Way for possessing heroin. Hom Way immediately threw in a Blackie Toy, owner of a laundry on Leavenworth Street, as the person he bought it from the day before. When Toy refused admittance to the agents coming to interview him, and slammed shut his door, about six of them just ran in, again without any warrants. The agents chased him to the living quarters, in the rear where his wife and children were sleeping, and he was arrested. He gave up *his* supplier as a Johnny Yee. *Payton v. New York* not having been decided yet (Chapter Two—warrant required to enter house for purposes of an arrest), the agents then went to and entered Yee's house (again, no mention of consent or paper), where Yee promptly surrendered his stash and laid it all on a Wong Sun, aka Sea Dog, as his supplier. Confused yet?

Now, the agents, after knocking on Wong Sun's door, barged past his wife as she opened it, entered the house, and arrested him. The record is barren of any request to enter, warrant, or consent given by Mrs. Wong Sun. I don't know how they did things in federal court in 1959, but I don't see much of a prosecution here besides Hom Way, who got caught with the dope, and that assumes a lawful arrest and search. In any event, the feds tried to make a case against all of them with their statements, which indicated that Blackie Toy's Chinese laundry was the

---

[14]*United States v. Ceccolini*, 435 U.S. 268, 274 (1978).

source of the heroin. However, the investigation was also pre-*Miranda* so maybe they had a case.

Considering all the hearsay by untested and unreliable co-defendants, and a big assumption they would agree to testify against their buddy,[15] that might have been the end of his case, but Wong Sun had another big problem and that caused him to be convicted at trial.

He made a statement to the federal agents a few days *after* his arrest. He wanted this suppressed as it was a result of, and flowed from, he claimed, not only his unlawful arrest and the unwarranted search of his house (which turned up no drugs) but also from the statements made by Blackie Toy and Johnny Yee, who were similarly arrested and searched illegally. He argued that his subsequent statement was the fruit of all these constitutional violations. Despite this case being pre-*Payton* and pre-*Miranda*, federal agents jeopardized any seizures made without complying with the Fourth Amendment pursuant to *Weeks v. United States*, the law in federal court since 1914.[16] Arrests are seizures (of the person), see Chapter Nine, and must be based upon probable cause.

After Wong Sun's conviction at trial, both the Court of Appeals and the Supreme Court found his arrest was not based upon probable cause. This supported the defendant's argument that his statement must fall due to the illegal arrest.

However, the final opinion states:

> In view of the fact that, after his unlawful arrest, petitioner Wong Sun had been lawfully arraigned and released on his own recognizance and had returned voluntarily several days later when he made his unsigned statement, the connection between his unlawful arrest and the making of that statement was *so attenuated* that the unsigned statement was not the fruit of the unlawful arrest and, therefore, it was properly admitted in evidence. *Wong Sun*, at 491.

Wong Sun's unsigned confession (as he could not read English) was not the product of his arrest (it did not flow directly from the illegal arrest) and was therefore properly admitted at trial. As for the alleged constitutional violations committed against Toy and Yee, those actions did not violate Wong Sun's rights and he had no standing to complain about them. His statement was attenuated—so distanced as to not be caused by the previous illegal conduct.

Many years later, I made a similar argument after a Miami judge found the arrest of one of our lesser known dope-rip-murderers, by a Newark, New Jersey, police officer to be illegal. Seems the guy's girl friend "dimed him out" and called 911 to report his warrant status. The Newark officer took the defendant on a five-minute ride to his station to verify that he was the one wanted in Miami for first-degree murder, after the defendant gave several different names. The learned trial court ruled

---

[15]Needless to say, both co-defendants invoked their rights at Wong Sun's trial and refused to testify.

[16]As no drugs were found on Wong Sun, and only statements were made, the charge was conspiracy to possess and distribute, and Ham Way's and Yee's dope was the corroboration needed.

that the Newark officer had no right to detain the defendant and should have done the computer check at the scene (Newark police cars had no computers in their cars then) *and* on a consensual basis. Fearing an appeal and a reversal on those rather shaky grounds, the court allowed me to argue that the defendant's statement, given two and a half days later to a Metro Dade homicide detective, after the waiving of *Miranda* rights, and the defendant having seen a judge in Newark, was "sufficiently distinguished/attenuated from the primary illegality so to be purged of its taint." Motion to suppress denied. Thank you, *Wong Sun*, and Detective James Gallagher, for taking two days to get there.

As seen above, if physical evidence or statements are the direct result of constitutional violations, the suppression of that evidence was thought to be the best way of deterring illegal activities by the police. If you can't use it, why take it? Suppression was clearly the only remedy available in earlier years. But today?

> We cannot assume that exclusion in this context is necessary deterrence simply because we found that it was necessary deterrence in different contexts and long ago. That would be forcing the public today to pay for the sins and inadequacies of a legal regime that existed almost half a century ago. Dollree Mapp (the defendant in *Mapp v. Ohio* whose home was invaded without a warrant in a search for pornography) could not turn to 42 U.S.C. § 1983 for meaningful relief (authorizing criminal penalties on police officers for knowingly violating her constitutional rights), . . . It would be another 17 years before the §1983 remedy was extended to reach the deep pocket of municipalities, *Monell v. New York City Dept. of Social Servs.*, 436 U.S. 658 (1978). Citizens whose Fourth Amendment rights were violated by federal officers could not bring suit until 10 years after *Mapp*, with this Court's decision in *Bivens v. Six Unknown Fed. Narcotics Agents*, 403 U.S. 388 (1971).
>
> (Complaints) that it would be very hard to find a lawyer to take a case such as this, (fail, as) 42 U.S.C. §1988(b) answers this objection. Since some civil-rights violations would yield damages too small to justify the expense of litigation, Congress has authorized attorney's fees for civil-rights plaintiffs.   *Hudson*, at 597.

The opinion goes on to discuss more modern methods of deterring improper police conduct that have been developed in the days since *Weeks* and *Mapp* were decided.

> (One) development over the past half-century that deters civil-rights violations is the increasing professionalism of police forces, including a new emphasis on internal police discipline. . . .

Another is:

> (There is also) increasing evidence that police forces across the United States take the constitutional rights of citizens seriously. There have been wide-ranging reforms in the education, training, and supervision

of police officers. . . . Numerous sources are now available to teach officers and their supervisors what is required of them under this Court's cases, how to respect constitutional guarantees in various situations, and how to craft an effective regime for internal discipline. *See, e.g., D. Waksman & D. Goodman, The Search and Seizure Handbook (2d ed. 2006). Hudson*, at 599.

Where does the court stand on the exclusionary rule now? Despite this 5–4 opinion, there was a concurring opinion by Justice Kennedy, concerned about the rule's continued existence.

The Court's decision should not be interpreted as suggesting that violations of the (Knock and Announce) requirement are trivial or beyond the law's concern. Second, the continued operation of the exclusionary rule, as settled and defined by our precedents, is not in doubt. Today's decision determines only that in the specific context of the knock-and-announce requirement, a violation is not sufficiently related to (is attenuated from) the later discovery of evidence to justify suppression. *Hudson*, at 602–3 (Kennedy, concurring in part and concurring in the judgment).[17]

The strong, four-justice dissent naturally disagreed with the majority opinion. They felt that this method of entry was a substantial violation of a Fourth Amendment protected interest and must be remedied by suppression. They cite some very interesting cases discussing the reasons for the knock-and-announce and exclusionary rules; however, the majority opinion now holds that violations of the knock-and-announce rule can be more effectively dealt with by civil rights lawsuits holding the departments and the jurisdictions liable for damages, internal administrative discipline, federal civil rights criminal penalties (who hasn't heard of the Rodney King case?), and the modern "education and training of police officers." An even more important deterrence for those of you in the field should be the first one mentioned by Justice Scalia:

One of those interests (of the knock and announce rule) is the protection of human life and limb, because an unannounced entry may provoke violence in supposed self-defense by the surprised resident. *Hudson*, at 594.

Getting in before the dope hit the toilet, or the bad guy gets a gun, is important, but him not knowing who you are can be just as dangerous. As we have seen through these cases, the court will protect you and the evidence if you are acting reasonably. That's what the Fourth Amendment is all about. Just don't get hurt applying it.

---

[17]Concurring means he agrees with the final result, but for different reasons. Justice Kennedy believed in the attenuation argument but wanted to make sure all knew the exclusionary rule was alive and well for *un*-attenuated violations. Had he merely *joined* the opinion, there might have been some argument that five justices had done away with the rule.

Before you get concerned that *Hudson* may suggest the end of the exclusionary rule, about three months before *Hudson*, in another opinion, Justice Scalia reminded us that it will live on:

> The Constitution protects property owners . . . by interposing (before-hand) the 'deliberate and impartial judgment of a judicial officer between the citizen and the police,' [citation omitted], and providing (afterwards) a right to suppress evidence improperly obtained and a cause of action for damages.   *U.S. v. Grubbs*, 547 U.S. 90, 99 (2006).

Shortly after *Hudson* came out, a SWAT commander called and asked if they no longer had to apply the knock-and-announce rule. The answer was succinct: The evidence may not be suppressed, but you might be, in more ways than one.

Discussion:

_____

_____

_____

_____

_____

_____

_____

_____

_____

_____

_____

_____

_____

_____

_____

_____

_____

_____

_____

_____

Notes:

_____

_____

_____

_____

_____

CHAPTER 9

Whaddaya Do Now?

Now that you have digested, analyzed, and learned what it takes lawyers two years to do in law school, let's see how you will handle the Fourth Amendment when you *hit the road*.

You are on patrol. You come across a car in a parking lot, or on a side street. It may not be parked exactly right. People wave you down. You listen to them as you see flies hover around the trunk.

Whaddaya do?

Can you enter the car? Are the flies an *exijentzy*? What is causing the flies to stay there? Starting to lose your appetite for lunch?

_____

_____

_____

_____

Are you authorized to force open the trunk? What are you likely to find here?

_____

_____

_____

_____

Is it possible that an injured person may be in there, bleeding to death? If so, get in there and save his life! Don't get too excited. Many times it is the BBQ meats for the weekend that someone forgot to take into the house, *a few days ago*!

Let's say it is a person. If he/she is still alive, do whatever it takes to save their life. That is why you took this job!

Questions:

What if the person is dead?

_____

_____

_____

_____

Remember *Mincey*, what can you do? This is a crime scene and someone may be prosecuted.

_____

_____

_____

_____

#1 Is the emergency over? You bet!!

#2 Need a warrant?[1]

The answer to that depends on whose car it is and where it is parked. If on the public street, let's find out who owns it. If in someone's garage, secure the scene and get out. The VIN # should be visible through the front windshield. The tag, if there is one, should also be visible. There is no reasonable expectation of privacy if those two identifiers are not covered up, and it's probably a violation of law if they are.

After you run the VIN and tag, and get a name, then whaddaya do?

If the car comes back to John Smith, does that tell you who is in the trunk? Depending upon the weather, someone might recognize your DOA. I once went to a homicide scene and saw *four* bodies in a car, off to the side of I-95. Two in the trunk and two in the rear seat. Every *Narc* in town came. Soon we recognized the bodies and didn't have to guess. Quite often in climates like South Florida, you will be unable to even determine the sex or race of your victim. Could be John Smith, or someone Smith killed and left in his car.

---

[1]Even though Chapter Two taught us the automobile exception, apply my grandmother's rule. Search warrants are like chicken soup, they can't hurt, if you have the time.

Whaddaya Do?

_____

_____

_____

_____

If you gamble the body is Smith, and you are wrong, Smith may get all your evidence from the trunk and the body suppressed. Do you want to explain that to the widow and children? How about the media? How about your chief?

Would knowing the approximate time of death be helpful in this investigation? Have the ME take a quick look and feel. Cases like this can be smelled from about forty feet away; but you'll get used to it after awhile.

What do you put in your search warrant affidavit? Before you look in Appendix B, remember what you learned so far. You were authorized to enter the vehicle, due to the exigent circumstances, so tell the judge what you saw while you were lawfully in the car.

Tell him who the car belongs to and the results of trying to find that person, or a co-owner, in order to get permission to search the car. Tell him why you want to enter the car. Why? The crime scene techs and the ME have a job to do.

If it turns out that it was Smith in the car, not only did you preserve his Fourth Amendment rights, he wasn't going anywhere anyway. However, if it was not Smith in the car, and Smith is missing, and Smith's fingerprints are found on the body, or on the wallet and credit card holder near the body, or on the knife still in the body, you are on your way to making a _nice collar_.

How's this scenario?

We responded (there I go, talking like a cop again). _We went_ to an apartment one evening after the occupant did not show for work on Monday and Tuesday. Instead of kicking in the door, the detectives asked the landlord/manager for a key. The exigency is not as strong as if the neighbors hear shots, but he could still be alive, after a serious injury or other medical condition.

As we entered, we saw that our first aid capabilities would not help the man on the floor. He was cold, stiff, and dead. Blood had leaked out of some holes in his chest.

Whaddaya do now? The first question in a _Whodunit_ is _Who is it_? If the neighbors tell you he is the tenant, can you begin searching? Somebody better look around to see if the shooter is still there, unlikely, but why take chances with your life. Anyone else shot? Does he need a paramedic or a funeral director? Is the _exijentzy_ over? Sounds like it.

Whaddaya do now?

Before you start searching, maybe you want to know who he lives with. The apartment I went to had an open bedroom closet, in the same room where the deceased was. One side of the closet had men's clothing, and the other side was empty. No suitcase above the clothes rack. Didn't mean too much until the neighbors asked us *where his wife was*.

Is she a potential suspect? Did she just pack up and chase after the killer? Until you know the answers to those questions, any searching for evidence would be foolish. Whaddaya do? Prepare a search warrant affidavit. What do you put in it? Everything you saw during your lawful search for *shooters, victims, and weapons*. Isn't that what *Mincey* taught us? Tell the judge about the body, the clothes, *the missing clothes*, the missing wife, and the loud argument the neighbors heard Sunday evening. If she comes back from her sister's on Wednesday morning, clothes, suitcase, and all and tells you she left after fighting with him when she learned he had a girlfriend, at least you didn't blow the search. She may not have killed him, but if she did, or had *her* boyfriend do it, your physical evidence is still intact and won't be suppressed.

One last war story before we send you on your way, to protect life and property (and the constitutional rights of us all).

Miami Homicide called one morning. They found a body, behind a building that had a bar on the first level. Drag marks could be seen from the rear door of the bar. They ended at the DOA's feet. It didn't take a brain surgeon to figure out where the body came from. Could there be other bodies still in the bar? Could they still be alive? Anybody willing to guarantee us that no one is not slowly bleeding to death? The landlord/manager was called. He let us in to search for the *shooter, victims, and weapons*. As we, very slowly, walked through the bar looking for other victims, notations were made as to what was seen. Overturned tables, glasses, and beer bottles on the floor, blood stains leading to the rear door, and general signs of a fight were clearly visible. After satisfying ourselves that there were no shooters or other victims present, the *exijentzy* was deemed over, and a search warrant affidavit was prepared. What did we tell the judge?

You tell me.

1. _____

2. _____

3. _____

4. _____

The warrant was signed, the crime scene was searched, and no evidence was suppressed. Had the killer been a customer at the next table, there probably would not have been a Fourth Amendment issue.

Why?

_____

_____

_____

_____

What if the bartender, who sleeps in the rear, or the owner of the bar were the killer? Until you know these answers, any searching for evidence must wait until the arrival of the search warrant.

When you arrive at a homicide scene, all you know is that someone is dead. You know almost nothing else. Don't assume and make mistakes that could be catastrophic to your case. Protect life and property, look for bad guys, and then step back and wait. That's why they gave you that big roll of yellow crime scene tape; use it!!

One final scenario (for real).

You get to the condo of an elderly couple. He does not know where his wife is, but her wheelchair is plainly visible in the kitchen, as are about twenty pill containers. You try to get his permission to look around, but his mind is wandering. He barely knows where he is. You know any issue of consent will never hold up in court.

By this time, you know you can walk around the apartment and look for her. You do not see her, but in the bathroom you see four knives, a carpenter's saw, and puddles of blood. Is she still alive? Is there still an *exijentzy*? You have already looked in all the places an adult could hide in. Still can't find her. There is blood trailing from the bathroom to the kitchen. There is some pooled blood in front of the refrigerator. If reason tells you she is still alive, can you open the fridge? Of course.

But what does common sense tell you?

_____

_____

_____

We go back to the husband and ask for his permission to search the entire condo. He asks again, "Where is my wife?" He is not clear-headed enough to make any important decision. Do you want to open the fridge and search for the body parts? Do you want to be responsible for the suppression of the evidence?

Get a warrant. What did we find in the refrigerator? What happened to the husband? That's in the next book:

Stories from the Crime Scene

Notes:

_____

_____

_____

_____

_____

_____

_____

_____

_____

_____

_____

_____

_____

_____

_____

_____

_____

_____

_____

_____

_____

_____

_____

_____

_____

_____

_____

_____

CHAPTER 10

You're Under Arrest!!

When we think of the Fourth Amendment, we usually think of the word *search*. That's because much of what has been written about that amendment deals with searches. However, when we read the amendment, we see that *seizures* must also be reasonable. We have discussed this earlier, but not in the context of arrests. An arrest is also seizure—of the person. Let's look at the amendment again.

> The right of the people to be secure in their *persons*, houses, papers, and effects, *against unreasonable* searches and *seizures*, *shall not be violated*, and *no warrants shall issue*, *but upon probable cause*, supported by oath or affirmation, and *particularly describing* the place to be searched, and *the persons* or things *to be seized*.   *The Fourth Amendment to the Constitution of the United States*

Did you ever wonder where your authority to arrest, and even more importantly, *to use force* to make the arrest, comes from? Regardless of whatever state statute you are working under, *the seizure of the person*, whether by warrant or not, must be reasonable under the Fourth Amendment. Arrests can be made either with or without a warrant.

Warrantless arrests have an ancient origin.

> The cases construing the Fourth Amendment thus reflect the ancient common-law rule that a peace officer was permitted to arrest without a warrant for a misdemeanor or felony committed in his presence as well as for a felony not committed in his presence *if there was reasonable ground for making the arrest*. 10 Halsbury's Laws of England 344–345 (3d ed. 1955); 4 W. Blackstone, Commentaries 292. This *has also been the prevailing rule under state constitutions and statutes*. 'The rule of the common law, that a peace officer or a private citizen may arrest a felon without a warrant, has been generally held by the courts of the several

States to be in force in cases of felony punishable by the civil tribunals.'
Kurtz v. Moffitt, 115 U.S. 487 (1885).[1]

The warrantless arrest must be for a violation of law that the officer has reasonable grounds for believing has occurred. The arrest by warrant must similarly allege a violation of law, but by sworn testimony, usually done by affidavit. Some jurisdictions allow warrants by telephone.

Take a look at this arrest warrant. Whadaya think about it? The defendant didn't care for it and petitioned for a writ of habeas corpus. Known as *The Great Writ*, it commands the person holding the body to come before the court and explain the legality of the detention.

Shortly after Christmas, in 1805, John Burford was arrested pursuant to a warrant signed by several judges in Alexandria, Virginia. He could not post bond, so he asked the U.S. Supreme Court to decide the legality of his confinement. Here's what the warrant said:

> Forasmuch as we are given to understand, from the information, testimony and complaint of many credible persons, that John A. Burford, of the said county, shop-keeper, *is not of good name and fame, nor of honest conversation, but an evil doer and disturber of the peace* of the United States, so that murder, homicide, strikes, discords, and other grievances and damages, amongst the citizens of the United States, concerning their bodies and property, *are likely to arise thereby.*

Chief Justice John Marshall, speaking for the court, granted the writ and discharged the prisoner, holding:

> The Judges of this court were unanimously of opinion, that the warrant of commitment was illegal, *for want of stating some good cause certain*, supported by oath.[2]

You have to allege that the person arrested committed some act *in violation of the law*. Recent pronouncements from the Supreme Court have stated it in more familiar language:

> An arrest warrant shall be issued only upon a written and sworn complaint (1) setting forth 'the essential facts constituting the offense charged,' and (2) showing 'that there is probable cause to believe that [such] an offense has been committed and that the defendant has committed it. . . .'[3]

---

[1] *U.S. v. Watson*, 423 U.S. 411 (1976).

[2] *Ex Parte Burford*, 7 U.S. 448 (1806).

[3] *Giordenello v. U.S.*, 357 U.S. 489 (1958).

In summary, you must allege, and swear to, either in your affidavit, applying for an arrest warrant, or in your arrest report, which follows the defendant as he goes to his first court appearance, the essential elements of a specific violation of a criminal statute and the identity of the person who committed it.[4]

As most arrests are made without a warrant, let's discuss the law relating to them first. As the early English law held, a police officer can make an arrest:

> *for a misdemeanor or felony committed in his presence as well as for a felony not committed in his presence if there were reasonable grounds for making the arrest.*

Once the arrest is announced, what happens if the subject tells you to "pound salt" and refuses to go along with the game plan? Whadaya do? What *can* you do?

In the leading case of *Graham v. Connor*,[5] the U.S. Supreme Court held that "our Fourth Amendment jurisprudence has long recognized that the right to make an arrest or investigatory stop necessarily carries with it the right to use some degree of physical coercion or threat to effect it," referring us back to *Terry v. Ohio*. See Chapter Two.

Connor, a police officer in Charlotte, North Carolina, saw Graham enter and quickly leave a convenience store. Being somewhat suspicious, our soon-to-be-sued police officer followed the car that Graham then entered and stopped it about one-half mile away. While there was no probable cause to make an arrest, this was your basic "investigatory stop" to maintain the status quo and fully investigate the suspicious behavior. As Officer Connor awaited back-up, he observed Graham exit the car, run around it twice, sit on the curb, and then pass out. The back-up officers arrived, and assuming this was your typical drunk, rather forcefully picked Graham up, carried him to the patrol car, and cuffed him. When Graham awoke, he tried to tell the officers he was a diabetic, and that they should look in his wallet for his "decal," and get him some sugar. The *drunk* was ignored and thrown, headfirst into the police car, rather unceremoniously.

While this was occurring, Officer Connor had gone to the convenience store to check on what had occurred there. After learning that Graham had done nothing wrong, he took him home and released him. There is no mention of an apology.

Because we are talking about it now, you know the story didn't end there.

According to the opinion (which means someone got sued), "at some point during his encounter with the police, Graham sustained a broken foot, cuts on his wrists, a bruised forehead, and an injured shoulder; he also claims to have developed a loud ringing in his right ear that continues to this day." He sued everyone there, including the city of Charlotte, alleging a violation of *his constitutional rights*, pursuant to that well-known section of federal law, the "1983 action." No specific provision of the Constitution was alleged to have been violated, just that "constitutionally excessive force" was used.

---

[4]In some states judges have signed "John Doe" arrest warrants only alleging that "DNA Profile # . . . " committed a specific offense. The subject is not further identified, as he is not known. These warrants were applied for as the statute of limitations was about to expire. Whether they will satisfy the "particularity" provision of the Fourth Amendment remains to be seen.

[5]490 U.S. 386 (1989) The opinion is in Appendix A.

The Supreme Court held that excessive force claims, arising out of arrests or investigatory stops, are to be decided under the Fourth Amendment, which as we know, "guarantees citizens the right 'to be secure in their persons . . . against unreasonable . . . seizures' of the person" (*Connor*, at p. 395).

Because the determination of reasonableness is not capable of a precise definition, the court directed the lower courts to examine:

> the facts and circumstances of each particular case, including the severity of the crime at issue, whether the suspect poses an immediate threat to the safety of the officers or others, and whether he is actively resisting arrest or attempting to evade arrest by flight. See *Tennessee v. Garner*, (the question is "whether the totality of the circumstances justifie[s] a particular sort of . . . seizure").[6]

What happened to Officer Connor and *his co-defendants*? Well, at the trial in federal court, the judge dismissed the charges after *the victim* rested his case. The judge ruled that the amount of force was "appropriate under the circumstances," that "there were no discernable injuries," and that the force used was not applied maliciously but in a "good faith effort to maintain or restore order in the face of a potentially explosive situation." The Court of Appeals affirmed, finding that a reasonable jury applying *that test* could not find that the force used was constitutionally excessive; however, it sent the case back for the trial judge to determine if the city and police department (known as *entity defendants*) were liable due to their policies the officer acted under. Generally speaking, if the individual officer follows a policy authorized by those he works for, he has qualified immunity (assuming he acted in good faith in carrying out that policy). The city and the department, though, enjoy no such immunity and may be held liable if any "unconstitutional municipal conduct flows from *a policy or custom*." See *Monell v. New York City Dept. of Social Services*, 436 U.S. 658 (1978).

Before that happened, the Supremes took the case and reversed, unanimously, requiring the lower court to decide the case under the Fourth Amendment's *reasonableness* requirement, not general principles.[7] After the reversal, the case was tried again. This time the judge applied the proper test and submitted the case to the jury. After the jury was instructed on the appropriate rule of law, they found that the police officers acted reasonably and ruled for the defendants. This opinion was based upon *Terry v. Ohio*, and *Tennessee v. Garner*, in which the court found fault with the amount of force used to *seize* an unarmed, 14-year-old burglar.

The court went on to tell us that the reasonableness of the force must be judged from the perspective of a reasonable officer *on the scene*, rather than with the 20/20 vision of hindsight. One bold federal appellate judge took that admonition to heart, in denying a *1983* claim made by the recipient of force used by a police officer in Monroe County, Alabama, one night.

---

[6]*Garner* is the fleeing felon case we will discuss shortly.

[7]They did not rule the cops were wrong, just that the judge applied the wrong test.

That case began during the evening hours of November 11, 1999. As a 911 call came in reporting a shooting; the shots could still be heard in the background. Monroe County Deputy Sheriff Jason Terry was dispatched, as the call was replayed for him. When the deputy and his backup arrived at the complainant's home in Beatrice, Alabama, they were directed to the nearby woods. A person was seen in the woods but the officers could not apprehend him. As they returned to talk to the complainant, an additional shot was heard, coming from a nearby house owned by our soon-to-be plaintiff, Willie J. Crosby.

As the deputies approached Crosby's home, they saw him with a shotgun and heard him rack the weapon and eject a round. Their exact testimony in court was of a "distinctive and threatening sound." Crosby was ordered to drop the gun and lie down, but he chose instead to enter his garage, place his shotgun there, and *then* lie down. Now, the gist of his complaint, and this great opinion, binding on all federal courts in Florida, Georgia, and Alabama, and *persuasive authority* in the other forty-seven!!

> Two of the officers got on top of Crosby, putting their knees in his back, and began to handcuff him. (As Crosby lost, his version of the facts is accepted here.) Crosby raised his head and asked why he was being arrested. Deputy Terry then placed his foot on the side of Crosby's face and neck and applied pressure. In response, Crosby jerked one hand away from the officers who were attempting to handcuff him, shoved Terry's foot off his face, cursed at Terry, and asked Terry if he was crazy. Crosby was then handcuffed and arrested. When the officers searched him, he was found to be carrying a .38 handgun. . . .

As we get into the opinion, we can see where the court is going.

> Deputy Terry was responding to a report of gunshots fired toward the home of Crosby's neighbor, Scott, shortly before the officers arrived. The officers knew that Scott, who had been there when the shots were fired, was in fear for his life. While on the scene, they heard a shot from the direction of Crosby's home. As they approached that area, the officers saw Crosby carrying a shotgun and heard the sound of him ejecting a shell from the weapon. Given these facts, *an officer in Terry's position reasonably could have believed that Crosby had fired multiple shots in the direction of his neighbor's house, including the shots they had heard while the neighbor was on the phone calling the sheriff's office for help, and that he had fired another shot after they arrived*. Because an officer in that position reasonably could have believed that Crosby had "create[d] a substantial risk of serious physical injury to another person," *there was . . . probable cause to arrest Crosby* for reckless endangerment as defined in (the Alabama statutes).
>
> Crosby argues that, even if there was probable cause to arrest him, *Deputy Terry used excessive force in making the arrest*. Although not happy about the way in which the officers held him down, Crosby's primary focus in making this claim is that at one point Terry put his foot on Crosby's face.

Except for that fact, this would be an easy case. *The Fourth Amendment encompasses the right to be free from the use of excessive force during an arrest.* As we have recently said, "[t]he 'reasonableness' inquiry in an excessive force case is an objective one: the question is whether the officer's actions are 'objectively reasonable' in light of the facts and circumstances confronting him, without regard to his underlying intent or motivation."

In making an excessive force inquiry, we are not to view the matter as judges from the comfort and safety of our chambers, fearful of nothing more threatening than the occasional paper cut as we read a cold record accounting of what turned out to be the facts. We must see the situation through the eyes of the officer on the scene who is hampered by incomplete information and forced to make a split-second decision between action and inaction in circumstances where inaction could prove fatal. See *Graham v. Connor*, 490 U.S. 386, 396–97. [Don't you just love him!!!]

From that perspective, *a reasonable officer could have believed that the force applied was reasonably necessary in the situation Deputy Terry found himself in that night.* The circumstances were fraught with danger for the officers.

The Supreme Court "has long recognized that the right to make an arrest . . . necessarily carries with it the right to use some degree of physical coercion or threat thereof to effect it." *Graham*, 490 U.S. at 397; *see also Garrett v. Athens-Clarke County*, 378 F.3d 1274 (11th Cir. 2004) (hit with baton, tackled, pepper-sprayed, and tied up); *Draper v. Reynolds*, 369 F.3d 1270 (11th Cir. 2004) (Taser gun); *Durruthy v. Pastor*, 351 F.3d 1080 (11th Cir. 2003) (knee in back).

Though Crosby was on the ground at the time Deputy Terry put his foot on Crosby's face, *he had not yet been handcuffed.* For all the officers knew, Crosby had other weapons concealed on his person—as it turned out, he actually did have another weapon on him—and raising his head to ask why he was being arrested could have been an attempt by Crosby to distract Terry and a prelude to actual resistance. Given the circumstances and the risks inherent in apprehending any suspect, *an officer in Terry's position reasonably could have concluded that it was imperative to keep Crosby, who had not been entirely cooperative, completely flat and immobile until he had been successfully handcuffed.* The fact that Crosby was able to wrestle his hand loose and push Terry's foot away indicates that he had not been subdued.

There is also the fact that the force about which Crosby complains, *while undignified in its placement, was not severe in amount.* See *Durruthy*, at 1094, stating that 'the application of de minimis force (that means a minimal amount), without more, will not support a claim for *excessive force* in violation of the Fourth Amendment . . . noting that one factor to be considered in evaluating excessive force claims is the relationship between the need and amount of force used.'

The district court's grant of summary judgment to Deputy Terry is AFFIRMED.[8] Carnes, Circuit Judge, U.S. Court of Appeals, for the Eleventh Circuit, for the court.

---

[8]*Crosby v. Monroe County and Jason Terry*, 394 F.3d 1328 (11th Cir. 2004).

Because of Crosby's potential for hurting someone, the court found the officer's conduct to be reasonable, under the Fourth Amendment. The force used was consistent with the dangers present and prevented an escalation and further possible injury to both the officer and the subject. As we learned from *Terry v. Ohio*, there is no bright line test for how much force is permitted during an investigatory stop. Each case turns on its particular facts.

Can you cuff someone who is not under arrest; for whom there is no probable cause to believe has committed a crime? Do the handcuffs turn the *Terry* patdown (which is merely an investigative stop and not an arrest) into an arrest? Remember, under *Terry*, you only have to have reasonable suspicion (less than PC) to make the stop. Do you have to subject yourself to unnecessary danger as you go about your duties? See below for a sampling of cases from across the country, both state and federal, finding the use of handcuffs (and more) during an investigative stop, under *Terry*, to have been reasonably necessary to protect the officers' safety or prevent the suspect from fleeing, due to the particular situation then facing the officer:

> *United States v. Crittendon*, 883 F.2d 326 (4th Cir.1989) (use of handcuffs during investigative stop reasonably necessary to maintain status quo and protect officer's safety); *United States v. Glenna*, 878 F.2d 967 (7th Cir.1989) (use of handcuffs during investigative stop not improper where police found ammunition and explosives on suspect); *United States v. Taylor*, 716 F.2d 701, 709 (9th Cir.1983) (use of handcuffs not improper where suspect made furtive movements with hands after refusing an order to put his hands in the air); *United States v. Bautista*, 684 F.2d 1286 (9th Cir.1982) (use of handcuffs during *Terry* stop upheld where an armed robbery suspect was still at large and handcuffs eliminated possibility of assault or escape attempt), *cert. denied*, 459 U.S. 1211; *Howard v. State*, 664 P.2d 603 (Alaska Ct.App.1983) (drawn guns and handcuffing do not necessarily turn investigative stop into arrest); *People v. Allen*, 73 N.Y.2d 378 (1989) (police justified in handcuffing armed robbery suspect to ensure their safety while moving him out of alley to conduct pat down); *State v. Wheeler*, 108 Wash.2d 230, (1987) (handcuffing suspected burglar for two-block ride to scene of burglary upheld). *See also*, *United States v. Kapperman*, 764 F.2d 786, 790, (11th Cir.1985) (neither handcuffing nor other restraints automatically convert *Terry* stop into an arrest requiring probable cause; *inquiry is reasonableness*). Likewise, we do not find *Terry* and its progeny to prohibit placing a suspect in handcuffs during the course of an investigative detention where the circumstances reasonably warrant such action. If an officer reasonably believes that an investigative stop can be carried out only in such a manner, it is not a court's place to substitute its judgment for that of the officer. *United States v. Sharpe*, 470 U.S. 675 (1985); *United States v. Glenna*, at 972–73.

What the cases seem to say is that whether such action is appropriate depends on whether it is a reasonable response to the demands of the situation.

What does *that* mean?—Do what you have to do . . . but no more.

When such restraint is used in the course of an investigative detention, *it must be temporary* and *last no longer than necessary to effectuate the purpose of the stop*. The methods employed must be *the least intrusive means reasonably available to verify or dispel in a short period of time the officers' suspicions that the suspect may be armed and dangerous*. Absent other threatening circumstances, once the pat down reveals the absence of weapons, the handcuffs should be removed.   *United States v. Glenna*, at 972.

So what should you do when they don't listen or if they may be armed and dangerous? Act reasonably based upon what you see and know about the situation. Remember Det. McFadden in Cleveland? Do your job but don't take unnecessary risks. If you are wrong, we lose whatever the search may have disclosed; don't worry about it.We'd rather lose a case than a cop!!

Let's discuss another use of force case that involved the use of a stun gun in making the arrest. Is 50,000 volts reasonable?

First the facts:

The Traffic Stop:

At approximately 11:30 p.m. on July 19, 2001, Deputy Sheriff Clinton D. Reynolds ("Reynolds") stopped a tractor-trailer truck (the "truck") driven by Plaintiff Stacy Allen Draper ("Draper"). While on patrol for the Sheriff's Office of Coweta County, Georgia, Reynolds observed Draper's truck traveling northbound on I-85 and stopped the truck allegedly because its tag light was not appropriately illuminated under Georgia law. After Draper pulled his truck to the side of the interstate, Reynolds stopped his patrol car directly behind the truck. Reynolds on foot approached the passenger side of the truck cab, as was his practice in all roadside stops. When Reynolds reached the truck cab, the engine was running, the passenger window was closed, and the cab was illuminated briefly by an interior light but then became dark. Draper observed Reynolds at the passenger side and believed that Reynolds was performing an inspection of the vehicle. From the passenger side, Reynolds shined his flashlight at the truck cab twice.

Draper was blinded by the flashlight the second time Reynolds shined it in the cab. Draper rolled down the passenger window and politely[9] asked Reynolds to stop shining the flashlight at him. Reynolds then "said something like god dammit, you don't worry about what I'm doing over here." Draper again politely asked Reynolds to stop shining the light at him. Reynolds replied, "I told you to get your f. . . . . . ass over here two times." Draper then told Reynolds to get his "god darn flashlight" out of his eyes.

---

[9]Once again, the plaintiff's version of the facts is taken as true. This is because the court ruled that, even if true, he has not made out a case to submit to the jury. The trial testimony had Reynolds "hotly" contesting many of those facts.

Reynolds then instructed Draper to meet him behind the truck, a location in view of a police camera that Reynolds had activated in his patrol car. Reynolds also unholstered his TASER[10] International ADVANCED TASER M26 ("taser gun"), which he kept in his hand through the remainder of the encounter. Draper got out of the truck cab and walked to the back of the truck. The police camera recorded the actions and sound from the encounter behind the truck.

Upon arrival behind the truck, Draper immediately began shouting and complaining about Reynolds' shining the flashlight in his face. Reynolds calmly asked Draper for his driver's license, but Draper continued to complain about Reynolds's prior use of the flashlight. Draper also insisted that he had done nothing wrong. *During the encounter, Draper was belligerent, gestured animatedly, continuously paced, appeared very excited, and spoke loudly.*

Reynolds repeatedly asked Draper to stop yelling and informed Draper that he would be taken to jail if he continued to yell. Reynolds told Draper that he also needed Draper's logbook and bill of lading. Draper began to walk toward the truck cab while asking Reynolds if he needed anything else, but then turned around and loudly accused Reynolds of harassing him. Reynolds replied that he needed Draper's license and insurance.

Draper handed his license to Reynolds and again began walking to the truck cab, but turned around when Reynolds told him *for the second time* to retrieve his bill of lading, proof of insurance, and log book. Draper still did not go to the truck cab but instead walked back toward Reynolds and accused him again of harassment.

For the third time, Reynolds told Draper to get the requested items, and Draper responded by exclaiming, "How 'bout you just go ahead and take me to f. . . . . . jail, then, man, you know, because I'm not going to kiss your damn ass because you're a police officer." Reynolds instructed Draper to calm down, but Draper protested loudly that he was calm. Reynolds explained that he believed Draper's actions were "threatening."

For the fourth time, Reynolds told Draper to retrieve the requested documents. Draper did not move to the truck cab to get them and loudly complained that Reynolds was treating him like a "child" and disrespecting him. Reynolds replied that he had not disrespected Draper, and then he signaled to his back up, which had just arrived, with his flashlight. Draper continued to yell and accuse Reynolds of disrespecting him.

For the fifth time, Reynolds told Draper to retrieve the documents and then promptly discharged his taser gun at Draper's chest. Draper fell to the ground out of the police camera's view. Reynolds told Draper to stay on the ground and threatened to discharge the taser gun again if Draper did not comply. Reynolds then yelled to his back-up officer who had just arrived: "Handcuff this son of a bitch." Draper was handcuffed, searched, and placed in the back of the police car.

---

[10]Named after its inventor, the Thomas A. Smith Electronic Rifle. The generic name is an *electronic control device* (ECD).

Now, the complaint:

Draper contends that Reynolds violated his Fourth Amendment rights by arresting him. Probable cause to arrest exists "when the facts and circumstances within the officer's knowledge, of which he or she has reasonably trustworthy information, would cause a prudent person to believe, under the circumstances shown, that the suspect has committed, is committing, or is about to commit an offense." *Durruthy,* at 1088 (quoting *McCormick v. City of Fort Lauderdale,* 333 F.3d 1234, 1243 (11th Cir.2003)). Reynolds had probable cause to stop Draper for a tag light violation, and that probable cause was also sufficient to permit Reynolds to arrest Draper for that violation (under Georgia law).[11]

Allegation #2:

Excessive Force

Draper also asserts that Reynolds used excessive force in effectuating the arrest by discharging a taser gun at Draper's chest. Draper argues that Reynolds did not need to use any force in arresting him because Draper gladly would have complied with Reynolds's arrest requests if Reynolds had just verbally told him he was under arrest.

The ruling:

In the circumstances of this case, Reynolds' use of the taser gun to effectuate the arrest of Draper was reasonably proportionate to the difficult, tense and uncertain situation that Reynolds faced in this traffic stop, and did not constitute excessive force. From the time Draper met Reynolds at the back of the truck, *Draper was hostile, belligerent, and uncooperative.* No less than five times, Reynolds asked Draper to retrieve documents from the truck cab, and each time Draper refused to comply. Rather, Draper accused Reynolds of harassing him and blinding him with the flashlight. *Draper used profanity, moved around and paced in agitation, and repeatedly yelled at Reynolds.* Because Draper repeatedly refused to comply with Reynolds' verbal commands, starting with a verbal arrest command was not required in these particular factual circumstances. More importantly, a verbal arrest command accompanied by attempted physical handcuffing, in these particular factual circumstances, *may well have, or would likely have, escalated a tense and difficult situation into a serious physical struggle in which either Draper or Reynolds would be seriously hurt.* Thus, there was a reasonable need for some use of force in this arrest.

Although being struck by a taser gun is an unpleasant experience, the amount of force Reynolds used—a single use of the taser gun causing a one-time shocking—was *reasonably proportionate* to *the need for force* and did not inflict any serious injury. Indeed, the police video shows that Draper was standing up, handcuffed, and coherent shortly after the taser gun stunned and calmed him. *The single use of the taser gun may well have*

---

[11]If that is not an arrestable offense in your state, follow the advice of my old sergeant in The Bronx, "He's in 'summons custody.' He stays until he gets the ticket. If he leaves, Lock 'em up!"

prevented a physical struggle and serious harm to either Draper or Reynolds. Under the "totality of the circumstances," Reynolds' use of the taser gun did not constitute excessive force, and Reynolds did not violate Draper's constitutional rights in this arrest.[12]

Let's try another area of the law. Our friends Crosby and Draper did not listen to the officers' commands, but at least they remained at the scene. One was under investigative detention (a *Terry* stop) and the other was about to be arrested. The force used to permit the officers to perform their duties was found to be reasonable under the Fourth Amendment. Let's change the facts a bit.

You get a burglary call about 11 p.m. in a residential neighborhood. The dispatcher says the prowler is inside. As you roll up, the next-door neighbor points to the adjacent house and says she heard glass breaking and *they* or *someone* is breaking in. As you go to the rear of the house you hear a door slam and see a figure run across the backyard. The unknown figure stops at a six-foot-high chain link fence. You shine your flashlight on him and see a person that appears to be seventeen or eighteen years old and about 5′5″ to 5′7″ tall. No weapons are seen and you are *reasonably sure* he is unarmed. The suspect is crouched at the base of the fence. You yell out "Police, Halt!" and start going toward him. With that, your younger and more energetic suspect starts climbing over the fence. You are carrying a lot of equipment and wearing heavy boots and know you will never make it over that fence and there is no way that you could catch him.

Do you have PC to arrest, or at least detain him?

If so, can you use a reasonable amount of force to prevent his escape and arrest him?

Does your state have a *Fleeing Felon* rule?

In simple terms, *Can you shoot him*?

This is what was going through the mind of Police Officer Elton Hymon of the Memphis, Tennessee, Police Department on the evening of October 3, 1974.

Hymon was relying on the state statute authorizing a police officer to "use all the necessary means to effect the arrest, if after notice of the intention to arrest the defendant, he either flees or forcibly resists."[13] His department had a similar policy that allowed the use of deadly force in cases of burglary.

Returning to that night in the backyard, the suspect, Edward Garner, who later turned out to be an eighth-grader, and only fifteen years old, 5′4″ tall and weighing in at about 100 pounds, began to climb over the fence. Officer Hymon, convinced that if Garner made it over the fence he would elude capture, fired one shot. The bullet hit Garner in the head. He died shortly thereafter. Ten dollars and a purse taken from the house were found on his body. Garner's father filed suit in federal court. Named as defendants, were the police officer, the police department, the chief, the mayor, and the city. He alleged the killing violated his son's rights under the

---

[12]*Draper v. Reynolds*, 369 F.3d 1270 (11th Cir. 2004).

[13]Although the statute does not specifically mention felonies, Tennessee law forbids the use of deadly force to make a misdemeanor arrest.

Fourth, Fifth, Sixth, Eighth, and Fourteenth Amendments to the U.S. Constitution.[14] After a short trial, the court dismissed the claim as:

> Hymon's actions were authorized by the Tennessee statute, which in turn was constitutional. Hymon had employed the only reasonable and practicable means of preventing Garner's escape. Garner had "recklessly and heedlessly attempted to vault over the fence to escape, thereby assuming the risk of being fired upon."

On appeal, the U.S. Court of Appeal for the Sixth Circuit issued a split opinion, affirming as to the officer, finding that Hymon had acted in good-faith reliance on the Tennessee statute and was therefore within the scope of his qualified immunity, and reversing, as the city, for allowing the officer to operate under what they called an unconstitutional statute. What they said was that "the killing of a fleeing suspect is a *seizure* under the Fourth Amendment, and is therefore constitutional only if *reasonable.*"

Before we get to the reasoning of the U.S. Supreme Court, let's see how they handled some of the arguments made by the parties. By this time the state of Tennessee joined the lawsuit, as they had written the statute. The court looked into two issues:

a. What was the common-law rule at the time the Fourth Amendment was adopted? and
b. Have there been any legal and technological changes, which would require the court *not to follow* what was in the minds of the framers of the amendment? (This is what is known as *original intent.*)

> (T)he common-law rule is best understood in light of the fact that it arose at a time when virtually *all* felonies were punishable by death. (Therefore) the killing of a resisting or fleeing felon resulted in no greater (penalty) than those authorized for the felony of which the individual was suspected. Courts have also justified the common-law rule by emphasizing the relative dangerousness of felons.[15]

Another reason for the harsh common-law rule was that:

> The common-law rule developed at a time when weapons were rudimentary. Deadly force could be inflicted almost solely in a hand-to-hand struggle during which, necessarily, *the safety of the arresting officer was at risk.* Handguns were not carried by police officers until the latter half of the last century. *L. Kennett & J. Anderson, The Gun in America 150–151 (1975).* Only then did it become possible to use deadly force from a

---

[14]Alleged were the actions of the defendants to deny the victim his right to due process of law (be tried before being punished) under the Fifth Amendment; the right to trial by jury under the Sixth Amendment; and the right to be free from cruel and unusual punishments under the Eighth Amendment, all being binding on the states through the Fourteenth Amendment.

[15]*Tennessee v. Garner*, 471 U.S. 1, at p. 15 (1985).

distance as a means of apprehension. As a practical matter, the use of deadly force under the standard articulation of the common-law rule has an altogether different meaning—and harsher consequences—now than in past centuries.[16]

Recognizing the changing technology was easy. The question of whether the common-law rule is still *reasonable* under the Fourth Amendment becomes doubtful when we see that the death penalty is only available to those convicted of first degree murder, and then only in about 37 states.

In evaluating the reasonableness of police procedures under the Fourth Amendment, we have also looked to prevailing rules in individual jurisdictions. The rules in the States are varied. Some 21 States have (followed) the common-law rule,[17] though in two of these the courts have significantly limited the statute. Eighteen others allow, in slightly varying language, the use of deadly force only if the suspect has committed a felony involving the use or threat of physical or deadly force, or is escaping with a deadly weapon, or is likely to endanger life or inflict serious physical injury if not arrested. The remaining States either have no relevant statute or case law, or have positions that are unclear.[18]

Considering that most of the states chose *not* to follow the common-law rule, was part of the analysis. However, the actions taken by most police departments and the commission that accredits them carried even more weight with the court. The court noted that the FBI and the NYPD "forbid the use of firearms except when necessary to prevent death or grievous bodily harm." Another study concluded that "the police department regulations in a majority of the large cities of the United States allowed the firing of a weapon only when a felon presented a threat of death or serious bodily harm."[19]

Under our modern statutes, there are many felonies that are far less dangerous than certain misdemeanors. Take for example, white-collar fraud, forgery, and grand larceny. These felonies pose a significantly lesser physical threat than DUI, usually a misdemeanor, or even simple assault. Where is the logic to shoot the felon and not the drunk driver, capable of seriously hurting many people by committing his misdemeanor?

The court then looked to their own precedents and pointed to cases where they had changed long-standing common-law rules. Two of such cases are discussed:

a. *Payton v. New York*—requiring an arrest warrant to force entry into a home to arrest a felon (there is also case law requiring a search warrant to enter a third party's home (to search for that felon) and

---

[16]*Garner*, at 15.

[17]A good example of changing times is the Florida Statute, 776.05, cited by the court as an example of a state following the common-law rule. In 1997, the Florida legislature amended the statute to comply with *Garner*.

[18]*Garner*, at 15–16.

[19]*Garner*, at 18.

b. *Katz v. United States*—bringing the telephone user within the purview of the Fourth Amendment, something clearly not in the contemplation of the framers.

Balancing the common-law history with the changes in law and technology, the decision of most states not to follow the common-law rule, and the modern trend of police administrators, the Supremes kept the rule, but severely limited its application:

> The use of deadly force to prevent the escape of *all* felony suspects, whatever the circumstances, is constitutionally *unreasonable*. It is not better that all felony suspects die than that they escape. Where the suspect poses no immediate threat to the officer and no threat to others, the harm resulting from failing to apprehend him does not justify the use of deadly force to do so. It is no doubt unfortunate when a suspect who is in sight escapes, but the fact that the police arrive a little late or are a little slower afoot does not always justify killing the suspect. A police officer *may not seize an unarmed, non-dangerous suspect by shooting him dead*. The Tennessee statute is unconstitutional insofar as it authorizes the use of deadly force against such fleeing suspects.
>
> It is not, however, unconstitutional on its face. Where the officer has probable cause to believe that the suspect poses a threat of serious physical harm, either to the officer or to others, it is not constitutionally unreasonable to prevent escape by using deadly force. Thus, if the suspect threatens the officer with a weapon or there is probable cause to believe that he has committed a crime involving the infliction or threatened *infliction of serious physical harm*, deadly force may be used if necessary to prevent escape, and if, where feasible, some warning has been given. As applied in such circumstances, the Tennessee statute would pass constitutional muster.[20]

Just to help us see how difficult and important cases are decided, let's examine the small, but powerful dissent. Justice Sandra Day O'Connor, joined by Chief Justice Warren Burger and Justice Rehnquist, reminded us of the "heavy burden" the court has before it changes police practices accepted when the Fourth Amendment was adopted. Their review of additional factors led them to believe that Officer Hymon did act *reasonably*. Justice O'Connor starts out with the recognition of *the difficult, split second decisions police officers must make in these circumstances.*

> For purposes of Fourth Amendment analysis, I agree with the Court that *Officer Hymon 'seized' Garner by shooting him*. Whether that seizure was reasonable and therefore permitted by the Fourth Amendment requires a careful balancing of the important public interest in crime prevention . . . and the nature and quality of the intrusion upon . . . the individual. In striking this balance here, it is crucial to acknowledge that police use of

---

[20]*Garner*, at 11.

deadly force to apprehend a fleeing criminal suspect falls within the 'rubric of police conduct . . . necessarily [involving] swift action predicated upon the on-the-spot observations of the officer on the beat.' *Terry v. Ohio*. The clarity of hindsight cannot provide the standard for judging the reasonableness of *police decisions made in uncertain and often dangerous circumstances*. Moreover, I am far more reluctant than is the Court to conclude that the Fourth Amendment prohibits a police practice that was accepted at the time of the adoption of the Bill of Rights and has continued to receive the support of many state legislatures.[21]

The public interest involved in the use of deadly force as a last resort to apprehend a fleeing burglary suspect relates primarily to the serious nature of the crime. Household burglaries not only represent the illegal entry into a person's home, but also pose real risk of serious harm to others. According to recent Department of Justice statistics, '[t]hree-fifths of all rapes in the home, three-fifths of all home robberies, and about a third of home aggravated and simple assaults are committed by burglars.' Bureau of Justice Statistics Bulletin, Household Burglary 1 (January 1985).

Citing to a learned legal text, the dissent argued that "burglary is among felonies that normally cause or threaten death or serious bodily harm;" and another that said, "Burglary is a dangerous felony that creates unreasonable risk of great personal harm."

Because burglary is a serious and dangerous felony, the public interest in its prevention . . . is of compelling importance. Where a police officer has probable cause to arrest a suspected burglar, the use of deadly force as a last resort might well be the only means of apprehending the suspect. Subsequent investigation simply cannot represent a substitute for immediate apprehension of the criminal suspect at the scene.

Although some law enforcement agencies may (disagree), the Tennessee statute reflects a legislative determination that the use of deadly force in (felony situations) will serve generally to protect the public. Such statutes assist the police in apprehending suspected perpetrators of serious crimes and provide notice that a lawful police order to stop and submit to arrest may not be ignored with impunity.

For purposes of this case, we must recall that the police officer, in the course of investigating a nighttime burglary, had reasonable cause to arrest the suspect and ordered him to halt. The officer's use of force resulted because the suspected burglar refused to heed this command and the officer reasonably believed that there was no means short of firing his weapon to apprehend the suspect. Without questioning the importance of a person's interest in his life, I do not think (it) encompasses a right to flee unimpeded from the scene of a burglary. The policeman's hands should

---

[21]Many . . . but still less than half.

not be tied merely because of the possibility that the suspect will fail to cooperate with legitimate actions by law enforcement personnel. The legitimate interests of the suspect in these circumstances are adequately accommodated by the Tennessee statute: to avoid the use of deadly force and the consequent risk to his life, *the suspect need merely obey the valid order to halt.*[22]

Despite the great support of three justices recognizing the important and dangerous work that police officers do under very trying circumstances, the first thing I learned in law school was simple math. *Six is more than three.* The majority opinion is the law we must follow.[23]

So when you respond to a situation that appears to be a felony and the suspect won't obey your command to stop, unless he's got a gun, or otherwise poses a threat of serious physical harm to you or others, or has inflicted or threatened serious physical harm to someone, *Let 'em go!* Some prosecutor will probably offer him probation anyway as part of a plea bargain!

A more recent case from the Supremes dealing with the amount of force which may be reasonably used came down in April of 2007, *Scott v. Harris.*[24] This case is more reminiscent of America's Greatest Car Chases and was so alluded to by the court.

Victor Harris, a nineteen-year-old driver with a suspended license, tried to elude the police when he was observed speeding in Coweta County, Georgia. He was seriously injured when he crashed after being struck in the rear by an officer using the "Precision Intervention Technique." This maneuver caused Harris' car to spin out and he was paralyzed in the ensuing accident. He brought suit in federal court, alleging the officers used unreasonable force in "seizing" him, in violation of *Tennessee v. Garner*, the fleeing felon case. Naturally, the lawsuit was based upon section 1983 of the U.S. Code.

When the federal court of appeals upheld the trial court's refusal to dismiss the civil lawsuit against the officers, allowing the case to go to trial, they accepted the plaintiff's version of the facts. For the first time in U.S. Supreme Court history, the court adopted the video from the front of the pursuing police cars into their opinion.

We are happy to allow the videotape to speak for itself. See Record 36, Exh. A, available at http://www.supremecourtus.gov/opinions/video/ scott_v_harris.rmvb and in Clerk of Court's case file. [You can view it too.]

The videotape tells quite a different story. There we see (plaintiff's) vehicle racing down narrow, two-lane roads in the dead of night at speeds

---

[22]*Garner*, at 26–27 (O'Connor, dissenting).

[23]Why do we read dissenting opinions if they are not the law? One reason is that they explain exactly what the majority said (in case we missed something) and their reasons for disagreeing. Many times when justices, philosophies, or votes change, the dissent becomes the basis for a majority opinion. See the dissenting opinions of Justices Brandeis and Holmes, in *Olmstead*, parts of which are quoted in the Introduction. They were adopted by the court almost forty years later in *Katz v. U.S.*

[24]550 U.S. 372 (2007), 127 S.Ct. 1769 (2007).

that are shockingly fast. We see it swerve around more than a dozen other cars, cross the double-yellow line, and force cars traveling in both directions to their respective shoulders to avoid being hit. We see it run multiple red lights and travel for considerable periods of time in the occasional center left-turn-only lane, chased by numerous police cars forced to engage in the same hazardous maneuvers just to keep up. Far from being the cautious and controlled driver the lower court depicts, what we see on the video more closely resembles a Hollywood-style car chase of the most frightening sort, placing police officers and innocent bystanders alike at great risk of serious injury.   *Harris,* at 378.

At issue here is whether Deputy Sheriff Timothy Scott used unreasonable force in seizing the plaintiff. Defining *seizure* once again, the court said:

Scott (acknowledges) that his decision to terminate the car chase by ramming his bumper into (plaintiff's) vehicle constituted a "seizure." "[A] Fourth Amendment seizure [occurs] . . . when there is a governmental termination of freedom of movement through means intentionally applied." Brower v. County of Inyo, 489 U.S. 593, 596–597 (1989).
It is also conceded, by both sides, that a claim of "excessive force in the course of making [a] . . . 'seizure' of [the] person . . . [is] properly analyzed under the Fourth Amendment's 'objective reasonableness' standard." Graham *v.* Connor. The question we need to answer is whether Scott's actions were objectively reasonable.

The plaintiff argued that in *Garner*, the court held that unarmed and nondangerous felons may not be *seized* by shooting and killing them, and that this was no different. The court made short shrift of that argument:

(T)he flight on foot of an unarmed suspect (is not) even remotely comparable to the extreme danger to human life posed by (plaintiff) in this case.

Then Justice Scalia, speaking for an 8–1 majority, balanced the danger to all in assessing the blame:

We think it appropriate in this process to take into account not only the number of lives at risk, but also their relative culpability. It was (the plaintiff), after all, who intentionally placed himself and the public in danger by unlawfully engaging in the reckless, high-speed flight that ultimately produced the choice between two evils that Scott confronted. Multiple police cars, with blue lights flashing and sirens blaring, had been chasing (him) for nearly 10 miles, but he ignored their warning to stop. By contrast, those who might have been harmed had Scott not taken the action he did were entirely innocent. We have little difficulty in concluding *it was reasonable for Scott to take the action that he did*.

Calling off the chase or hoping Harris would stop on his own were considered and rejected by the court. First, they concluded, there was no certainty that the driver would slow down had the police deactivated their emergency equipment and stopped the pursuit. Secondly,

> We are loath to lay down a rule requiring the police to allow fleeing suspects to get away whenever they drive so recklessly that they put other people's lives in danger. It is obvious the perverse incentives such a rule would create: Every fleeing motorist would know that escape is within his grasp, if only he accelerates to 90 miles per hour, crosses the double-yellow line a few times, and runs a few red lights. The Constitution assuredly does not impose this invitation to impunity-earned-by-recklessness. Instead, we lay down a more sensible rule: A police officer's attempt to terminate a dangerous high-speed car chase that threatens the lives of innocent bystanders does not violate the Fourth Amendment, even when it places the fleeing motorist at risk of serious injury or death. *Scott v. Harris*, at 382.

The end result is another decision protecting police officers when they act reasonably to protect the public. However, keep in mind that many jurisdictions have prohibited such pursuits due to the very dangers presented here, to both the general public and the police officers. Always remember that to protect and serve you have to be able to. You are of no help to anyone when you and your patrol car are wrapped around a tree or a light pole on the side of the roadway. A safe alternative is to get his tag number and pay him a visit the next day. Should it be a stolen vehicle, found abandoned later, his prints, and DNA, should be all over the inside of the car. While this has nothing to do with the Fourth Amendment, it may keep you alive, which is one of the other goals of this book.

Be safe out there as you go about protecting life and property. Remember, the life you save may be your own! I'll see you *"On the Road."*

David Waksman
Miami, Florida
2009

APPENDIX A

Leading Cases

Stop and Frisk

   a. Terry v. Ohio
   b. State v. Ramos

Search Warrants

   c. Mincey v. Arizona
   d. Michigan v. Tyler
   e. Thompson v. Louisiana
   f. Arizona v. Hicks
   g. People v. Defore (*Should the Criminal Go Free Because. . . .*)

Use of Force

   h. Graham v. Connor
   i. Tennessee v. Garner
   j. Draper v. Reynolds

U.S. Supreme Court
TERRY v. OHIO
392 U.S. 1 (1968)

CERTIORARI TO THE SUPREME COURT OF OHIO

Argued December 12, 1967
Decided June 10, 1968

MR. CHIEF JUSTICE WARREN delivered the opinion of the Court.

This case presents serious questions concerning the role of the Fourth Amendment in the confrontation on the street between the citizen and the policeman investigating suspicious circumstances.

Petitioner Terry was convicted of carrying a concealed weapon and sentenced to the statutorily prescribed term of one to three years in the penitentiary. Following the denial of a pretrial motion to suppress, the prosecution introduced in evidence two revolvers and a number of bullets seized from Terry and a codefendant, Richard Chilton, by Cleveland Police Detective Martin McFadden. At the hearing on the motion to suppress this evidence, Officer McFadden testified that while he was patrolling in plain clothes in downtown Cleveland at approximately 2:30 in the afternoon of October 31, 1963, his attention was attracted by two men, Chilton and Terry, standing on the corner of Huron Road and Euclid Avenue. He had never seen the two men before, and he was unable to say precisely what first drew his eye to them. However, he testified that he had been a policeman for 39 years and a detective for 35 and that he had been assigned to patrol this vicinity of downtown Cleveland for shoplifters and pickpockets for 30 years. He explained that he had developed routine habits of observation over the years and that he would "stand and watch people or walk and watch people at many intervals of the day." He added: "Now, in this case when I looked over they didn't look right to me at the time."

His interest aroused, Officer McFadden took up a post of observation in the entrance to a store 300 to 400 feet away from the two men. "I get more purpose to watch them when I seen their movements," he testified. He saw one of the men leave the other one and walk southwest on Huron Road, past some stores. The man paused for a moment and looked in a store window, then walked on a short distance, turned around and walked back toward the corner, pausing once again to look in the same store window. He rejoined his companion at the corner, and the two conferred briefly. Then the second man went through the same series of motions, strolling down Huron Road, looking in the same window, walking on a short distance, turning back, peering in the store window again, and returning to confer with the first man at the corner. The two men repeated this ritual alternately between five and six times apiece—in all, roughly a dozen trips. At one point, while the two were standing together on the corner, a third man approached them and engaged them briefly in conversation. This man then left the two others and walked west on Euclid Avenue. Chilton and Terry resumed their measured pacing, peering, and conferring. After this had gone on for 10 to 12 minutes, the two men walked off together, heading west on Euclid Avenue, following the path taken earlier by the third man.

By this time Officer McFadden had become thoroughly suspicious. He testified that after observing their elaborately casual and oft-repeated reconnaissance of the store window on Huron Road, he suspected the two men of "casing a job, a stickup," and that he considered it his duty as a police officer to investigate further. He added that he feared "they may have a gun." Thus, Officer McFadden followed Chilton and Terry and saw them stop in front of Zucker's store to talk to the same man who had conferred with them earlier on the street corner. Deciding that the situation was ripe for direct action. Officer McFadden approached the three men, identified himself as a police officer and asked for their names. At this point his knowledge was confined to what he had observed. He was not acquainted with any of the three men by name or by sight, and he had received no information concerning them from any other source. When the men "mumbled something" in response to his inquiries, Officer McFadden grabbed petitioner Terry, spun him around so that they were facing the other two, with Terry between McFadden and the others, and patted down the outside of his clothing. In the left breast pocket of Terry's overcoat Officer McFadden felt a pistol. He reached inside the overcoat pocket, but was unable to remove the gun. At this point, keeping Terry between himself and the others, the officer ordered all three men to enter Zucker's store. As they went in, he removed Terry's overcoat completely, removed a .38-caliber revolver from the pocket and ordered all three men to face the wall with their hands raised. Officer McFadden proceeded to pat down the outer clothing of Chilton and the third man, Katz. He discovered another revolver in the outer pocket of Chilton's overcoat, but no weapons were found on Katz. The officer testified that he only patted the men down to see whether they had weapons, and that he did not put his hands beneath the outer garments of either Terry or Chilton until he felt their guns. So far as appears from the record, he never placed his hands beneath Katz' outer garments. Officer McFadden seized Chilton's gun, asked the proprietor of the store to call a police wagon, and took all three men to the station, where Chilton and Terry were formally charged with carrying concealed weapons.

On the motion to suppress the guns the prosecution took the position that they had been seized following a search incident to a lawful arrest. The trial court rejected this theory, stating that it "would be stretching the facts beyond reasonable comprehension" to find that Officer McFadden had had probable cause to arrest the men before he patted them down for weapons. However, the court denied the defendants' motion on the ground that Officer McFadden, on the basis of his experience, "had reasonable cause to believe . . . that the defendants were conducting themselves suspiciously, and some interrogation should be made of their action." Purely for his own protection, the court held, the officer had the right to pat down the outer clothing of these men, who he had reasonable cause to believe might be armed. The court distinguished between an investigatory "stop" and an arrest, and between a "frisk" of the outer clothing for weapons and a full-blown search for evidence of crime. The frisk, it held, was essential to the proper performance of the officer's investigatory duties, for without it "the answer to the police officer may be a bullet, and a loaded pistol discovered during the frisk is admissible."

After the court denied their motion to suppress, Chilton and Terry waived jury trial and pleaded not guilty. The court adjudged them guilty, and the Court of Appeals for the Eighth Judicial District, Cuyahoga County, affirmed. State v. Terry,

5 Ohio App. 2d 122, 214 N. E. 2d 114 (1966). The Supreme Court of Ohio dismissed their appeal on the ground that no "substantial constitutional question" was involved. We granted certiorari, 387 U.S. 929 (1967), to determine whether the admission of the revolvers in evidence violated petitioner's rights under the Fourth Amendment, made applicable to the States by the Fourteenth. Mapp v. Ohio, 367 U.S. 643 (1961). We affirm the conviction.

I.

The Fourth Amendment provides that "the right of the people to be secure in their persons, houses, papers, and effects, against unreasonable searches and seizures, shall not be violated. . . . " This inestimable right of [392 U.S. 1, 9] personal security belongs as much to the citizen on the streets of our cities as to the homeowner closeted in his study to dispose of his secret affairs. For, as this Court has always recognized,

> "No right is held more sacred, or is more carefully guarded, by the common law, than the right of every individual to the possession and control of his own person, free from all restraint or interference of others, unless by clear and unquestionable authority of law." Union Pac. R. Co. v. Botsford, 141 U.S. 250, 251 (1891).

We have recently held that "the Fourth Amendment protects people, not places," Katz v. United States, 389 U.S. 347, 351 (1967), and wherever an individual may harbor a reasonable "expectation of privacy," id., at 361 (MR. JUSTICE HARLAN, concurring), he is entitled to be free from unreasonable governmental intrusion. Of course, the specific content and incidents of this right must be shaped by the context in which it is asserted. For "what the Constitution forbids is not all searches and seizures, but unreasonable searches and seizures." Elkins v. United States, 364 U.S. 206, 222 (1960). Unquestionably petitioner was entitled to the protection of the Fourth Amendment as he walked down the street in Cleveland. The question is whether in all the circumstances of this on-the-street encounter, his right to personal security was violated by an unreasonable search and seizure.

We would be less than candid if we did not acknowledge that this question thrusts to the fore difficult and troublesome issues regarding a sensitive area of police activity—issues which have never before been squarely presented to this Court. Reflective of the tensions involved are the practical and constitutional arguments pressed with great vigor on both sides of the public debate over the power of the police to "stop and frisk"—as it is sometimes euphemistically termed—suspicious persons.

On the one hand, it is frequently argued that in dealing with the rapidly unfolding and often dangerous situations on city streets the police are in need of an escalating set of flexible responses, graduated in relation to the amount of information they possess. For this purpose it is urged that distinctions should be made between a "stop" and an "arrest" (or a "seizure" of a person), and between a "frisk" and a "search." Thus, it is argued, the police should be allowed to "stop" a person and detain him briefly for questioning upon suspicion that he may be connected with criminal activity. Upon suspicion that the person may be armed, the police should have the power to "frisk" him for weapons. If the "stop" and the "frisk" give rise to probable cause to believe that the suspect has committed a crime, then the police should be empowered to make a formal "arrest," and a full incident "search" of the person. This scheme is justified in part upon the notion that a "stop" and a "frisk" amount to a mere "minor inconvenience and petty indignity," which can properly be imposed upon the citizen in the interest of effective law enforcement on the basis of a police officer's suspicion.

On the other side the argument is made that the authority of the police must be strictly circumscribed by the law of arrest and search as it has developed to date in the traditional jurisprudence of the Fourth Amendment. It is contended with some force that there is not—and cannot be—a variety of police activity which does not depend solely upon the voluntary cooperation of the citizen and yet which stops short of an arrest based upon probable cause to make such an arrest. The heart of the Fourth Amendment, the argument runs, is a severe requirement of specific justification for any intrusion upon protected personal security, coupled with a highly developed system of judicial controls to enforce upon the agents of the State the commands of the Constitution. Acquiescence by the courts in the compulsion inherent in the field interrogation practices at issue here, it is urged, would constitute an abdication of judicial control over, and indeed an encouragement of, substantial interference with liberty and personal security by police officers whose judgment is necessarily colored by their primary involvement in "the often competitive enterprise of ferreting out crime" Johnson v. United States, 333 U.S. 10, 14 (1948). This, it is argued, can only serve to exacerbate police-community tensions in the crowded centers of our Nation's cities.

In this context we approach the issues in this case mindful of the limitations of the judicial function in controlling the myriad daily situations in which policemen and citizens confront each other on the street. The State has characterized the issue here as "the right of a police officer . . . to make an on-the-street stop, interrogate and pat down for weapons (known in street vernacular as 'stop and frisk')." But this is only partly accurate. For the issue is not the abstract propriety of the police conduct, but the admissibility against petitioner of the evidence uncovered by the search and seizure. Ever since its inception, the rule excluding evidence seized in violation of the Fourth Amendment has been recognized as a principal mode of discouraging lawless police conduct. See Weeks v. United States, 232 U.S. 383, 391–393 (1914). Thus its major thrust is a deterrent one, see Linkletter v. Walker, 381 U.S. 618, 629–635 (1965), and experience has taught that it is the only effective deterrent to police misconduct in the criminal context, and that without it the constitutional guarantee against unreasonable searches and seizures would be a mere "form of words." Mapp v. Ohio, 367 U.S. 643, 655 (1961). The rule also serves another vital function—"the imperative of judicial integrity." Courts which sit under our Constitution cannot and will not be made party to lawless invasions of the constitutional rights of citizens by permitting unhindered governmental use of the fruits of such invasions. Thus in our system evidentiary rulings provide the context in which the judicial process of inclusion and exclusion approves some conduct as comporting with constitutional guarantees and disapproves other actions by state agents. A ruling admitting evidence in a criminal trial, we recognize, has the necessary effect of legitimizing the conduct which produced the evidence, while an application of the exclusionary rule withholds the constitutional imprimatur.

The exclusionary rule has its limitations, however, as a tool of judicial control. It cannot properly be invoked to exclude the products of legitimate police investigative techniques on the ground that much conduct which is closely similar involves unwarranted intrusions upon constitutional protections. Moreover, in some contexts the rule is ineffective as a deterrent. Street encounters between citizens and police officers are incredibly rich in diversity. They range from wholly friendly exchanges of pleasantries or mutually useful information to hostile confrontations of armed men involving arrests, or injuries, or loss of life. Moreover, hostile confrontations are not all of a piece. Some of them begin in a friendly enough manner, only to take a different turn upon the injection of some unexpected element into the conversation. Encounters are initiated by the police for a wide variety of purposes, some of which are wholly unrelated to a desire to prosecute for crime. Doubtless some police "field interrogation" conduct violates the Fourth Amendment. But a stern refusal by this Court to condone such activity does not necessarily render it responsive to the exclusionary rule. Regardless of how effective the rule may be where obtaining convictions is an important objective of the police, it is powerless to deter invasions of constitutionally guaranteed rights where the police either have no interest in prosecuting or are willing to forgo successful prosecution in the interest of serving some other goal.

Proper adjudication of cases in which the exclusionary rule is invoked demands a constant awareness of these limitations. The wholesale harassment by certain elements of the police community, of which minority groups, particularly Negroes, frequently complain, will not be stopped by the exclusion of any evidence from any criminal trial. Yet a rigid and unthinking application of the exclusionary rule, in futile protest against practices which it can never be used effectively to control, may exact a high toll in human injury and frustration of efforts to prevent crime. No judicial opinion can comprehend the protean variety of the street encounter, and we can only judge the facts of the case before us. Nothing we say today is to be taken as indicating approval of police conduct outside the legitimate investigative sphere. Under our decision, courts still retain their traditional responsibility to guard against police conduct which is overbearing or harassing, or which trenches upon personal security without the objective evidentiary justification which the Constitution requires. When such conduct is identified, it must be condemned by the judiciary and its fruits must be excluded from evidence in criminal trials. And, of course, our approval of legitimate and restrained investigative conduct undertaken on the basis of ample factual justification should in no way discourage the employment of other remedies than the exclusionary rule to curtail abuses for which that sanction may prove inappropriate.

Having thus roughly sketched the perimeters of the constitutional debate over the limits on police investigative conduct in general and the background against which this case presents itself, we turn our attention to the quite narrow question posed by the facts before us: whether it is always unreasonable for a policeman to seize a person and subject him to a limited search for weapons unless there is probable cause for an arrest. Given the narrowness of this question, we have no occasion to canvass in detail the constitutional limitations upon the scope of a policeman's power when he confronts a citizen without probable cause to arrest him.

II.

Our first task is to establish at what point in this encounter the Fourth Amendment becomes relevant. That is, we must decide whether and when Officer McFadden "seized" Terry and whether and when he conducted a "search." There is some suggestion in the use of such terms as "stop" and "frisk" that such police conduct is outside the purview of the Fourth Amendment because neither action rises to the level of a "search" or "seizure" within the meaning of the Constitution. We emphatically reject this notion. It is quite plain that the Fourth Amendment governs "seizures" of the person which do not eventuate in a trip to the station house and prosecution for crime—"arrests" in traditional terminology. It must be recognized that whenever a police officer accosts an individual and restrains his freedom to walk away, he has "seized" that person. And it is nothing less than sheer torture of the English language to suggest that a careful exploration of the outer surfaces of a person's clothing all over his or her body in an attempt to find weapons is not a "search." Moreover, it is simply fantastic to urge that such a procedure performed in public by a policeman while the citizen stands helpless, perhaps facing a wall with his hands raised, is a "petty indignity." It is a serious intrusion upon the sanctity of the person, which may inflict great indignity and arouse strong resentment, and it is not to be undertaken lightly.

The danger in the logic which proceeds upon distinctions between a "stop" and an "arrest," or "seizure" of the person, and between a "frisk" and a "search" is two-fold. It seeks to isolate from constitutional scrutiny the initial stages of the contact between the policeman and the citizen. And by suggesting a rigid all-or-nothing model of justification and regulation under the Amendment, it obscures the utility of limitations upon the scope, as well as the initiation, of police action as a means of constitutional regulation. This Court has held in the past that a search which is reasonable at its inception may violate the Fourth Amendment by virtue of its intolerable intensity and scope. The distinctions of classical "stop-and-frisk" theory thus serve to divert attention from the central inquiry under the Fourth Amendment—the reasonableness in all the circumstances of the particular governmental invasion of a citizen's personal security. "Search" and "seizure" are not talismans. We therefore reject the notions that the Fourth Amendment does not come into play at all as a limitation upon police conduct if the officers stop short of something called a "technical arrest" or a "full-blown search."

In this case there can be no question, then, that Officer McFadden "seized" petitioner and subjected him to a "search" when he took hold of him and patted down the outer surfaces of his clothing. We must decide whether at that point it was reasonable for Officer McFadden to have interfered with petitioner's personal security as he did. And in determining whether the seizure and search were "unreasonable" our inquiry is a dual one—whether the officer's action was justified at its inception, and whether it was reasonably related in scope to the circumstances which justified the interference in the first place.

III.

If this case involved police conduct subject to the Warrant Clause of the Fourth Amendment, we would have to ascertain whether "probable cause" existed to justify the search and seizure which took place. However, that is not the case. We do not retreat from our holdings that the police must, whenever practicable, obtain advance judicial approval of searches and seizures through the warrant procedure, see, e.g., Katz v. United States, 389 U.S. 347 (1967); Beck v. Ohio, 379 U.S. 89, 96 (1964); Chapman v. United States, 365 U.S. 610 (1961), or that in most instances failure to comply with the warrant requirement can only be excused by exigent circumstances, see, e.g., Warden v. Hayden, 387 U.S. 294 (1967) (hot pursuit); cf. Preston v. United States, 376 U.S. 364, 367–368 (1964). But we deal here with an entire rubric of police conduct—necessarily swift action predicated upon the on-thespot observations of the officer on the beat—which historically has not been, and as a practical matter could not be, subjected to the warrant procedure. Instead, the conduct involved in this case must be tested by the Fourth Amendment's general proscription against unreasonable searches and seizures.

Nonetheless, the notions which underlie both the warrant procedure and the requirement of probable cause remain fully relevant in this context. In order to assess the reasonableness of Officer McFadden's conduct as a general proposition, it is necessary "first to focus upon the governmental interest which allegedly justifies official intrusion upon the constitutionally protected interests of the private citizen," for there is "no ready test for determining reasonableness other than by balancing the need to search [or seize] against the invasion which the search [or seizure] entails." Camara v. Municipal Court, 387 U.S. 523, 534–535, 536–537 (1967). And in justifying the particular intrusion the police officer must be able to point to specific and articulable facts which, taken together with rational inferences from those facts, reasonably warrant that intrusion. The scheme of the Fourth Amendment becomes meaningful only when it is assured that at some point the conduct of those charged with enforcing the laws can be subjected to the more detached, neutral scrutiny of a judge who must evaluate the reasonableness of a particular search or seizure in light of the particular circumstances. And in making that assessment it is imperative that the facts be judged against an objective standard: would the facts available to the officer at the moment of the seizure or the search "warrant a man of reasonable caution in the belief" that the action taken was appropriate? Anything less would invite intrusions upon constitutionally guaranteed rights based on nothing more substantial than inarticulate hunches, a result this Court has consistently refused to sanction. And simple "'good faith on the part of the arresting officer is not enough.' . . . If subjective good faith alone were the test, the protections of the Fourth Amendment would evaporate, and the people would be 'secure in their persons, houses, papers, and effects,' only in the discretion of the police." Applying these principles to this case, we consider first the nature and extent of the governmental interests involved. One general interest is of course that of effective crime prevention and detection; it is this interest which underlies the recognition that a police officer may in appropriate circumstances and in an appropriate manner approach a person for purposes of investigating possibly criminal behavior even though there is no probable cause to make an arrest. It was this legitimate investigative function Officer McFadden was discharging when he decided to approach petitioner and his companions. He had observed Terry, Chilton, and Katz go through a series of acts, each of them perhaps innocent in itself, but which taken together warranted further investigation. There is nothing unusual in two men standing together on a street corner, perhaps waiting for someone. Nor is there anything suspicious about people in such circumstances strolling up and down the street, singly or in pairs. Store windows, moreover, are made to be looked in. But the story in quite different where, as here, two men hover about a street corner for an extended period of time, at the end of which it becomes apparent that they are not waiting for anyone or anything; where these men pace alternately along an identical route, pausing to stare in the same store window roughly 24 times; where each completion of this route is followed immediately by a conference between the two men on the corner; where they are joined in one of these conferences by a third man who leaves swiftly; and where the two men finally follow the third and rejoin him a couple of blocks away. It would have been poor police work indeed for an officer of 30 years' experience in the detection of thievery from stores in this same neighborhood to have failed to investigate this behavior further.

The crux of this case, however, is not the propriety of Officer McFadden's taking steps to investigate petitioner's suspicious behavior, but rather, whether there was justification for McFadden's invasion of Terry's personal security by searching him for weapons in the course of that investigation. We are now concerned with more than the governmental interest in investigating crime; in addition, there is the more immediate interest of the police officer in taking steps to assure himself that the person with whom he is dealing is not armed with a weapon that could unexpectedly and fatally be used against him. Certainly it would be unreasonable to require that police officers take unnecessary risks in the performance of their duties. American criminals have a long tradition of armed violence, and every year in this country many law enforcement officers are killed in the line of duty, and thousands more are wounded. Virtually all of these deaths and a substantial portion of the injuries are inflicted with guns and knives.[1]

In view of these facts, we cannot blind ourselves to the need for law enforcement officers to protect themselves and other prospective victims of violence in situations where they may lack probable cause for an arrest. When an officer is justified in believing that the individual whose suspicious behavior he is investigating at close range is armed and presently dangerous to the officer or to others, it would appear to be clearly unreasonable to deny the officer the power to take necessary measures to determine whether the person is in fact carrying a weapon and to neutralize the threat of physical harm.

We must still consider, however, the nature and quality of the intrusion on individual rights which must be accepted if police officers are to be conceded the right to search for weapons in situations where probable cause to arrest for crime is lacking. Even a limited search of the outer clothing for weapons constitutes a severe, though brief, intrusion upon cherished personal security, and it must surely be an annoying, frightening, and perhaps humiliating experience. Petitioner contends that such an

---

[1]Fifty-seven law enforcement officers were killed in the line of duty in this country in 1966, bringing the total to 335 for the seven-year period beginning with 1960. Also in 1966, there were 23,851 assaults on police officers, 9,113 of which resulted in injuries to the policeman. Fifty-five of the 57 officers killed in 1966 died from gunshot wounds, 41 of them inflicted by handguns easily secreted about the person. The remaining two murders were perpetrated by knives. See Federal Bureau of Investigation, Uniform Crime Reports for the United States—1966, at 45–48, 152 and Table 51.

intrusion is permissible only incident to a lawful arrest, either for a crime involving the possession of weapons or for a crime the commission of which led the officer to investigate in the first place. However, this argument must be closely examined.

Petitioner does not argue that a police officer should refrain from making any investigation of suspicious circumstances until such time as he has probable cause to make an arrest; nor does he deny that police officers in properly discharging their investigative function may find themselves confronting persons who might well be armed and dangerous. Moreover, he does not say that an officer is always unjustified in searching a suspect to discover weapons. Rather, he says it is unreasonable for the policeman to take that step until such time as the situation evolves to a point where there is probable cause to make an arrest. When that point has been reached, petitioner would concede the officer's right to conduct a search of the suspect for weapons, fruits or instrumentalities of the crime, or "mere" evidence, incident to the arrest.

There are two weaknesses in this line of reasoning, however. First, it fails to take account of traditional limitations upon the scope of searches, and thus recognizes no distinction in purpose, character, and extent between a search incident to an arrest and a limited search for weapons. The former, although justified in part by the acknowledged necessity to protect the arresting officer from assault with a concealed weapon, is also justified on other grounds, ibid., and can therefore involve a relatively extensive exploration of the person. A search for weapons in the absence of probable cause to arrest, however, must, like any other search, be strictly circumscribed by the exigencies which justify its initiation. Warden v. Hayden, 387 U.S. 294, 310 (1967) (MR. JUSTICE FORTAS, concurring). Thus it must be limited to that which is necessary for the discovery of weapons which might be used to harm the officer or others nearby, and may realistically be characterized as something less than a "full" search, even though it remains a serious intrusion.

A second, and related, objection to petitioner's argument is that it assumes that the law of arrest has already worked out the balance between the particular interests involved here—the neutralization of danger to the policeman in the investigative circumstance and the sanctity of the individual. But this is not so. An arrest is a wholly different kind of intrusion upon individual freedom from a limited search for weapons, and the interests each is designed to serve are likewise quite different. An arrest is the initial stage of a criminal prosecution. It is intended to vindicate society's interest in having its laws obeyed, and it is inevitably accompanied by future interference with the individual's freedom of movement, whether or not trial or conviction ultimately follows. The protective search for weapons, on the other hand, constitutes a brief, though far from inconsiderable, intrusion upon the sanctity of the person. It does not follow that because an officer may lawfully arrest a person only when he is apprised of facts sufficient to warrant a belief that the person has committed or is committing a crime, the officer is equally unjustified, absent that kind of evidence, in making any intrusions short of an arrest. Moreover, a perfectly reasonable apprehension of danger may arise long before the officer is possessed of adequate information to justify taking a person into custody for the purpose of prosecuting him for a crime. Petitioner's reliance on cases which have worked out standards of reasonableness with regard to "seizures" constituting arrests and searches incident thereto is thus misplaced. It assumes that the interests sought to be vindicated and the invasions of personal security may be equated in the two cases, and thereby ignores a vital aspect of the analysis of the reasonableness of particular types of conduct under the Fourth Amendment. See Camara v. Municipal Court, supra.

Our evaluation of the proper balance that has to be struck in this type of case leads us to conclude that there must be a narrowly drawn authority to permit a reasonable search for weapons for the protection of the police officer, where he has reason to believe that he is dealing with an armed and dangerous individual, regardless of whether he has probable cause to arrest the individual for a crime. The officer need not be absolutely certain that the individual is armed; the issue is whether a reasonably prudent man in the circumstances would be warranted in the belief that his safety or that of others was in danger. And in determining whether the officer acted reasonably in such circumstances, due weight must be given, not to his inchoate and unparticularized suspicion or "hunch," but to the specific reasonable inferences which he is entitled to draw from the facts in light of his experience.

IV.

We must now examine the conduct of Officer McFadden in this case to determine whether his search and seizure of petitioner were reasonable, both at their inception and as conducted. He had observed Terry, together with Chilton and another man, acting in a manner he took to be preface to a "stick-up." We think on the facts and circumstances Officer McFadden detailed before the trial judge a reasonably prudent man would have been warranted in believing petitioner was armed and thus presented a threat to the officer's safety while he was investigating his suspicious behavior. The actions of Terry and Chilton were consistent with McFadden's hypothesis that these men were contemplating a daylight robbery—which, it is reasonable to assume, would be likely to involve the use of weapons—and nothing in their conduct from the time he first noticed them until the time he confronted them and identified himself as a police officer gave him sufficient reason to negate that hypothesis. Although the trio had departed the original scene, there was nothing to indicate abandonment of an intent to commit a robbery at some point. Thus, when Officer McFadden approached the three men gathered before the display window at Zucker's store he had observed enough to make it quite reasonable to fear that they were armed; and nothing in their response to his hailing them, identifying himself as a police officer, and asking their names served to dispel that reasonable belief. We cannot say his decision at that point to seize Terry and pat his clothing for weapons was the product of a volatile or inventive imagination, or was undertaken simply as an act of harassment; the record evidences the tempered act of a policeman who in the course of an investigation had to make a quick decision as to how to protect himself and others from possible danger, and took limited steps to do so.

The manner in which the seizure and search were conducted is, of course, as vital a part of the inquiry as whether they were warranted at all. The Fourth Amendment proceeds as much by limitations upon the scope of governmental action as by imposing preconditions upon its initiation. Compare Katz v. United States, 389 U.S. 347, 354–356 (1967). The entire deterrent purpose of the rule excluding evidence seized in violation of the Fourth Amendment rests on the assumption that "limitations upon the fruit to be gathered tend to limit the quest itself." Thus, evidence may not be introduced if it was discovered by means of a seizure and search which were not reasonably related in scope to the justification for their initiation.

V.

We conclude that the revolver seized from Terry was properly admitted in evidence against him. At the time he seized petitioner and searched him for weapons, Officer McFadden had reasonable grounds to believe that petitioner was armed and dangerous, and it was necessary for the protection of himself and others to take swift measures to discover the true facts and neutralize the threat of harm if it materialized. The policeman carefully restricted his search to what was appropriate to the discovery of the particular items which he sought. Each case of this sort will, of course, have to be decided on its own facts. We merely hold today that where a police officer observes unusual conduct which leads him reasonably to conclude in light of his experience that criminal activity may be afoot and that the persons with whom he is dealing may be armed and presently dangerous, where in the course of investigating this behavior he identifies himself as a policeman and makes reasonable inquiries, and where nothing in the initial stages of the encounter serves to dispel his reasonable fear for his own or others' safety, he is entitled for the protection of himself and others in the area to conduct a carefully limited search of the outer clothing of such persons in an attempt to discover weapons which might be used to assault him. Such a search is a reasonable search under the Fourth Amendment, and any weapons seized may properly be introduced in evidence against the person from whom they were taken.

Affirmed.

District Court of Appeal of Florida, Third District.
The STATE of Florida, Appellant
v.
Raunel RAMOS, Appellee
378 So.2d 1294 (Fla. 3rd DCA)

No. 79-332
Dec. 28, 1979
Rehearing Denied Jan. 28, 1980

Reversed and remanded

Before HENDRY, HUBBART and NESBITT, JJ.

HUBBART, Judge.

The central question presented for review is whether a police officer's observation of a person (a) with a bulge protruding from under such person's clothing which is consistent with, but does not reveal the actual outline of a firearm, (b) wearing unseasonably long and heavy clothing on a hot day, and (c) with a prior arrest record for illegal possession of firearms, constitutes a reasonable basis to temporarily seize such person and conduct a carefully limited search of the outer clothing of such person to discover the presence of weapons under the Fourth and Fourteenth Amendments to the United States Constitution and Article I, Section 12 of the Florida Constitution. We hold that: (1) such a temporary seizure and limited search of the person is reasonable within the meaning of the above constitutional provisions, and (2) the discovery and seizure of a concealed firearm in such a limited search constitutes a reasonable basis for a subsequent arrest of the person for carrying a concealed firearm, and a full-blown search of such person incident thereto, within the meaning of the above constitutional provisions. We, accordingly, reverse the order under review which suppressed the evidence seized in this cause in both the limited and full-blown search.

I

The facts pertaining to the above issue are as follows. On June 3, 1978, at approximately 3:00 p.m., Detective Orlando Martinez of the Miami Police Department, attached to the robbery division, was on duty at a car lot located at 1565 Flagler Street, Miami, Florida. It was an extremely warm day and his purpose in being at the car lot was to have his police car serviced as it was not cooling well. While there, he observed the defendant Raunel Ramos waiting for his pickup truck to be washed in a car wash facility at the rear of the car lot. At first, Detective Martinez saw only the back of the defendant, but was attracted to the defendant because he was wearing unusually long and heavy clothing for the weather. The defendant had on a dark brown leisure suit with a long-sleeved shirt and coat and was standing under a hot sun. At that point, the defendant turned to face Detective Martinez who, in turn, recognized the defendant as having a prior criminal arrest record for illegal possession of firearms. A few minutes later, the defendant again turned revealing the presence of a bulge under his clothing which was consistent with, but did not reveal the actual outline of a firearm. Under the circumstances, Detective Martinez thought the defendant might be armed, radioed this information to his police dispatcher and asked for a backup police unit.

About this time, the defendant got in his truck and drove to a nearby laundromat. Detective Martinez followed the defendant in a police car. Upon arriving at this location, Detective Martinez was joined by Officer Luis Soler of the Miami Police Department who arrived in another police car. Officer Soler briefly conferred with Detective Martinez and then approached the defendant who was about to get into his pickup truck having just paid for and picked up his laundry at the laundromat. The defendant still had a large bulge under his leisure suit. Officer Soler stopped the defendant and advised him that he wanted to ask him a few questions and to check his clothing for firearms. Whereupon Officer Soler patted the outside of the bulge of the defendant's clothing which revealed the presence of a firearm. Officer Soler ordered the defendant to put his hands on the top of the truck and retrieved a .45 caliber firearm. The defendant was thereupon placed under arrest by Officer Soler for carrying a concealed firearm and a complete search of his person was made which revealed the presence of a vial of cocaine, nine live rounds of .38 caliber ammunition, a fully loaded clip with the .45 caliber firearm.

The defendant was subsequently charged by information with carrying a concealed firearm (s 790.01(2), Fla.Stat. (1977)) and possession of a controlled substance, to wit: cocaine (s 893.13(1)(e), Fla.Stat. (1977)). The defendant through counsel entered a plea of not guilty and filed a motion to suppress all of the evidence seized by the police from his person on the ground that such evidence was obtained as a result of an unreasonable search and seizure. The parties then submitted depositions of Detective Martinez and Officer Soler to the trial court as constituting the evidence on the motion to suppress. Those depositions revealed the existence of the above-stated facts. After reviewing these depositions and hearing argument of counsel, the trial court entered an order suppressing the evidence. The state appeals that order, which appeal we have jurisdiction to entertain.

The Fourth Amendment to the United States Constitution and Article I, Section 12 of the Florida Constitution guarantee to the people the right "to be secure in their persons, houses, papers and effects against unreasonable searches and seizures." By their very terms, these constitutional provisions protect every person against "unreasonable searches and seizures" of their "persons." United States v. Brignoni-Ponce, 422 U.S. 873, 878, 95 S.Ct. 2574, 45 L.Ed.2d 607 (1975). "(A) police officer is not entitled to seize and search every person whom he sees on the street or of whom he makes inquiries. Before he places a hand on the person of a citizen in search of anything, he must have constitutionally adequate, reasonable grounds for doing so." Sibron v. New York, 392 U.S. 40, 64, 88 S.Ct. 1889, 1903, 20 L.Ed.2d 917 (1968). Unlike the search of private premises, however, there is no general constitutional requirement that a police officer obtain a search or arrest warrant before he may seize and search a person. United States v. Watson, 423 U.S. 411, 96 S.Ct. 820, 46 L.Ed.2d 598 (1976); United States v. Santana, 427 U.S. 38, 96 S.Ct. 2406, 49 L.Ed.2d 300 (1976); State v. Perez, 277 So.2d 778 (Fla.1973). Compare: Camara v. Municipal Court, 387 U.S. 523, 528–29, 87 S.Ct. 1727, 18 L.Ed.2d 930 (1967); Hornblower v.

State, 351 So.2d 716 (Fla.1977). A person has been seized within the meaning of the above constitutional provisions "whenever a police officer accosts an individual and restrains his freedom to walk away . . . ". Terry v. Ohio, 392 U.S. 1, 16, 88 S.Ct. 1868, 1876, 20 L.Ed.2d 889 (1968). There are, in turn, two types of police seizures of a person which act to restrain personal liberty. The first is a temporary detention on the street for investigatory purposes; the second is formal arrest which necessitates a trip to the police station for booking or for further questioning. Both are serious invasions of personal privacy and should not be lightly undertaken. "Nothing is more clear than that the Fourth Amendment was meant to prevent wholesale intrusions upon the personal security of the citizenry, whether these intrusions be termed 'arrests' or 'investigatory detentions.' "Davis v. Mississippi, 394 U.S. 721, 726, 89 S.Ct. 1394, 1397, 22 L.Ed.2d 676 (1969). A temporary detention on the street is, however, a less intrusive invasion of privacy than a formal arrest and, therefore, may be constitutionally accomplished based on articulable or founded suspicion of criminal activity. Terry v. Ohio, 392 U.S. 1, 88 S.Ct. 1868, 20 L.Ed.2d 889 (1968); Adams v. Williams, 407 U.S. 143, 92 S.Ct. 1921, 32 L.Ed.2d 612 (1972); Ingram v. State, 264 So.2d 109 (Fla.4th DCA 1972); Thomas v. State, 250 So.2d 15 (Fla.1st DCA 1971); s 901.151, Fla.Stat. (1977). A formal arrest, on the other hand, involves a more intrusive invasion of personal privacy, and, consequently, requires a greater evidentiary showing in order to be reasonable, to wit: probable cause to believe that the person arrested has committed a felony. Henry v. United States, 361 U.S. 98, 80 S.Ct. 168, 4 L.Ed.2d 134 (1959); Brown v. State, 62 So.2d 348 (Fla.1952); s 901.15, Fla.Stat. (1977).

The right to conduct a search subsequent to a reasonable police seizure of a person depends, in part, on the nature of the seizure. If the seizure is a formal arrest, the police have an automatic right, without any further evidentiary showing, to conduct a full-blown search of the person arrested and the physical area into which he might reach in order to grab a weapon or destroy evidentiary items. Gustafson v. Florida, 414 U.S. 260, 94 S.Ct. 488, 38 L.Ed.2d 456 (1973), affirming State v. Gustafson, 258 So.2d 1 (Fla.1972); Chimel v. California, 395 U.S. 752, 89 S.Ct. 2034, 23 L.Ed.2d 685 (1969); s 905.21, Fla.Stat. (1977). Indeed, such a scope of search is essential for the police to perfect the arrest and prevent the destruction of evidence by the arrestee. Preston v. United States, 376 U.S. 364, 84 S.Ct. 881, 11 L.Ed.2d 777 (1964). On the other hand, if the seizure is a temporary detention for investigation, there is never any right to conduct such a full-blown search of the person detained, as such is not necessary to accomplish the detention. The police may only conduct a carefully limited, self-protective search of the outer clothing of such person to discover the presence of weapons; moreover, this limited search does not automatically follow upon a valid temporary detention, but can only be accomplished based on articulable or founded suspicion that the person detained is armed. Terry v. Ohio, 392 U.S. 1, 16, 88 S.Ct. 1868, 20 L.Ed.2d 889 (1968); Sibron v. New York, 392 U.S. 40, 88 S.Ct. 1889, 20 L.Ed.2d 917 (1968); State v. Lundy, 334 So.2d 671 (Fla.4th DCA 1976). Such a showing is made, however, where the basis for the prior valid temporary detention is articulable or founded suspicion of criminal activity involving an actual or potential threat of violence. Terry v. Ohio, 392 U.S. 1, 16, 88 S.Ct. 1868, 20 L.Ed.2d 889 (1968); Adams v. Williams, 407 U.S. 143, 92 S.Ct. 1921, 32 L.Ed.2d 612 (1972); State v. Brooks, 281 So.2d 55 (Fla.2d DCA 1973); State v. Woodard, 280 So.2d 700 (Fla.2d DCA 1973). This limited basis for, and scope of search is tailored specifically for the police to accomplish the temporary detention, freeze the criminal situation and investigate further without unnecessarily endangering the police officer involved.

III

In the instant case, we deal with a temporary detention of a defendant on the street followed by a carefully limited, self-protective search of the outer clothing of his person for the purpose of discovering the presence of weapons. Subsequent to this stop and frisk, a concealed firearm was seized from the defendant which, in turn, formed the basis for an arrest of the defendant for the felony of carrying a concealed firearm and a subsequent full-blown search incident thereto. This full-blown search revealed the presence of cocaine, a firearm clip, and ammunition. The trial court suppressed the firearm seized in the limited search and the cocaine, firearm clip, and ammunition seized in the full-blown search apparently on the theory, urged by the defendant, that the initial temporary stop of the defendant was not based on articulable or founded suspicion of criminal activity, and that the invalid stop, in turn, tainted the subsequent frisk, arrest and full-blown search. We cannot agree.

It is well-settled in this state that the presence of a bulge under a person's clothing which is consistent with, but does not reveal the actual outline of a firearm or other weapon constitutes, when coupled with other incriminating circumstances, articulable or founded suspicion of criminal activity for the police to temporarily detain the person involved and thereafter conduct a carefully limited, self-protective search of the outer clothing of the person involved for concealed weapons. McNamara v. State, 357 So.2d 410 (Fla.1978); State v. Francois, 355 So.2d 127 (Fla.3d DCA 1978); Williams v. State, 294 So.2d 37 (Fla.3d DCA 1974); State v. Woodard, 280 So.2d 700 (Fla.2d DCA 1973); Thomas v. State, 250 So.2d 15 (Fla.1st DCA 1971). These decisions rest on sound ground as the police must be able, based on limited evidentiary showings, to act swiftly to disarm people carrying concealed weapons on the street; the possession of these firearms all too often leads to crimes of violence including murder. The governmental interest in suppressing the illegal possession of firearms is too great in this area to impose artificial restrictions on police conduct; yet, at the same time, a blanket authority to stop and frisk cannot be countenanced herein as important privacy interests are involved. A delicate balance must be struck.

In the instant case, the police observed the defendant with a bulge under his clothing which was suspiciously consistent with the presence of a firearm. This suspicion was further supported by the fact that (a) the defendant was wearing unseasonably long and heavy clothing which tended to indicate that this clothing was being used to hide something on his person from public view, and (b) the defendant had a prior criminal arrest record for illegally possessing firearms. Under these limited circumstances, we believe the police had an articulable or founded suspicion to believe that the defendant was carrying a concealed firearm. Although insufficient to constitute probable cause for arrest, it was certainly no inchoate or inarticulated hunch that caused the police to act as swiftly as they did in this case. As such, the stop and frisk of the defendant in the instant case was reasonable.

After the firearm was obtained from the defendant pursuant to a reasonable stop and frisk, it is clear that the police had probable cause to arrest the defendant for a felony, to wit: carrying a concealed firearm, and to thereafter conduct a full-blown search of the person of the defendant wherein they discovered cocaine, a firearm clip, and ammunition. The seizure of this additional evidence was reasonable as it was made incident to a valid arrest of the defendant. Moreover, no search or arrest warrant was obtained for the defendant and none was required.

The trial court committed reversible error in granting the defendant's motion to suppress the evidence seized by the police from his person. All of this evidence was reasonably seized from the defendant consistent with his right to be free from unreasonable searches and seizures under the Fourth and Fourteenth Amendments to the United States Constitution and <u>Article I, Section 12</u> of the Florida Constitution. The order under review must, accordingly, be reversed and the cause remanded for further proceedings.

Reversed and remanded
Fla.App., 1979
State v. Ramos
378 So.2d 1294

Supreme Court of the United States
437 U.S. 385
Rufus Junior MINCEY, Petitioner
v.
State of ARIZONA

No. 77-5353
Argued Feb. 21, 1978
Decided June 21, 1978

Mr. Justice STEWART delivered the opinion of the Court.

On the afternoon of October 28, 1974, undercover police officer Barry Headricks of the Metropolitan Area Narcotics Squad knocked on the door of an apartment in Tucson, Ariz., occupied by the petitioner, Rufus Mincey. Earlier in the day, Officer Headricks had allegedly arranged to purchase a quantity of heroin from Mincey and had left, ostensibly to obtain money. On his return he was accompanied by nine other plainclothes policemen and a deputy county attorney. The door was opened by John Hodgman, one of three acquaintances of Mincey who were in the living room of the apartment. Officer Headricks slipped inside and moved quickly into the bedroom. Hodgman attempted to slam the door in order to keep the other officers from entering, but was pushed back against the wall. As the police entered the apartment, a rapid volley of shots was heard from the bedroom. Officer Headricks emerged and collapsed on the floor. When other officers entered the bedroom they found Mincey lying on the floor, wounded and semiconscious. Officer Headricks died a few hours later in the hospital.

The petitioner was indicted for murder, assault, and three counts of narcotics offenses. He was tried at a single trial and convicted on all the charges. At his trial and on appeal, he contended that evidence used against him had been unlawfully seized from his apartment without a warrant and that statements used to impeach his credibility were inadmissible because they had not been made voluntarily. The Arizona Supreme Court reversed the murder and assault convictions on state-law grounds, but affirmed the narcotics convictions. It held that the warrantless search of a homicide scene is permissible under the Fourth and Fourteenth Amendments and that Mincey's statements were voluntary. We granted certiorari to consider these substantial constitutional questions.

The first question presented is whether the search of Mincey's apartment was constitutionally permissible. After the shooting, the narcotics agents, thinking that other persons in the apartment might have been injured, looked about quickly for other victims. They found a young woman wounded in the bedroom closet and Mincey apparently unconscious in the bedroom, as well as Mincey's three acquaintances (one of whom had been wounded in the head) in the living room. Emergency assistance was requested, and some medical aid was administered to Officer Headricks. But the agents refrained from further investigation, pursuant to a Tucson Police Department directive that police officers should not investigate incidents in which they are involved. They neither searched further nor seized any evidence; they merely guarded the suspects and the premises.

Within 10 minutes, however, homicide detectives who had heard a radio report of the shooting arrived and took charge of the investigation. They supervised the removal of Officer Headricks and the suspects, trying to make sure that the scene was disturbed as little as possible, and then proceeded to gather evidence. Their search lasted four days, during which period the entire apartment was searched, photographed, and diagrammed. The officers opened drawers, closets, and cupboards, and inspected their contents; they emptied clothing pockets; they dug bullet fragments out of the walls and floors; they pulled up sections of the carpet and removed them for examination. Every item in the apartment was closely examined and inventoried, and 200 to 300 objects were seized. In short, Mincey's apartment was subjected to an exhaustive and intrusive search. No warrant was ever obtained.

Since the investigating homicide detectives knew that Officer Headricks was seriously injured, they began the search promptly upon their arrival at the apartment, and searched only for evidence either establishing the circumstances of death or "relevant to motive and intent or knowledge (narcotics, e.g.)," the court found that the warrantless search of the petitioner's apartment had not violated the Fourth and Fourteenth Amendments.

We cannot agree. The Fourth Amendment proscribes all unreasonable searches and seizures, and it is a cardinal principle that "searches conducted outside the judicial process, without prior approval by judge or magistrate, are per se unreasonable under the Fourth Amendment—subject only to a few specifically established and well-delineated exceptions." Katz v. United States, 389 U.S. 347 (footnotes omitted); see also South Dakota v. Opperman, 428 U.S. 364 (POWELL, J., concurring); Coolidge v. New Hampshire, 403 U.S. 443, Vale v. Louisiana, 399 U.S. 30, Terry v. Ohio, 392 U.S. 1. The Arizona Supreme Court did not hold that the search of the petitioner's apartment fell within any of the exceptions to the warrant requirement previously recognized by this Court, but rather that the search of a homicide scene should be recognized as an additional exception.

Several reasons are advanced by the State to meet its "burden . . . to show the existence of such an exceptional situation" as to justify creating a new exception to the warrant requirement. None of these reasons, however, persuades us of the validity of the generic exception delineated by the Arizona Supreme Court.

The first contention is that the search of the petitioner's apartment did not invade any constitutionally protected right of privacy. See Katz v. United States, supra. This argument appears to have two prongs. On the one hand, the State urges that by shooting Officer Headricks, Mincey forfeited any reasonable expectation of privacy in his apartment. We have recently rejected a similar waiver argument in Michigan v. Tyler, 436 U.S. 499, it suffices here to say that this reasoning would impermissibly convict the suspect even before the evidence against him was gathered. On the other hand, the State contends that the police entry to arrest Mincey was so great an invasion of his privacy that the additional intrusion caused by the search was constitutionally irrelevant. But this claim is hardly tenable in light of the extensive nature of this search. It is one thing to say that one who is legally taken into police custody has a lessened right of privacy in his person. It is quite another to argue that he also has a lessened right of privacy in his entire house. Indeed this very argument was rejected when it was advanced to support the warrantless search of a dwelling where a search occurred as "incident" to the arrest of its occupant.

<u>Chimel v. California, 395 U.S. 752.</u> Thus, this search cannot be justified on the ground that no constitutionally protected right of privacy was invaded.

The State's second argument in support of its categorical exception to the warrant requirement is that a possible homicide presents an emergency situation demanding immediate action. We do not question the right of the police to respond to emergency situations. Numerous state and federal cases have recognized that the Fourth Amendment does not bar police officers from making warrantless entries and searches when they reasonably believe that a person within is in need of immediate aid. Similarly, when the police come upon the scene of a homicide they may make a prompt warrantless search of the area to see if there are other victims or if a killer is still on the premises. <u>Michigan v. Tyler, supra,</u> "The need to protect or preserve life or avoid serious injury is justification for what would be otherwise illegal absent an exigency or emergency." And the police may seize any evidence that is in plain view during the course of their legitimate emergency activities. <u>Michigan v. Tyler, supra,</u> <u>Coolidge v. New Hampshire, 403 U.S., at 465</u>.

*But a warrantless search must be "strictly circumscribed by the exigencies which justify its initiation," <u>Terry v. Ohio, 392 U.S., at 25–26,</u> and it simply cannot be contended that this search was justified by any emergency threatening life or limb. All the persons in Mincey's apartment had been located before the investigating homicide officers arrived there and began their search. And a four-day search that included opening dresser drawers and ripping up carpets can hardly be rationalized in terms of the legitimate concerns that justify an emergency search.

Third, the State points to the vital public interest in the prompt investigation of the extremely serious crime of murder. No one can doubt the importance of this goal. But the public interest in the investigation of other serious crimes is comparable. If the warrantless search of a homicide scene is reasonable, why not the warrantless search of the scene of a rape, a robbery, or a burglary? "No consideration relevant to the Fourth Amendment suggests any point of rational limitation" of such a doctrine. Chimel v. California, at 766.

Moreover, the mere fact that law enforcement may be made more efficient can never by itself justify disregard of the Fourth Amendment. Cf. <u>Coolidge v. New Hampshire, supra, at 481, 91 S.Ct., at 2045.</u> The investigation of crime would always be simplified if warrants were unnecessary. But the Fourth Amendment reflects the view of those who wrote the Bill of Rights that the privacy of a person's home and property may not be totally sacrificed in the name of maximum simplicity in enforcement of the criminal law. See <u>United States v. Chadwick, 433 U.S. 1.</u> For this reason, warrants are generally required to search a person's home or his person unless "the exigencies of the situation" make the needs of law enforcement so compelling that the warrantless search is objectively reasonable under the Fourth Amendment. Chimel v. California, supra (search of arrested suspect and area within his control for weapons or evidence); <u>Warden v. Hayden, 387 U.S. 294</u> ("hot pursuit" of fleeting suspect); <u>Schmerber v. California, 384 U.S. 757, 770–771</u> (imminent destruction of evidence); see also supra, at 2413–2414.

*Except for the fact that the offense under investigation was a homicide, there were no exigent circumstances in this case, as, indeed, the Arizona Supreme Court recognized. 115 Ariz., at 482. There was no indication that evidence would be lost, destroyed, or removed during the time required to obtain a search warrant. Indeed, the police guard at the apartment minimized that possibility. And there is no suggestion that a search warrant could not easily and conveniently have been obtained. We decline to hold that the seriousness of the offense under investigation itself creates exigent circumstances of the kind that under the Fourth Amendment justify a warrantless search.

"The point of the Fourth Amendment, which often is not grasped by zealous officers, is not that it denies law enforcement the support of the usual inferences which reasonable men draw from evidence. Its protection consists in requiring that those inferences be drawn by a neutral and detached magistrate instead of being judged by the officer engaged in the often competitive enterprise of ferreting out crime." Johnson v. United States, supra, at 13–14.

In sum, we hold that the "murder scene exception" created by the Arizona Supreme Court is inconsistent with the Fourth and Fourteenth Amendments—that the warrantless search of Mincey's apartment was not constitutionally permissible simply because a homicide had recently occurred there.

Since there will presumably be a new trial in this case, it is appropriate to consider also the petitioner's contention that statements he made from a hospital bed were involuntary, and therefore could not constitutionally be used against him at his trial.

Statements made by a defendant in circumstances violating the strictures of Miranda v. Arizona, supra, are admissible for impeachment if their "trustworthiness . . . satisfies legal standards." Harris v. New York, 401 U.S. 224, Oregon v. Hass, 420 U.S. 714. But any criminal trial use against a defendant of his involuntary statement is a denial of due process of law, "even though there is ample evidence aside from the confession to support the conviction." Jackson v. Denno, 378 U.S. supra, at 376. If therefore, Mincey's statements to Detective Hust were not "the product of a rational intellect and a free will," Townsend v. Sain, 372 U.S. 293, his conviction cannot stand.

It is hard to imagine a situation less conducive to the exercise of "a rational intellect and a free will" than Mincey's. He had been seriously wounded just a few hours earlier, and had arrived at the hospital "depressed almost to the point of coma," according to his attending physician. Although he had received some treatment, his condition at the time of Hust's interrogation was still sufficiently serious that he was in the intensive care unit. He complained to Hust that the pain in his leg was "unbearable." He was evidently confused and unable to think clearly about either the events of that afternoon or the circumstances of his interrogation, since some of his written answers were on their face not entirely coherent. Finally, while Mincey was being questioned he was lying on his back on a hospital bed, encumbered by tubes, needles, and breathing apparatus. He was, in short, "at the complete mercy" of Detective Hust, unable to escape or resist the thrust of Hust's interrogation.

It is apparent from the record in this case that Mincey's statements were not "the product of his free and rational choice." Greenwald v. Wisconsin, 390 U.S. 519, 521, 88 S.Ct. 1152, 1154, 20 L.Ed.2d 77. To the contrary, the undisputed evidence makes clear that Mincey wanted *not* to answer Detective Hust. But Mincey was weakened by pain and shock, isolated from family, friends, and legal counsel, and barely conscious, and his will was simply overborne. Due process of law requires that statements obtained as these were cannot be used in any way against a defendant at his trial.

U.S. Supreme Court
MICHIGAN v. TYLER, 436 U.S. 499 (1978)

CERTIORARI TO THE SUPREME COURT OF MICHIGAN
Argued January 10, 1978

MR. JUSTICE STEWART delivered the opinion of the Court.

The respondents, Loren Tyler and Robert Tompkins, were convicted in a Michigan trial court of conspiracy to burn real property in violation of Mich. Comp. Laws 750.157a (1970). Various pieces of physical evidence and testimony based on personal observation, all obtained through unconsented and warrantless entries by police and fire officials onto the burned premises, were admitted into evidence at the respondents' trial. On appeal, the Michigan Supreme Court reversed the convictions, holding that "the warrantless searches were unconstitutional and that the evidence obtained was therefore inadmissible" 399 Mich. 564, 584 (1977). We granted certiorari to consider the applicability of the Fourth and Fourteenth Amendments to official entries onto fire-damaged premises.

Shortly before midnight on January 21, 1970, a fire broke out at Tyler's Auction, a furniture store in Oakland County, Mich. The building was leased to respondent Loren Tyler, who conducted the business in association with respondent Robert Tompkins. According to the trial testimony of various witnesses, the fire department responded to the fire and was "just watering down smoldering embers" when Fire Chief See arrived on the scene around 2 a.m. It was Chief See's responsibility "to determine the cause and make out all reports." Chief See was met by Lt. Lawson, who informed him that two plastic containers of flammable liquid had been found in the building. Using portable lights, they entered the gutted store, which was filled with smoke and steam, to examine the containers. Concluding that the fire "could possibly have been an arson," Chief See called Police Detective Webb, who arrived around 3:30 a.m. Detective Webb took several pictures of the containers and of the interior of the store, but finally abandoned his efforts because of the smoke and steam. Chief See briefly "[l]ooked throughout the rest of the building to see if there was any further evidence, to determine what the cause of the fire was." By 4 a.m. The fire had been extinguished and the firefighters departed. See and Webb took the two containers to the fire station, where they were turned over to Webb for safe-keeping. There was neither consent nor a warrant for any of these entries into the building, nor for the removal of the containers. The respondents challenged the introduction of these containers at trial, but abandoned their objection in the State Supreme Court. Four hours after he had left Tyler's Auction, Chief See returned with Assistant Chief Somerville, whose job was to determine the "origin of all fires that occur within the Township." The fire had been extinguished and the building was empty. After a cursory examination they left, and Somerville returned with Detective Webb around 9 a.m. In Webb's words, they discovered suspicious "burn marks in the carpet, which [Webb] could not see earlier that morning, because of the heat, steam, and the darkness." They also found "pieces of tape, with burn marks, on the stairway." After leaving the building to obtain tools, they returned and removed pieces of the carpet and sections of the stairs to preserve these bits of evidence suggestive of a fuse trial. Somerville also searched through the rubble "looking for any other signs or evidence that showed how this fire was caused." Again, there was neither consent nor a warrant for these entries and seizures. Both at trial and on appeal, the respondents objected to the introduction of evidence thereby obtained.

On February 16 Sergeant Hoffman of the Michigan State Police Arson Section returned to Tyler's Auction to take photographs. During this visit or during another at about the same time, he checked the circuit breakers, had someone inspect the furnace, and had a television repairman examine the remains of several television sets found in the ashes. He also found a piece of fuse. Over the course of his several visits, Hoffman secured physical evidence and formed opinions that played a substantial role at trial in establishing arson as the cause of the fire and in refuting the respondents' testimony about what furniture had been lost. His entries into the building were without warrants or Tyler's consent, and were for the sole purpose "of making an investigation and seizing evidence." At the trial, respondents' attorney objected to the admission of physical evidence obtained during these visits, and also moved to strike all of Hoffman's testimony "because it was got in an illegal manner."

The Michigan Supreme Court held that with only a few exceptions, any entry onto fire-damaged private property by fire or police officials is subject to the warrant requirements of the Fourth and Fourteenth Amendments. "[Once] the blaze [has been] extinguished and the firefighters have left the premises, a warrant is required to reenter and search the premises, unless there is consent or the premises have been abandoned." Applying this principle, the court ruled that the series of warrantless entries that began after the blaze had been extinguished at 4 a.m. on January 22 violated the Fourth and Fourteenth Amendments. It found that the "record does not factually support a conclusion that Tyler had abandoned the fire-damaged premises" and accepted the lower court's finding that "[c]onsent for the numerous searches was never obtained from defendant Tyler." Accordingly, the court reversed the respondents' convictions and ordered a new trial.

II

The decisions of this Court firmly establish that the Fourth Amendment extends beyond the paradigmatic entry into a private dwelling by a law enforcement officer in search of the fruits or instrumentalities of crime. As this Court stated in Camara v. Municipal Court, 387 U.S. 523, 528, the "basic purpose of this Amendment . . . is to safeguard the privacy and security of individuals against arbitrary invasions by governmental officials." The officials may be health, fire, or building inspectors. Their purpose may be to locate and abate a suspected public nuisance, or simply to perform a routine periodic inspection. The privacy that is invaded may be sheltered by the walls of a warehouse or other commercial establishment not open to the public. See v. Seattle, 387 U.S. 541. These deviations from the typical police search are thus clearly within the protection of the Fourth Amendment.

Thus, there is no diminution in a person's reasonable expectation of privacy nor in the protection of the Fourth Amendment simply because the official conducting the search wears the uniform of a firefighter rather than a policeman, or because his purpose is to ascertain the cause of a fire rather than to look for evidence of a crime, or because the fire might have been started deliberately. Searches for administrative purposes, like searches for evidence of crime, are encompassed by the Fourth Amendment. And under that Amendment, "one governing principle, justified by history and by current experience, has consistently been followed: except in certain carefully defined classes of cases, a search of private property without proper consent is 'unreasonable' unless it has been authorized by a valid search warrant." Camara, supra, at 528–529. The showing of probable cause necessary to secure a warrant may vary with the object and intrusiveness of the search, but the necessity for the warrant persists.

In the context of investigatory fire searches, which are not programmatic but are responsive to individual events, a more particularized inquiry may be necessary. The number of prior entries, the scope of the search, the time of day when it is proposed to be made, the lapse of time since the fire, the continued use of the building, and the owner's efforts to secure it against intruders might all be relevant factors. Even though a fire victim's privacy must normally yield to the vital social objective of ascertaining the cause of the fire, the magistrate can perform the important function of preventing harassment by keeping that invasion to a minimum.

In addition, even if fire victims can be deemed aware of the factual justification for investigatory searches, it does not follow that they will also recognize the legal authority for such searches. As the Court stated in Camara, "when the inspector demands entry [without a warrant], the occupant has no way of knowing whether enforcement of the municipal code involved requires inspection of his premises, no way of knowing the lawful limits of the inspector's power to search, and no way of knowing whether the inspector himself is acting under proper authorization." Thus, a major function of the warrant is to provide the property owner with sufficient information to reassure him of the entry's legality. See United States v. Chadwick, supra, at 9.

In short, the warrant requirement provides significant protection for fire victims in this context, just as it does for property owners faced with routine building inspections. As a general matter, then, official entries to investigate the cause of a fire must adhere to the warrant procedures of the Fourth Amendment. In the words of the Michigan Supreme Court: "Where the cause [of the fire] is undetermined, and the purpose of the investigation is to determine the cause and to prevent such fires from occurring or recurring, a . . . search may be conducted pursuant to a warrant issued in accordance with reasonable legislative or administrative standards or, absent their promulgation, judicially prescribed standards; if evidence of wrongdoing is discovered, it may, of course, be used to establish probable cause for the issuance of a criminal investigative search warrant or in prosecution." But "[i]f the authorities are seeking evidence to be used in a criminal prosecution, the usual standard [of probable cause] will apply." Since all the entries in this case were "without proper consent" and were not "authorized by a valid search warrant," each one is illegal unless it falls within one of the "certain carefully defined classes of cases" for which warrants are not mandatory. Camara, 387 U.S., at 528–529.

III

Our decisions have recognized that a warrantless entry by criminal law enforcement officials may be legal when there is compelling need for official action and no time to secure a warrant. Warden v. Hayden, 387 U.S. 294 (warrantless entry of house by police in hot pursuit of armed robber); Ker v. California, <u>374 U.S. 23</u> (warrantless and unannounced entry of dwelling by police to prevent imminent destruction of evidence). Similarly, in the regulatory field, our cases have recognized the importance of "prompt inspections, even without a warrant, . . . in emergency situations." Camara, supra, at 539, citing North American Cold Storage Co. v. Chicago, <u>211 U.S. 306</u> (seizure of unwholesome food); Jacobson v. Massachusetts, <u>197 U.S. 11</u> (compulsory smallpox vaccination); Compagnie Francaise v. Board of Health, <u>186 U.S. 380</u> (health quarantine).

A burning building clearly presents an exigency of sufficient proportions to render a warrantless entry "reasonable." Indeed, it would defy reason to suppose that firemen must secure a warrant or consent before entering a burning structure to put out the blaze. And once in a building for this purpose, firefighters may seize evidence of arson that is in plain view. Coolidge v. New Hampshire, 403 U.S. 443, 465–466. Thus, the Fourth and Fourteenth Amendments were not violated by the entry of the firemen to extinguish the fire at Tyler's Auction, nor by Chief See's removal of the two plastic containers of flammable liquid found on the floor of one of the showrooms.

Although the Michigan Supreme Court appears to have accepted this principle, its opinion may be read as holding that the exigency justifying a warrantless entry to fight a fire ends, and the need to get a warrant begins, with the dousing of the last flame. We think this view of the firefighting function is unrealistically narrow, however. Fire officials are charged not only with extinguishing fires, but with finding their causes. *Prompt determination of the fire's origin may be necessary to prevent its recurrence, as through the detection of continuing dangers such as faulty wiring or a defective urnace.* Immediate investigation may also be necessary to preserve evidence from intentional or accidental destruction. And, of course, the sooner the officials complete their duties, the less will be their subsequent interference with the privacy and the recovery efforts of the victims. *For these reasons, officials need no warrant to remain in a building for a reasonable time to investigate the cause of a blaze after it has been extinguished.* And if the warrantless entry to put out the fire and determine its cause is constitutional, the warrantless seizure of evidence while inspecting the premises for these purposes also is constitutional.

The respondents argue, however, that the Michigan Supreme Court was correct in holding that the departure by the fire officials from Tyler's Auction at 4 a.m. ended any license they might have had to conduct a warrantless search. Hence, they say that even if the firemen might have been entitled to remain in the building without a warrant to investigate the cause of the fire, their re-entry four hours after their departure required a warrant.

On the facts of this case, we do not believe that a warrant was necessary for the early morning re-entries on January 22. As the fire was being extinguished, Chief See and his assistants began their investigation, but visibility was severely hindered by darkness, steam, and smoke. Thus they departed at 4 a.m. and returned shortly after daylight to continue their investigation. Little purpose would have been served by their remaining in the building, except to remove any doubt about the legality of the warrantless search and seizure later that same morning. Under these circumstances, we find that the morning entries were no more than an actual continuation of the first, and the lack of a warrant thus did not invalidate the resulting seizure of evidence.

The entries occurring after January 22, however, were clearly detached from the initial exigency and warrantless entry. Since all of these searches were conducted without valid warrants and without consent, they were invalid under the Fourth and Fourteenth Amendments, and any evidence obtained as a result of those entries must, therefore, be excluded at the respondents' retrial.

In summation, we hold that an entry to fight a fire requires no warrant, and that once in the building, officials may remain there for a reasonable time to investigate the cause of the blaze. Thereafter, additional entries to investigate the cause of the fire must be made pursuant to the warrant procedures governing administrative searches. See Camara, 387 U.S., at 534–539. Evidence of arson discovered in the course of such investigations is admissible at trial, but if the investigating officials find probable cause to believe that arson has occurred and require further access to gather evidence for a possible prosecution, they may obtain a warrant only upon a traditional showing of probable cause applicable to searches for evidence of crime. United States v. Ventresca, 380 U.S. 102.

These principles require that we affirm the judgment of the Michigan Supreme Court ordering a new trial.

Affirmed.

U.S. Supreme Court
THOMPSON v. LOUISIANA
469 U.S. 17 (1984)

THOMPSON v. LOUISIANA
ON PETITION FOR WRIT OF CERTIORARI TO THE SUPREME COURT
OF LOUISIANA
No. 83-6775
Decided November 26, 1984

PER CURIAM.

In this case, the Louisiana Supreme Court upheld the validity of a warrantless "murder scene" search of petitioner's home. Because this holding is in direct conflict with our opinion in Mincey v. Arizona, 437 U.S. 385 (1978), we reverse.

I

The Louisiana Supreme Court states the facts as follows:

> "On May 18, 1982, several deputies from the Jefferson parish Sheriff's Department arrived at [petitioner's] home in response to a report by the [petitioner's] daughter of a homicide. The deputies entered the house, made a cursory search and discovered [petitioner's] husband dead of a gunshot wound in a bedroom and the [petitioner] lying unconscious in another bedroom due to an apparent drug overdose. According to the [petitioner's] daughter, the [petitioner] had shot her husband, then ingested a quantity of pills in a suicide attempt, and then, changing her mind, called her daughter, informed her of the situation and requested help. The daughter then contacted the police. Upon their arrival, the daughter admitted them into the house and directed them to the rooms containing the [petitioner] and the victim.
>
> The deputies immediately transported the then unconscious [petitioner] to a hospital and secured the scene. Thirty-five minutes later two members of the homicide unit of the Jefferson Parish Sheriff's Office arrived and conducted a follow-up investigation of the homicide and attempted suicide.
>
> "The homicide investigators entered the residence and commenced what they described at the motion to suppress hearing as a 'general exploratory search for evidence of a crime.' During their search, which lasted approximately two hours, the detectives examined each room of the house" 448 So.2d 666, 668 (1984).

Petitioner was subsequently indicted for the second-degree murder of her husband. She moved to suppress three items of evidence discovered during the search, including a pistol found inside a chest of drawers in the same room as the deceased's body, a torn up note found in a wastepaper basket in an adjoining bathroom, and another letter (alleged to be a suicide note) found folded up inside an envelope containing a Christmas card on the top of a chest of drawers. All of this evidence was found in the "general exploratory search for evidence" conducted by two homicide investigators who arrived at the scene approximately 35 minutes after petitioner was sent to the hospital. See ibid. By the time those investigators arrived, the officers who originally arrived at the scene had already searched the premises for other victims or suspects. See Mincey, supra, at 392. The investigators testified that they had time to secure a warrant before commencing the search, and that no one had given consent to the search (See transcript of testimony of Detectives Zinna and Masson at suppression hearing).

The trial court originally denied petitioner's motion to suppress. However, the trial court then granted petitioner's motion for reconsideration and partially reversed its former decision, holding that the gun and the suicide letter found in the Christmas card were obtained in violation of the Fourth Amendment and therefore must be suppressed. The Louisiana Court of Appeal denied the State's application for a writ of review. A sharply divided Louisiana Supreme Court subsequently held all of the evidence seized to be admissible.

II

As we stated in United States v. Chadwick, 433 U.S. 1, 9 (1977), "in this area we do not write on a clean slate." In a long line of cases, this Court has stressed that "searches conducted outside the judicial process, without prior approval by judge or magistrate, are per se unreasonable under the Fourth Amendment—subject only to a few specifically established and well delineated exceptions." Katz v. United States, 389 U.S. 347, 357 (1967) (footnotes omitted). This was not a principle freshly coined for the occasion in Katz, but rather represented this Court's longstanding understanding of the relationship between the two Clauses of the Fourth Amendment. See Katz, supra, at 357. Since the time of Katz, this Court has recognized the existence of additional exceptions. South Dakota v. Opperman, 428 U.S. 364 (1976). However, we have consistently reaffirmed our understanding that in all cases outside the exceptions to the warrant requirement the Fourth Amendment requires the interposition of a neutral and detached magistrate between the police and the "persons, houses, papers, and effects" of citizens.

Although the homicide investigators in undisputed this case may well have had probable cause to search the premises, it is that they did not obtain a warrant. Therefore, for the search to be valid, it must fall within one of the narrow and specifically delineated exceptions to the warrant requirement. In Mincey v. Arizona, 437 U.S. 385 (1978), we unanimously rejected the contention that one of the exceptions to the Warrant Clause is a "murder scene exception." Although we noted that police may make warrantless entries on premises where "they reasonably believe that a person within is in need of immediate aid," id., at 392, and that "they may make a prompt warrantless search of the area to see if there are other victims or if a killer is still on the premises," ibid., we held that "the 'murder scene exception' . . . is inconsistent with the Fourth and Fourteenth Amendments—that the warrantless search of Mincey's apartment was not constitutionally permissible simply because a homicide had recently occurred there." Id., at 395. Mincey is squarely on point in the instant case.

The Louisiana Supreme Court attempted to distinguish Mincey in several ways. The court noted that Mincey involved a 4-day search of the premises, while the search in this case took only two hours and was conducted on the same day as the murder. See 448 So.2d, at 671. Although we agree that the scope of the intrusion was certainly greater in Mincey than here, nothing in Mincey turned on the length of time taken in the search or the date on which it was conducted. A 2-hour general search remains a significant intrusion on petitioner's privacy and therefore may only be conducted subject to the constraints—including the warrant requirement—of the Fourth Amendment.

The Louisiana Supreme Court also believed that petitioner had a "diminished" expectation of privacy in her home, thus validating a search that otherwise would have been unconstitutional. 448 So.2d, at 671. The court noted that petitioner telephoned her daughter to request assistance. The daughter then called the police and let them in the residence. These facts, according to the court, demonstrated a diminished expectation of privacy in petitioner's dwelling and therefore legitimated the warrantless search.

Petitioner's attempt to get medical assistance does not evidence a diminished expectation of privacy on her part. To be sure, this action would have justified the authorities in seizing evidence under the plain-view doctrine while they were in petitioner's house to offer her assistance. In addition, the same doctrine may justify seizure of evidence obtained in the limited "victim-or-suspect" search discussed in Mincey. However, the evidence at issue here was not discovered in plain view while the police were assisting petitioner to the hospital, nor was it discovered during the "victim-or-suspect" search that had been completed by the time the homicide investigators arrived. Petitioner's call for help can hardly be seen as an invitation to the general public that would have converted her home into the sort of public place for which no warrant to search would be necessary. Therefore, the Louisiana Supreme Court's diminished-expectation-of-privacy argument fails to distinguish this case from Mincey. The State contends that there was a sufficient element of consent in this case to distinguish it from the facts of Mincey. The Louisiana Supreme Court's decision does not attempt to validate the search as consensual, although it attempts to support its diminished-expectation-of-privacy argument by reference to the daughter's "apparent authority" over the premises when she originally permitted the police to enter. 448 So.2d, at 671. Because the issue of consent is ordinarily a factual issue unsuitable for our consideration in the first instance, we express no opinion as to whether the search at issue here might be justified as consensual. However, we note that both homicide investigators explicitly testified that they had received no consent to search. Any claim of valid consent in this case would have to be measured against the standards of United States v. Matlock, 415 U.S. 164 (1974), and Schneckloth v. Bustamonte, 412 U.S. 218 (1973).

III

For the reasons stated above, petitioner's motion for leave to proceed in forma pauperis is granted, the petition for writ of certiorari is granted, the judgment of the Louisiana Supreme Court is reversed, and the cause is remanded for further proceedings not inconsistent with this opinion.

It is so ordered.

**U.S. Supreme Court
ARIZONA v. HICKS,
480 U.S. 321 (1987)**

CERTIORARI TO THE COURT OF APPEALS OF ARIZONA
No. 85-1027.
Argued December 8, 1986
Decided March 3, 1987

JUSTICE SCALIA delivered the opinion of the Court.

In Coolidge v. New Hampshire, 403 U.S. 443 (1971), we said that in certain circumstances a warrantless seizure by police of an item that comes within plain view during their lawful search of a private area may be reasonable under the Fourth Amendment. See id., at 465–471 (plurality opinion); id., at 505–506 (Black, J., concurring and dissenting); id., at 521–522 (WHITE, J., concurring and dissenting). We granted certiorari, 475 U.S. 1107 (1986), in the present case to decide whether this "plain view" doctrine may be invoked when the police have less than probable cause to believe that the item in question is evidence of a crime or is contraband.

I

On April 18, 1984, a bullet was fired through the floor of respondent's apartment, striking and injuring a man in the apartment below. Police officers arrived and entered respondent's apartment to search for the shooter, for other victims, and for weapons. They found and seized three weapons, including a sawed-off rifle, and in the course of their search also discovered a stocking-cap mask.

One of the policemen, Officer Nelson, noticed two sets of expensive stereo components, which seemed out of place in the squalid and otherwise ill-appointed four-room apartment. Suspecting that they were stolen, he read and recorded their serial numbers—moving some of the components, including a Bang and Olufsen turntable, in order to do so—which he then reported by phone to his headquarters. On being advised that the turntable had been taken in an armed robbery, he seized it immediately. It was later determined that some of the other serial numbers matched those on other stereo equipment taken in the same armed robbery, and a warrant was obtained and executed to seize that equipment as well. Respondent was subsequently indicted for the robbery.

The state trial court granted respondent's motion to suppress the evidence that had been seized. The Court of Appeals of Arizona affirmed. It was conceded that the initial entry and search, although warrantless, were justified by the exigent circumstance of the shooting. The Court of Appeals viewed the obtaining of the serial numbers, however, as an additional search, unrelated to that exigency. Relying upon a statement in Mincey v. Arizona, 437 U.S. 385 (1978), that a "warrantless search must be 'strictly circumscribed by the exigencies which justify its initiation,'" id., at 393 (citation omitted), the Court of Appeals held that the police conduct violated the Fourth Amendment, requiring the evidence derived from that conduct to be excluded. 146 Ariz. 533, 534–535, 707 P.2d 331, 332–333 (1985). Both courts—the trial court explicitly and the Court of Appeals by necessary implication—rejected the State's contention that Officer Nelson's actions were justified under the "plain view" doctrine of Coolidge v. New Hampshire, supra. The Arizona Supreme Court denied review, and the State filed this petition.

II

As an initial matter, the State argues that Officer Nelson's actions constituted neither a "search" nor a "seizure" within the meaning of the Fourth Amendment. We agree that the mere recording of the serial numbers did not constitute a seizure. To be sure, that was the first step in a process by which respondent was eventually deprived of the stereo equipment. In and of itself, however, it did not "meaningfully interfere" with respondent's possessory interest in either the serial numbers or the equipment, and therefore did not amount to a seizure. See Maryland v. Macon, 472 U.S. 463, 469 (1985).

Officer Nelson's moving of the equipment, however, did constitute a "search" separate and apart from the search for the shooter, victims, and weapons that was the lawful objective of his entry into the apartment.

Merely inspecting those parts of the turntable that came into view during the latter search would not have constituted an independent search, because it would have produced no additional invasion of respondent's privacy interest. See Illinois v. Andreas, 463 U.S. 765, 771 (1983). *But taking action, unrelated to the objectives of the authorized intrusion, which exposed to view concealed portions of the apartment or its contents, did produce a new invasion of respondent's privacy unjustified by the exigent circumstance that validated the entry.* This is why, contrary to JUSTICE POWELL'S suggestion, post, at 333, the "distinction between 'looking' at a suspicious object in plain view and 'moving' it even a few inches" is much more than trivial for purposes of the Fourth Amendment. It matters not that the search uncovered nothing of any great personal value to respondent—serial numbers rather than (what might conceivably have been hidden behind or under the equipment) letters or photographs. A search is a search, even if it happens to disclose nothing but the bottom of a turntable.

III

The remaining question is whether the search was "reasonable" under the Fourth Amendment.

On this aspect of the case we reject, at the outset, the apparent position of the Arizona Court of Appeals that because the officers' action directed to the stereo equipment was unrelated to the justification for their entry into respondent's apartment, it was ipso facto unreasonable. That lack of relationship always exists with regard to action validated under the "plain view" doctrine; where action is taken for the purpose justifying the entry, invocation of the doctrine is superfluous. Mincey v. Arizona, supra, in saying that a warrantless search must be "strictly circumscribed by the exigencies which justify its initiation," 437 U.S., at 393 (citation omitted), was addressing only the scope of the primary [480 U.S. 321, 326] search itself, and was not overruling by implication the many cases acknowledging that the "plain view" doctrine can legitimate action beyond that scope.

We turn, then, to application of the doctrine to the facts of this case. "It is well established that under certain circumstances the police may seize evidence in plain view without a warrant," Coolidge v. New Hampshire, <u>403 U.S., at 465</u> (plurality opinion) (emphasis added). Those circumstances include situations "[w]here the initial intrusion that brings the police within plain view of such [evidence] is supported . . . by one of the recognized exceptions to the warrant requirement," ibid., such as the exigent-circumstances intrusion here. It would be absurd to say that an object could lawfully be seized and taken from the premises, but could not be moved for closer examination. It is clear, therefore, that the search here was valid if the "plain view" doctrine would have sustained a seizure of the equipment.

There is no doubt it would have done so if Officer Nelson had probable cause to believe that the equipment was stolen. The State has conceded, however, that he had only a "reasonable suspicion," by which it means something less than probable cause. See Brief for Petitioner 18-19. We have not ruled on the question whether probable cause is required in order to invoke the "plain view" doctrine. Dicta in Payton v. New York, <u>445 U.S. 573, 587</u> (1980), suggested that the standard of probable cause must be met, but our later opinions in Texas v. Brown, <u>460 U.S. 730</u> (1983), explicitly regarded the issue as unresolved, see id., at 742, n. 7 (plurality opinion); id., at 746 (STEVENS, J., concurring in judgment).

We now hold that probable cause is required. To say otherwise would be to cut the "plain view" doctrine loose from its theoretical and practical moorings. The theory of that doctrine consists of extending to nonpublic places such as the home, where searches and seizures without a warrant are presumptively unreasonable, the police's longstanding authority to make warrantless seizures in public places of such objects as weapons and contraband. See Payton v. New York, supra, at 586–587. And the practical justification for that extension is the desirability of sparing police, whose viewing of the object in the course of a lawful search is as legitimate as it would have been in a public place, the inconvenience and the risk—to themselves or to preservation of the evidence—of going to obtain a warrant. See Coolidge v. New Hampshire, supra, at 468 (plurality opinion). Dispensing with the need for a warrant is worlds apart from permitting a lesser standard of cause for the seizure than a warrant would require, i.e., the standard of probable cause. No reason is apparent why an object should routinely be seizable on lesser grounds, during an unrelated search and seizure, than would have been needed to obtain a warrant for that same object if it had been known to be on the premises.

We do not say, of course, that a seizure can never be justified on less than probable cause. We have held that it can—where, for example, the seizure is minimally intrusive and operational necessities render it the only practicable means of detecting certain types of crime. See, e. g., United States v. Cortez, <u>449 U.S. 411</u> (1981) (investigative detention of vehicle suspected to be transporting illegal aliens); United States v. Brignoni-Ponce, <u>422 U.S. 873</u> (1975) (same); United States v. Place, <u>462 U.S. 696, 709</u>, and n. 9 (1983) (dictum) (seizure of suspected drug dealer's luggage at airport to permit exposure to specially trained dog). No special operational necessities are relied on here, however—but rather the mere fact that the items in question came lawfully within the officer's plain view. That alone cannot supplant the requirement of probable cause.

The same considerations preclude us from holding that, even though probable cause would have been necessary for a seizure, the search of objects in plain view that occurred here [480 U.S. 321, 328] could be sustained on lesser grounds.

A dwelling-place search, no less than a dwelling-place seizure, requires probable cause, and there is no reason in theory or practicality why application of the "plain view" doctrine would supplant that requirement. Although the interest protected by the Fourth Amendment injunction against unreasonable searches is quite different from that protected by its injunction against unreasonable seizures, see Texas v. Brown, supra, at 747–748 (STEVENS, J., concurring in judgment), neither the one nor the other is of inferior worth or necessarily requires only lesser protection. We have not elsewhere drawn a categorical distinction between the two insofar as concerns the degree of justification needed to establish the reasonableness of police action, and we see no reason for a distinction in the particular circumstances before us here. Indeed, to treat searches more liberally would especially erode the plurality's warning in Coolidge that "the 'plain view' doctrine may not be used to extend a general exploratory search from one object to another until something incrimination at last emerges" 403 U.S., at 466. In short, whether legal authority to move the equipment could be found only as an inevitable concomitant of the authority to seize it, or also as a consequence of some independent power to search certain objects in plain view, probable cause to believe the equipment was stolen was required.

JUSTICE O'CONNOR'S dissent suggests that we uphold the action here on the ground that it was a "cursory inspection" rather than a "full-blown search," and could therefore be justified by reasonable suspicion instead of probable cause. As already noted, a truly cursory inspection—one that involves merely looking at what is already exposed to view, without disturbing it—is not a "search" for Fourth Amendment purposes, and therefore does not even require reasonable suspicion. We are unwilling to send police and judges into a new thicket of Fourth Amendment law, to seek a creature of uncertain description that is neither a "plain view" inspection nor yet a "full-blown search." Nothing in the prior opinions of this Court supports such a distinction, not even the dictum from Justice Stewart's concurrence in Stanley v. Georgia, 394 U.S. 557, 571 (1969), whose reference to a "mere inspection" describes, in our view, close observation of what lies in plain sight.

JUSTICE POWELL'S dissent reasonably asks what it is we would have had Officer Nelson do in these circumstances. Post, at 332. The answer depends, of course, upon whether he had probable cause to conduct a search, a question that was not preserved in this case. If he had, then he should have done precisely what he did. If not, then he should have followed up his suspicions, if possible, by means other than a search—just as he would have had to do if, while walking along the street, he had noticed the same suspicious stereo equipment sitting inside a house a few feet away from him, beneath an open window. It may well be that, in such circumstances, no effective means short of a search exist. But there is nothing new in the realization that *the Constitution sometimes insulates the criminality of a few in order to protect the privacy of us all.* Our disagreement with the dissenters pertains to where the proper balance should be struck; we choose to adhere to the textual and traditional standard of probable cause.

The State contends that, even if Officer Nelson's search violated the Fourth Amendment, the court below should have admitted the evidence thus obtained under the "good faith" exception to the exclusionary rule. That was not the question on which certiorari was granted, and we decline to consider it.

For the reasons stated, the judgment of the Court of Appeals of Arizona is Affirmed.

JUSTICE WHITE, concurring.

I write only to emphasize that this case does not present, and we have no occasion to address, the so-called "inadvertent discovery" prong of the plain-view exception to the Warrant Clause. See Coolidge v. New Hampshire, 403 U.S. 443, 469–471 (1971) (plurality opinion). This "requirement" of the plain-view doctrine has never been accepted by a judgment supported by a majority of this Court, and I therefore do not accept JUSTICE O'CONNOR'S dissent's assertion that evidence seized in plain view must have been inadvertently discovered in order to satisfy the dictates of the Fourth Amendment. See post, at 334. I join the majority opinion today without regard to the inadvertence of the officers' discovery of the stereo components' serial numbers. The police officers conducted a search of respondent's stereo equipment absent probable cause that the equipment was stolen. It is for this reason that the judgment of the Court of Appeals of Arizona must be affirmed.

JUSTICE POWELL, with whom THE CHIEF JUSTICE and JUSTICE O'CONNOR join, dissenting.

I join JUSTICE O'CONNOR'S dissenting opinion, and write briefly to highlight what seem to me the unfortunate consequences of the Court's decision.

Today the Court holds for the first time that the requirement of probable cause operates as a separate limitation on the application of the plain-view doctrine. 1 The plurality opinion in Coolidge v. New Hampshire, 403 U.S. 443 (1971), required only that it be "immediately apparent to the police that they have evidence before them; the 'plain view' doctrine may not be used to extend a general exploratory search from one object to another until something incriminating at last emerges." Id., at 466 (citation omitted). There was no general exploratory search in this case, and I would not approve such a search. All the pertinent objects were in plain view and could be identified as objects frequently stolen. There was no looking into closets, opening of drawers or trunks, or other "rummaging around." JUSTICE O'CONNOR properly emphasizes that the moving of a suspicious object in plain view results in a minimal invasion of privacy. Post, at 338. The Court nevertheless holds that "merely looking at" an object in plain view is lawful, ante, at 328, but "moving" or "disturbing" the object to investigate a reasonable suspicion is not, ante, at 324, 328. The facts of this case well illustrate the unreasonableness of this distinction.

The officers' suspicion that the stereo components at issue were stolen was both reasonable and based on specific, articulable facts. Indeed, the State was unwise to concede the absence of probable cause. The police lawfully entered respondent's apartment under exigent circumstances that arose when a bullet fired through the floor of the apartment struck a man in the apartment below. What they saw in the apartment hardly suggested that it was occupied by lawabiding citizens. A .25-caliber automatic pistol lay in plain view on the living room floor. During a concededly lawful search, the officers found a .45-caliber automatic, a .22-caliber, sawed-off rifle, and a stocking-cap mask. The apartment was littered with drug paraphernalia. App. 29. The officers also observed two sets of expensive stereo components of a type that frequently was stolen It is fair to ask what Officer Nelson should have done in these circumstances. Accepting the State's concession that he lacked probable cause, he could not have obtained a warrant to seize the stereo components. Neither could he have remained on the premises and forcibly prevented their removal. Officer Nelson's testimony indicates that he was able to read some of the serial numbers without moving the components. $\underline{3}$ To read the serial number on a Bang and Olufsen turntable, however, he had to "turn it around or turn it upside down" Id., at 19. Officer Nelson noted the serial numbers on the stereo components and telephoned the National Crime Information Center to check them against the Center's computerized listing of stolen property. The computer confirmed his suspicion that at least the Bang and Olufsen turntable had been stolen. On the basis of this information, the officers obtained a warrant to seize the turntable and other stereo components that also proved to be stolen.

The Court holds that there was an unlawful search of the turntable. It agrees that the "mere recording of the serial numbers did not constitute a seizure" Ante, at 324. Thus, if the computer had identified as stolen property a component with a visible serial number, the evidence would have been admissible. But the Court further holds that "Officer Nelson's moving of the equipment . . . did constitute a 'search'. . . . " Ibid. It perceives a constitutional distinction between reading a serial number on an object and moving or picking up an identical object to see its serial number. To make its position unmistakably clear, the Court concludes that a "search is a search, even if it happens to disclose nothing but the bottom of a turntable" Ante, at 325. With all respect, this distinction between "looking" at a suspicious object in plain view and "moving" it even a few inches trivializes the Fourth Amendment. The Court's new rule will cause uncertainty, and could deter conscientious police officers from lawfully obtaining evidence necessary to convict guilty persons. Apart from the importance of rationality in the interpretation of the Fourth Amendment, today's decision may handicap law enforcement without enhancing privacy interests.

Accordingly, I dissent.

THE PEOPLE OF THE STATE OF NEW YORK, Respondent
v.
JOHN DEFORE, Appellant
242 N.Y. 13 (1926)

Court of Appeals of New York
Argued December 1, 1925
Decided January 12, 1926

CARDOZO, J.

A police officer arrested the defendant on a charge that he had stolen an overcoat. The crime, if committed, was petit larceny, a misdemeanor, for the value of the coat was not over fifty dollars (Penal Law, §§ 1296, 1298; Cons. Laws, ch. 40). The defendant when taken into custody was in the hall of his boarding house. The officer after making the arrest entered the defendant's room and searched it. The search produced a bag, and in the bag was a blackjack. The defendant after trial at Special Sessions was acquitted of the larceny. In the meantime he had been indicted as a second offender for the possession of the weapon (Penal Law, § 1897). He made a motion before trial to suppress the evidence obtained through search without a warrant. The motion was denied. He made objection again upon the trial when the bag and the contents, i.e., the blackjack and a hat, were offered in evidence by the People. The objection was overruled. *He contends* that through these rulings he has suffered a denial of his rights under the statute against unreasonable search and seizure (Civil Rights Law, § 8; Cons. Laws, ch. 6); a denial of his rights under the provision of the State Constitution which gives immunity against compulsory self-incrimination; and a denial of his rights under the due process clause of the Fourteenth Amendment to the Constitution of the United States.

(1) The search was unreasonable "in the light of common law traditions." A different conclusion might be necessary if the defendant had been lawfully arrested. As an incident to such an arrest, his person might have been searched for the fruits or evidences of crime. So, it seems, might the place where the arrest was made. But the arrest was not lawful. One who, acting without a warrant, arrests for a misdemeanor, exceeds the bounds of privilege, whether he be a private person or an officer, unless the crime has been committed or attempted in his presence. The defendant had neither committed the crime of petit larceny in the presence of the officer, nor there attempted to commit it. He had not committed nor attempted it anywhere. There was no lawful arrest to which the search could be an incident.

The People stress the fact that the weapon was contraband, a nuisance subject to destruction (Penal Law, § 1899). This might have justified the seizure, the abatement of the nuisance, if the weapon had been exposed to view. It might even have justified the refusal to return the weapon, though discovered by unlawful means. It did not justify the search. There is no rule that homes may be ransacked without process to discover the fruits or the implements of crime. To make such inquisitions lawful, there must be the support of a search warrant issued upon probable cause. Search even then is "confined under our statute [Code Crim. Pro. § 792] to property stolen or embezzled, or used as the means of committing a felony, or held with the intent to use it as an instrument of crime". The warrant does not issue for things of evidential value merely. What would be a wrong with a warrant is not innocent without one. To dispense with process in the pursuit of contraband is to dispense with it in the one case in which it may ever issue in the pursuit of anything. Means unlawful in their inception do not become lawful by relation when suspicion ripens into discovery.

We hold, then, with the defendant that the evidence against him was the outcome of a trespass. The officer might have been resisted, or sued for damages, or even prosecuted for oppression (Penal Law, §§ 1846, 1847). He was subject to removal or other discipline at the hands of his superiors. These consequences are undisputed. The defendant would add another. *We must determine whether evidence of criminality, procured by an act of trespass, is to be rejected as incompetent for the misconduct of the trespasser.* The question is not a new one. It was put to us more than twenty years ago in People v. Adams (176 N.Y. 351), and there deliberately answered. A search warrant had been issued against the proprietor of a gambling house for the seizure of gambling implements. The police did not confine themselves to the things stated in the warrant. Without authority of law, they seized the defendant's books and papers. We held that the documents did not cease to be competent evidence against him though the seizure was unlawful. In support of that holding, we cited many authorities, and notably a series of decisions by the courts of Massachusetts. "A trespasser may testify to pertinent facts observed by him, or may put in evidence pertinent articles or papers found by him while trespassing. For the trespass, he may be held responsible civilly, and perhaps criminally, but his testimony is not thereby incompetent." The ruling thus broadly made is decisive, while it stands, of the case before us now. It is at variance, however, with later judgments of the Supreme Court of the United States. Those judgments do not bind us (*Not then, but they do now!!*), for they construe provisions of the Federal Constitution, the Fourth and Fifth Amendments, not applicable to the States. Even though not binding, they merit our attentive scrutiny. Weeks v. U.S. (232 U.S. 383) held that articles wrongfully seized by agents of the Federal government should have been returned to the defendant or excluded as evidence if a timely motion to compel return had been made before the trial. Silverthorne Lumber Co. v. U.S. (251 U.S. 385) held that copies of the things so seized, in that case books and papers, must share the fate of the originals. Gouled v. U.S. (255 U.S. 298) and Amos v. U.S. (255 U.S. 313) held that a motion before trial was unnecessary if the defendant had no knowledge until the trial that an illegal seizure had been made. Burdeau v. McDowell (256 U.S. 465) held that a Federal prosecutor might make such use as he pleased of documents or other information acquired from a trespasser if persons other than Federal officers were guilty of the trespass. Hester v. U.S. (265 U.S. 57) and Carroll v. U.S. (267 U.S. 132) drew a distinction between search and seizure in a house and search and seizure in the fields or in automobiles or other vehicles. Finally Agnello v. U.S. (269 U.S. 20) held that the evidence must be excluded though the things seized were contraband and though there had been no motion before trial if the facts were undisputed. This means that the Supreme Court has overruled its own judgment in Adams v. New York, for the facts were undisputed there. The procedural condition of a preliminary motion has been substantially abandoned, or, if now enforced at all, is an exceptional requirement.

There has been no blinking the consequences. The criminal is to go free because the constable has blundered.

**The new doctrine has already met the scrutiny of courts of sister States. The decisions have been brought together for our guidance through the industry of counsel. In forty-five States (exclusive of our own) the subject has been considered. Fourteen States have adopted the rule of the Weeks case either as there laid down or as subsequently broadened. Thirty-one have rejected it. To what is there written, little of value can be added. The controversy, starting with the courts, has been taken up by the commentators, and with them has been the theme of animated argument. For the most part, there has been adherence to the older doctrine. With authority thus divided, it is only some overmastering consideration of principle or of policy that should move us to a change. The balance is not swayed until something more persuasive than uncertainty is added to the scales.

We find nothing in the statute (<u>Civil Rights Law, § 8</u>) whereby official trespasses and private are differentiated in respect of the legal consequences to follow them. All that the statute does is to place the two on an equality. In times gone by, officialdom had arrogated to itself a privilege of indiscriminate inquisition. The statute declares that the privilege shall not exist. Thereafter, all alike, whenever search is unreasonable, must answer to the law. For the high intruder and the low, the consequences become the same. Evidence is not excluded because the private litigant who offers it has gathered it by lawless force. By the same token, the State, when prosecuting an offender against the peace and order of society, incurs no heavier liability.

The Federal rule as it stands is either too strict or too lax. A Federal prosecutor may take no benefit from evidence collected through the trespass of a Federal officer. The thought is that in appropriating the results, he ratifies the means. He does not have to be so scrupulous about evidence brought to him by others. How finely the line is drawn is seen when we recall that marshals in the service of the nation are on one side of it, and police in the service of the States on the other. The nation may keep what the servants of the States supply. We must go farther or not so far. The professed object of the trespass rather than the official character of the trespasser should test the rights of government. The incongruity of other tests gains emphasis from the facts of the case before us. The complainant, the owner of the overcoat, co-operated with the officer in the arrest and the attendant search. Their powers were equal, since the charge was petit larceny, a misdemeanor (Code Crim. Pro. §§ 177, 183). If one spoke or acted for the State, so also did the other. A government would be disingenuous, if, in determining the use that should be made of evidence drawn from such a source, it drew a line between them. This would be true whether they had acted in concert or apart. We exalt form above substance when we hold that the use is made lawful because the intruder is without a badge of office. We break with precedent altogether when we press the prohibition farther.

The truth indeed is that the statute says nothing about consequences. It does no more than deny a privilege. Denying this, it stops. Intrusion without privilege has certain liabilities and penalties. The statute does not assume to alter or increase them. No scrutiny of its text can ever evoke additional consequences by a mere process of construction. We must attach them, if at all, because some public policy, adequately revealed, would otherwise be thwarted. But adequate revelation of such a policy it is surely hard to see. This would have been true in the beginning before the courts had spoken. It is more plainly true to-day. In this State the immunity is the creature, not of constitution, but of statute (Civil Rights Law, § 8). The Legislature, which created it, has acquiesced in the ruling of this court that the prohibition of the search did not anathematize the evidence yielded through the search. If we had misread the statute or misconceived the public policy, a few words of amendment would have quickly set us right. The process of amendment is prompt and simple. It is without the delays or obstructions that clog the change of constitutions. In such circumstances silence itself is the declaration of a policy. We scan the statute in vain for any token of intention that search by intruders wearing a badge of office shall have any different consequences in respect of the law of evidence than search by intruders generally.

**We are confirmed in this conclusion when we reflect how far-reaching in its effect upon society the new consequences would be. *The pettiest peace officer would have it in his power through overzeal or indiscretion to confer immunity upon an offender for crimes the most flagitious. A room is searched against the law, and the body of a murdered man is found. If the place of discovery may not be proved, the other circumstances may be insufficient to connect the defendant with the crime. The privacy of the home has been infringed, and the murderer goes free.* Another search, once more against the law, discloses counterfeit money or the implements of forgery. The absence of a warrant means the freedom of the forger. Like instances can be multiplied. *We may not subject society to these dangers until the Legislature has spoken with a clearer voice.* In so holding, we are not unmindful of the argument that unless the evidence is excluded, the statute becomes a form and its protection an illusion. This has a strange sound when the immunity is viewed in the light of its origin and history. The rule now embodied in the statute was received into English law as the outcome of the prosecution of Wilkes and Entick. Wilkes sued the messengers who had ransacked his papers, and recovered a verdict of £4,000 against one and £1,000 against the other. Entick, too, had a substantial verdict (Boyd v. U.S., 116 U.S. 616, at p. 626; Entick v. Carrington, 19 Howell State Trials, 1030. We do not know whether the public, represented by its juries, is to-day more indifferent to its liberties than it was when the immunity was born. If so, the change of sentiment without more does not work a change of remedy. Other sanctions, penal and disciplinary, supplementing the right to damages, have already been enumerated. No doubt the protection of the statute would be greater from the point of view of the individual whose privacy had been invaded if the government were required to ignore what it had learned through the invasion. *The question is whether protection for the individual would not be gained at a disproportionate loss of protection for society. On the one side is the social need that crime shall be repressed. On the other, the social need that law shall not be flouted by the insolence of office.* There are dangers in any choice. The rule of the Adams case strikes a balance between opposing interests. We must hold it to be the law until those organs of government by which a change of public policy is normally effected, shall give notice to the courts that the change has come to pass.

The judgment of conviction should be affirmed.

HISCOCK, Ch. J.; POUND, MCLAUGHLIN; CRANE, ANDREWS; and LEHMAN, JJ. concur. Judgment affirmed.

Supreme Court of the United States
Dethorne GRAHAM, Petitioner v. M.S. CONNOR et al.
490 U.S. 386 (1989)

Argued Feb. 21, 1989
Decided May 15, 1989

REHNQUIST, C.J., delivered the opinion of the Court, in which WHITE, STEVENS; O'CONNOR, SCALIA; and KENNEDY, JJ. joined. BLACKMUN, J., filed an opinion concurring in part and concurring in the judgment, in which BRENNAN and MARSHALL, JJ., joined.

Chief Justice REHNQUIST delivered the opinion of the Court.

This case requires us to decide what constitutional standard governs a free citizen's claim that law enforcement officials used excessive force in the course of making an arrest, investigatory stop, or other "seizure" of his person. We hold that such claims are properly analyzed under the Fourth Amendment's "objective reasonableness" standard.

In this action under 42 U.S.C. § 1983, petitioner Dethorne Graham seeks to recover damages for injuries allegedly sustained when law enforcement officers used physical force against him during the course of an investigatory stop. On November 12, 1984, Graham, a diabetic, felt the onset of an insulin reaction. He asked a friend, William Berry, to drive him to a nearby convenience store so he could purchase some orange juice to counteract the reaction. Berry agreed, but when Graham entered the store, he saw a number of people ahead of him in the check-outline. Concerned about the delay, he hurried out of the store and asked Berry to drive him to a friend's house instead.

[Defendant] Connor, an officer of the Charlotte, North Carolina, Police Department, saw Graham hastily enter and leave the store. The officer became suspicious that something was amiss and followed Berry's car. About one-half mile from the store, he made an investigative stop. Although Berry told Connor that Graham was simply suffering from a "sugar reaction," the officer ordered Berry and Graham to wait while he found out what, if anything, had happened at the convenience store. When Officer Connor returned to his patrol car to call for backup assistance, Graham got out of the car, ran around it twice, and finally sat down on the curb, where he passed out briefly.

In the ensuing confusion, a number of other Charlotte police officers arrived on the scene in response to Officer Connor's request for backup. One of the officers rolled Graham over on the sidewalk and cuffed his hands tightly behind his back, ignoring Berry's pleas to get him some sugar. Another officer said: "I've seen a lot of people with sugar diabetes that never acted like this. Ain't nothing wrong with the M.F. but drunk. Lock the S.B. up." Several officers then lifted Graham up from behind, carried him over to Berry's car, and placed him face down on its hood. Regaining consciousness, Graham asked the officers to check in his wallet for a diabetic decal that he carried. In response, one of the officers told him to "shut up" and shoved his face down against the hood of the car. Four officers grabbed Graham and threw him headfirst into the police car. A friend of Graham's brought some orange juice to the car, but the officers refused to let him have it. Finally, Officer Connor received a report that Graham had done nothing wrong at the convenience store, and the officers drove him home and released him.

At some point during his encounter with the police, Graham sustained a broken foot, cuts on his wrists, a bruised forehead, and an injured shoulder; he also claims to have developed a loud ringing in his right ear that continues to this day. He commenced this action under 42 U.S.C. § 1983 against the individual officers involved in the incident, all of whom are respondents here, alleging that they had used excessive force in making the investigatory stop, in violation of "rights secured to him under the Fourteenth Amendment to the United States Constitution and 42 U.S.C. § 1983."

The case was tried before a jury. At the close of [the plaintiff's] evidence, [the defendant police officers] moved for a directed verdict. In ruling on that motion, the District Court considered the following four factors, which it identified as "[t]he factors to be considered in determining when the excessive use of force gives rise to a cause of action under § 1983": (1) the need for the application of force; (2) the relationship between that need and the amount of force that was used; (3) the extent of the injury inflicted; and (4) "[w]hether the force was applied in a good faith effort to maintain and restore discipline or maliciously and sadistically for the very purpose of causing harm" 644 F.Supp. 246, 248 (WDNC 1986). Finding that the amount of force used by the officers was "appropriate under the circumstances," that "[t]here was no discernable injury inflicted," and that the force used "was not applied maliciously or sadistically for the very purpose of causing harm," but in "a good faith effort to maintain or restore order in the face of a potentially explosive situation," the District Court granted [defendants'] motion for a directed verdict. (What this means is that the judge decided there was nothing for a *reasonable* jury to decide and took the case away from them, or in the vernacular of the courtroom, directed them to return a verdict of Not Guilty.)

*Determining whether the force used to effect a particular seizure is "reasonable" under the Fourth Amendment requires a careful balancing of "the nature and quality of the intrusion on the individual's Fourth Amendment interests" against the countervailing governmental interests at stake. *Id.*, at 8, 105 S.Ct., at 1699, quoting *United States v. Place,* 462 U.S. 696, 703 (1983). *Our Fourth Amendment jurisprudence has long recognized that the right to make an arrest or investigatory stop necessarily carries with it the right to use some degree of physical coercion or threat thereof to effect it. See Terry v. Ohio,* 392 U.S., at 22–27. *Because "[t]he test of reasonableness under the Fourth Amendment is not capable of precise definition or mechanical application,"* Bell v. Wolfish, 441 U.S. 520, 559 (1979), however, its proper application requires careful attention to *the facts and circumstances of each particular case,* including the severity of the crime at issue, whether the suspect poses an immediate threat to the safety of the officers or others, and whether he is actively resisting arrest or attempting to evade arrest by flight. See *Tennessee v. Garner,* 471 U.S., at 8–9 (the question is "whether the totality of the circumstances justifie[s] a particular sort of . . . seizure").

The "reasonableness" of a particular use of force must be judged from the perspective of a reasonable officer on the scene, rather than with the 20/20 vision of hindsight. See Terry v. Ohio, supra, 392 U.S., at 20–22. The Fourth Amendment is not violated by an arrest based on probable cause, even though the wrong person is arrested, *Hill v. California,* 401 U.S. 797 (1971), nor by the mistaken execution of a valid search warrant on the wrong premises, *Maryland v. Garrison,* 480 U.S. 79 (1987). With respect to a claim of excessive force, the same standard of reasonableness at the moment applies:

"Not every push or shove, even if it may later seem unnecessary in the peace of a judge's chambers," Johnson v. Glick, 481 F.2d, at 1033, *violates the Fourth Amendment.* The calculus of reasonableness must embody allowance for the fact that *police officers are often forced to make split-second judgments-in circumstances that are tense, uncertain, and rapidly evolving-about the amount of force that is necessary in a particular situation.*

As in other Fourth Amendment contexts, however, the "reasonableness" inquiry in an excessive force case is an objective one: the question is whether the officers' actions are "objectively reasonable" in light of the facts and circumstances confronting them, without regard to their underlying intent or motivation. See Scott v. United States, 436 U.S. 128, 137–139 (1978); see also Terry v. Ohio, supra, 392 U.S., at 21 (in analyzing the reasonableness of a particular search or seizure, "it is imperative that the facts be judged against an objective standard"). An officer's evil intentions will not make a Fourth Amendment violation out of an objectively reasonable use of force; nor will an officer's good intentions make an objectively unreasonable use of force constitutional. See Scott v. United States, supra, 436 U.S., at 138, citing United States v. Robinson, 414 U.S. 218 (1973).

Because the Court of Appeals reviewed the District Court's ruling on the motion for directed verdict under an erroneous view of the governing substantive law, its judgment must be vacated and the case remanded to that court for reconsideration of that issue under the proper Fourth Amendment standard. (The Supremes did not say the police officers acted wrongly, just that the judge applied the wrong test in determining that they did not.)

It is so ordered.

Supreme Court of the United States
TENNESSEE, Appellant
v.
Cleamtee GARNER

MEMPHIS POLICE DEPARTMENT et al., Petitioners
v.
Cleamtee GARNER

471 U.S. 1
Argued Oct. 30, 1984
Decided March 27, 1985

Justice WHITE delivered the opinion of the Court.

This case requires us to determine the constitutionality of the use of deadly force to prevent the escape of an apparently unarmed suspected felon. We conclude that such force may not be used unless it is necessary to prevent the escape and the officer has probable cause to believe that the suspect poses a significant threat of death or serious physical injury to the officer or others.

   At about 10:45 p.m. on October 3, 1974, Memphis Police Officers Elton Hymon and Leslie Wright were dispatched to answer a "prowler inside call." Upon arriving at the scene they saw a woman standing on her porch and gesturing toward the adjacent house.[1] She told them she had heard glass breaking and that "they" or "someone" was breaking in next door. While Wright radioed the dispatcher to say that they were on the scene, Hymon went behind the house. He heard a door slam and saw someone run across the backyard. The fleeing suspect, who was appellee-respondent's decedent, Edward Garner, stopped at a 6-feet-high chain link fence at the edge of the yard. With the aid of a flashlight, Hymon was able to see Garner's face and hands. He saw no sign of a weapon, and, though not certain, was "reasonably sure" and "figured" that Garner was unarmed. He thought Garner was 17 or 18 years old and about 5'5" or 5'7" tall.[2] While Garner was crouched at the base of the fence, Hymon called out "police, halt" and took a few steps toward him. Garner then began to climb over the fence. Convinced that if Garner made it over the fence he would elude capture,[3]

---

[1]The owner of the house testified that no lights were on in the house, but that a back door light was on. Record 160. Officer Hymon, though uncertain, stated in his deposition that there were lights on in the house. *Id.*, at 209.

[2]In fact, Garner, an eighth-grader, was 15. He was 5'4" tall and weighed somewhere around 100 or 110 pounds.

[3]When asked at trial why he fired, Hymon stated:"Well, first of all it was apparent to me from the little bit that I knew about the area at the time that he was going to get away because, number 1, I couldn't get to him. My partner then couldn't find where he was because, you know, he was late coming around. He didn't know where I was talking about. I couldn't get to him because of the fence here, I couldn't have jumped this fence and come up, consequently jumped this fence and caught him before he got away because he was already up on the fence, just one leap and he was already over the fence, and so there is no way that I could have caught him." He also stated that the area beyond the fence was dark, that he could not have gotten over the fence easily because he was carrying a lot of equipment and wearing heavy boots, and that Garner, being younger and more energetic, could have outrun him.

Hymon shot him. The bullet hit Garner in the back of the head. Garner was taken by ambulance to a hospital, where he died on the operating table. Ten dollars and a purse taken from the house were found on his body.[4]

In using deadly force to prevent the escape, Hymon was acting under the authority of a Tennessee statute and pursuant to Police Department policy. The statute provides that "[i]f, after notice of the intention to arrest the defendant, he either flee or forcibly resist, the officer may use all the necessary means to effect the arrest" Tenn.Code Ann. § 40-7-108 (1982).[5] The Department policy was slightly more restrictive than the statute, but still allowed the use of deadly force in cases of burglary. App. 140–144. The incident was reviewed by the Memphis Police Firearm's Review Board and presented to a grand jury. Neither took any action. *Id.*, at 57.

Garner's father then brought this action in the Federal District Court for the Western District of Tennessee, seeking damages under 42 U.S.C. § 1983 for asserted violations of Garner's constitutional rights. The complaint alleged that the shooting violated the Fourth, Fifth, Sixth, Eighth, and Fourteenth Amendments of the United States Constitution. It named as defendants Officer Hymon, the Police Department, its Director, and the Mayor and city of Memphis. After a 3-day bench trial, the District Court entered judgment for all defendants. It dismissed the claims against the Mayor and the Director for lack of evidence. It then concluded that Hymon's actions were authorized by the Tennessee statute, which in turn was constitutional. Hymon had employed the only reasonable and practicable means of preventing Garner's escape. Garner had "recklessly and heedlessly attempted to vault over the fence to escape, thereby assuming the risk of being fired upon."

The State of Tennessee, which had intervened to defend the statute, see 28 U.S.C. § 2403(b), appealed to this Court. The city filed a petition for certiorari. We noted probable jurisdiction in the appeal and granted the petition.

Whenever an officer restrains the freedom of a person to walk away, he has seized that person. *United States v. Brignoni-Ponce,* 422 U.S. 873, 878 (1975). While it is not always clear just when minimal police interference becomes a seizure, see *United States v. Mendenhall,* 446 U.S. 544 (1980), there can be no question that apprehension by the use of deadly force is a seizure subject to the reasonableness requirement of the Fourth Amendment.

A police officer may arrest a person if he has probable cause to believe that person committed a crime. *United States v. Watson,* 423 U.S. 411 (1976). Petitioners and appellant argue that if this requirement is satisfied the Fourth Amendment has nothing to say about *how* that seizure is made. This submission ignores the many cases in which this Court, by balancing the extent of the intrusion against the need for it, has examined the reasonableness of the manner in which a search or seizure is conducted. To determine the constitutionality of a seizure "[w]e must balance the nature and quality of the intrusion on the individual's Fourth Amendment interests against the importance of the governmental interests alleged to justify the intrusion" *United States v.*

---

[4]Garner had rummaged through one room in the house, in which, in the words of the owner, "[a]ll the stuff was out on the floors, all the drawers was pulled out, and stuff was scattered all over." *Id.*, at 34. The owner testified that his valuables were untouched but that, in addition to the purse and the 10 dollars, one of his wife's rings was missing. The ring was not recovered.

[5]Although the statute does not say so explicitly, Tennessee law forbids the use of deadly force in the arrest of a misdemeanant. See *Johnson v. State,* 173 Tenn. 134 (1938).

Place, 462 U.S. 696 (1983). We have described "the balancing of competing interests" as "the key principle of the Fourth Amendment." Because one of the factors is the extent of the intrusion, it is plain that _reasonableness depends_ on not only when a seizure is made, _but also how it is carried out. Terry v. Ohio_, 392 U.S. 1, 28–29 (1968).

Applying these principles to particular facts, the Court has held that governmental interests did not support a lengthy detention of luggage, _United States v. Place, supra_, an airport seizure not "carefully tailored to its underlying justification," _Florida v. Royer_, 460 U.S. 491, 500 (1983) (plurality opinion), surgery under general anesthesia to obtain evidence, _Winston v. Lee_, 470 U.S. 753 (1985), or detention for fingerprinting without probable cause, _Davis v. Mississippi_, 394 U.S. 721 (1969); _Hayes v. Florida_, 470 U.S. 811 (1985). _On the other hand_, under the same approach it has upheld the taking of fingernail scrapings from a suspect, _Cupp v. Murphy_, 412 U.S. 291 (1973), an unannounced entry into a home to prevent the destruction of evidence, _Ker v. California_, 374 U.S. 23 (1963), administrative housing inspections without probable cause to believe that a code violation will be found, _Camara v. Municipal Court, supra_, and a blood test of a drunken-driving suspect, _Schmerber v. California_, 384 U.S. 757 (1966). In each of these cases, the question was whether the totality of the circumstances justified a particular sort of search or seizure.

The same balancing process applied in the cases cited above demonstrates that, notwithstanding probable cause to seize a suspect, an officer may not always do so by killing him. The intrusiveness of a seizure by means of deadly force is unmatched. The suspect's fundamental interest in his own life need not be elaborated upon. The use of deadly force also frustrates the interest of the individual, and of society, in judicial determination of guilt and punishment. Against these interests are ranged governmental interests in effective law enforcement.[8] It is argued that overall violence will be reduced by encouraging the peaceful submission of suspects who know that they may be shot if they flee. Effectiveness in making arrests requires the resort to deadly force, or at least the meaningful threat thereof. "Being able to arrest such individuals is a condition precedent to the state's entire system of law enforcement."

In lamenting the inadequacy of later investigation, the dissent relies on the report of the President's Commission on Law Enforcement and Administration of Justice. It is worth noting that, notwithstanding its awareness of this problem, the Commission itself proposed a policy for use of deadly force arguably even more stringent than the formulation we adopt today. See President's Commission on Law Enforcement and Administration of Justice, Task Force Report: The Police 189 (1967). The Commission proposed that deadly force be used only to apprehend "perpetrators who, in the course of their crime threatened the use of deadly force, or if the officer believes there is a substantial risk that the person whose arrest is sought will cause death or serious bodily harm if his apprehension is delayed." In addition, the officer would have "to know, as a virtual certainty, that the suspect committed an offense for which the use of deadly force is permissible."

---

[8]The dissent emphasizes that subsequent investigation cannot replace immediate apprehension. Thus, we proceed on the assumption that subsequent arrest is not likely. Nonetheless, it should be remembered that failure to apprehend at the scene does not necessarily mean that the suspect will never be caught.

Without in any way disparaging the importance of these goals, we are not convinced that the use of deadly force is a sufficiently productive means of accomplishing them to justify the killing of nonviolent suspects. The use of deadly force is a self-defeating way of apprehending a suspect and so setting the criminal justice mechanism in motion. If successful, it guarantees that that mechanism will not be set in motion. And while the meaningful threat of deadly force might be thought to lead to the arrest of more live suspects by discouraging escape attempts, the presently available evidence does not support this thesis.[9] The fact is that a majority of police departments in this country have forbidden the use of deadly force against nonviolent suspects. If those charged with the enforcement of the criminal law have abjured the use of deadly force in arresting nondangerous felons, there is a substantial basis for doubting that the use of such force is an essential attribute of the arrest power in all felony cases. Petitioners and appellant have not persuaded us that shooting nondangerous fleeing suspects is so vital as to outweigh the suspect's interest in his own life.

The use of deadly force to prevent the escape of all felony suspects, whatever the circumstances, is constitutionally unreasonable. It is not better that all felony suspects die than that they escape. Where the suspect poses no immediate threat to the officer and no threat to others, *the harm resulting from failing to apprehend him does not justify the use of deadly force to do so.* It is no doubt unfortunate when a suspect who is in sight escapes, but the fact that the police arrive a little late or are a little slower afoot does not always justify killing the suspect. *A police officer may not seize an unarmed, nondangerous suspect by shooting him dead.* The Tennessee statute is unconstitutional insofar as it authorizes the use of deadly force against such fleeing suspects.

It is not, however, unconstitutional on its face. Where the officer has probable cause to believe that the suspect poses a threat of serious physical harm, either to the officer or to others, it is not constitutionally unreasonable to prevent escape by using deadly force. Thus, if the suspect threatens the officer with a weapon or there is probable cause to believe that he has committed a crime involving the infliction or threatened infliction of serious physical harm, deadly force may be used if necessary to prevent escape, and if, where feasible, some warning has been given. As applied in such circumstances, the Tennessee statute would pass constitutional muster.

It is insisted that the Fourth Amendment must be construed in light of the common-law rule, which allowed the use of whatever force was necessary to effect the arrest of a fleeing felon, though not a misdemeanant. As stated in Hale's posthumously published Pleas of the Crown:

"[I]f persons that are pursued by these officers for felony or the just suspicion thereof . . . shall not yield themselves to these officers, but shall either resist or fly before they are apprehended or being apprehended shall rescue themselves and resist or fly, so that they cannot be otherwise apprehended, and are upon necessity slain therein, because they cannot be otherwise taken, it is no felony (on the part of the shooting officer)." 2 M. Hale, Historia Placitorum Coronae 85 (1736). See also 4 W. Blackstone, Commentaries 289.

---

[9]See Sherman, Reducing Police Gun Use, in Control in the Police Organization 98, 120–123 (M. Punch ed. 1983); Fyfe, Observations on Police Deadly Force, 27 Crime & Delinquency 376, 378–381 (1981); W. Geller & K. Karales, Split-Second Decisions 67 (1981); App. 84 (affidavit of William Bracey, Chief of Patrol, New York City Police Department). See generally Brief for Police Foundation et al. as *Amici Curiae.*

The State and city argue that because this was the prevailing rule at the time of the adoption of the Fourth Amendment and for some time thereafter, and is still in force in some States, use of deadly force against a fleeing felon must be "reasonable." It is true that this Court has often looked to the common law in evaluating the reasonableness, for Fourth Amendment purposes, of police activity. See, e.g., *United States v. Watson, Carroll v. United States,* 267 U.S. 132, 149–153 (1925). On the other hand, it "has not simply frozen into constitutional law those law enforcement practices that existed at the time of the Fourth Amendment's passage." *Payton v. New York,* 445 U.S. 573, 591, n. 33 (1980). Because of sweeping change in the legal and technological context, reliance on the common-law rule in this case would be a mistaken literalism that ignores the purposes of a historical inquiry.

It has been pointed out many times that the common-law rule is best understood in light of the fact that it arose at a time when virtually all felonies were punishable by death.[10] "Though effected without the protections and formalities of an orderly trial and conviction, the killing of a resisting or fleeing felon resulted in no greater consequences than those authorized for punishment of the felony of which the individual was charged or suspected." American Law Institute, Model Penal Code § 3.07, Comment 3, p. 56 (Tentative Draft No. 8, 1958) (hereinafter Model Penal Code Comment). Courts have also justified the common-law rule by emphasizing the relative dangerousness of felons.

Neither of these justifications makes sense today. Almost all crimes formerly punishable by death no longer are or can be. See *Enmund v. Florida,* 458 U.S. 782 (1982); *Coker v. Georgia,* 433 U.S. 584 (1977). And while in earlier times "the gulf between the felonies and the minor offences was broad and deep," 2 Pollock & Maitland 467, n. 3, today the distinction is minor and often arbitrary. Many crimes classified as misdemeanors, or nonexistent, at common law are now felonies. Wilgus, 22 Mich.L.Rev., at 572–573. These changes have undermined the concept, which was questionable to begin with, that use of deadly force against a fleeing felon is merely a speedier execution of someone who has already forfeited his life. They have also made the assumption that a "felon" is more dangerous than a misdemeanant untenable. Indeed, numerous misdemeanors involve conduct more dangerous than many felonies.[11]

There is an additional reason why the common-law rule cannot be directly translated to the present day. The common-law rule developed at a time when weapons were rudimentary. Deadly force could be inflicted almost solely in a hand-to-hand struggle during which, necessarily, the safety of the arresting officer was at

---

[10]The roots of the concept of a "felony" lie not in capital punishment but in forfeiture. 2 F. Pollock & F. Maitland, The History of English Law 465 (2nd ed. 1909) (hereinafter Pollock & Maitland). Not all felonies were always punishable by death. See *id.,* at 466–467, n. 3. Nonetheless, the link was profound. Blackstone was able to write: "The idea of felony is indeed so generally connected with that of capital punishment, that we find it hard to separate them; and to this usage the interpretations of the law do now conform. And therefore if a statute makes any new offence felony, the law implies that is shall be punished with death, *viz.* by hanging, as well as with forfeiture. . . ."4 W. Blackstone, Commentaries 98. See also R. Perkins & R. Boyce, Criminal Law 14–15 (3rd ed. 1982); 2 Pollock & Maitland 511.

[11]White-collar crime, for example, poses a less significant physical threat than, say, drunken driving.

risk. Handguns were not carried by police officers until the latter half of the last century. L. Kennett & J. Anderson, The Gun in America 150–151 (1975). Only then did it become possible to use deadly force from a distance as a means of apprehension. As a practical matter, the use of deadly force under the standard articulation of the common-law rule has an altogether different meaning—and harsher consequences—now than in past centuries. See Wechsler & Michael, A Rationale for the Law of Homicide: I, 37 Colum.L.Rev. 701, 741 (1937).[12]

In evaluating the reasonableness of police procedures under the Fourth Amendment, we have also looked to prevailing rules in individual jurisdictions. See, e.g., *United States v. Watson.* The rules in the States are varied. Some 19 States have codified the common-law rule,[13] though in two of these the courts have significantly limited the statute.[14] Four States, though without a relevant statute, apparently retain the common-law rule.[15] Two States have adopted the Model Penal Code's provision verbatim.[16] Eighteen others allow, in slightly varying language, the use of deadly force only if the suspect has committed a felony involving the use or threat of physical or deadly force, or is escaping with a deadly weapon, or is likely to

---

[12]It has been argued that sophisticated techniques of apprehension and increased communication between the police in different jurisdictions have made it more likely that an escapee will be caught than was once the case, and that this change has also reduced the "reasonableness" of the use of deadly force to prevent escape. E.g., Sherman, Execution Without Trial: Police Homicide and the Constitution, 33 Vand.L.Rev. 71, 76 (1980). We are unaware of any data that would permit sensible evaluation of this claim. Current arrest rates are sufficiently low, however, that we have some doubt whether in past centuries the failure to arrest at the scene meant that the police had missed their only chance in a way that is not presently the case. In 1983, 21% of the offenses in the Federal Bureau of Investigation crime index were cleared by arrest. Federal Bureau of Investigation, Uniform Crime Reports, Crime in the United States 159 (1984). The clearance rate for burglary was 15%. *Ibid.*

[13]Ala.Code § 13A-3-27 (1982); Ark.Stat.Ann. § 41–510 (1977); Cal.Penal Code Ann. § 196 (West 1970); Conn.Gen.Stat. § 53a–22 (1972); Fla.Stat. § 776.05 (1983); Idaho Code § 19–610 (1979); Ind.Code § 35-413-3 (1982); Kan.Stat.Ann. § 21–3215 (1981); Miss.Code Ann. § 97-3-15(d) (Supp.1984); Mo.Rev.Stat. § 563.046 (1979); Nev.Rev.Stat. § 200.140 (1983); N.M.Stat.Ann. § 30-2-6 (1984); Okla.Stat., Tit. 21, § 732 (1981); R.I.Gen.Laws § 12-7-9 (1981); S.D. Codified Laws §§ 22-16-32, 22-16-33 (1979); Tenn.Code Ann. § 40-7-108 (1982); Wash.Rev.Code § 9A.16.040(3) (1977). Oregon limits use of deadly force to violent felons, but also allows its use against any felon if "necessary." Ore.Rev.Stat. § 161.239 (1983). Wisconsin's statute is ambiguous, but should probably be added to this list. Wis.Stat. § 939.45(4) (1981–1982) (officer may use force necessary for "a reasonable accomplishment of a lawful arrest"). But see *Clark v. Ziedonis*, 368 F.Supp. 544 (ED Wis.1973), aff'd on other grounds, 513 F.2d 79 (CA7 1975).

[14]In California, the police may use deadly force to arrest only if the crime for which the arrest is sought was "a forcible and atrocious one which threatens death or serious bodily harm," or there is a substantial risk that the person whose arrest is sought will cause death or serious bodily harm if apprehension is delayed. *Kortum v. Alkire*, 69 Cal.App.3d 325, 333, 138 Cal.Rptr. 26, 30–31 (1977). See also *People v. Ceballos*, 12 Cal.3d 470, 476–484, 116 Cal.Rptr. 233, 237–242, 526 P.2d 241, 245–250 (1974); *Long Beach Police Officers Assn. v. Long Beach*, 61 Cal.App.3d 364, 373–374, 132 Cal.Rptr. 348, 353–354 (1976). In Indiana, deadly force may be used only to prevent injury, the imminent danger of injury or force, or the threat of force. It is not permitted simply to prevent escape. *Rose v. State*, 431 N.E.2d 521 (Ind.App.1982).

[15]These are Michigan, Ohio, Virginia, and West Virginia. *Werner v. Hartfelder*, 113 Mich.App. 747, 318 N.W.2d 825 (1982); *State v. Foster*, 60 Ohio Misc. 46, 59–66, 396 N.E.2d 246, 255–258 (Com.Pl.1979) (citing cases); *Berry v. Hamman*, 203 Va. 596, 125 S.E.2d 851 (1962); *Thompson v. Norfolk & W.R. Co.*, 116 W.Va. 705, 711–712, 182 S.E. 880, 883–884 (1935).

[16]Haw.Rev.Stat. § 703–307 (1976); Neb.Rev.Stat. § 28–1412 (1979). Massachusetts probably belongs in this category. Though it once rejected distinctions between felonies, *Uraneck v. Lima*, 359 Mass. 749, 750 (1971), it has since adopted the Model Penal Code limitations with regard to private citizens, *Commonwealth v. Klein*, 372 Mass. 823 (1977), and seems to have extended that decision to police officers, *Julian v. Randazzo*, 380 Mass. 391 (1980).

endanger life or inflict serious physical injury if not arrested.[17] Louisiana and Vermont, though without statutes or case law on point, do forbid the use of deadly force to prevent any but violent felonies.[18] The remaining States either have no relevant statute or case law, or have positions that are unclear.[19]

It cannot be said that there is a constant or overwhelming trend away from the common-law rule. In recent years, some States have reviewed their laws and expressly rejected abandonment of the common-law rule.[20] Nonetheless, the long-term movement has been away from the rule that deadly force may be used against any fleeing felon, and that remains the rule in less than half the States.

This trend is more evident and impressive when viewed in light of the policies adopted by the police departments themselves. Overwhelmingly, these are more restrictive than the common-law rule. C. Milton, J. Halleck, J. Lardner, & G. Abrecht, Police Use of Deadly Force 45–46 (1977). The Federal Bureau of Investigation and the New York City Police Department, for example, both forbid the use of firearms except when necessary to prevent death or grievous bodily harm. *Id.,* at 40–41; App. 83. For accreditation by the Commission on Accreditation for Law Enforcement Agencies, a department must restrict the use of deadly force to situations where "the officer reasonably believes that the action is in defense of human life . . . or in defense of any person in immediate danger of serious physical injury." Commission on Accreditation for Law Enforcement Agencies, Inc., Standards for Law Enforcement Agencies 1–2 (1983) (italics deleted). A 1974 study reported that the police department regulations in a majority of the large cities of the United States allowed the firing of a weapon only when a felon presented a threat of death or serious bodily harm. Boston Police Department, Planning & Research Division, The Use of Deadly Force by Boston Police Personnel (1974). Overall, only 7.5% of departmental and municipal policies explicitly

---

[17]Alaska Stat.Ann. § 11.81.370(a) (1983); Ariz.Rev.Stat.Ann. § 13–410 (1978); Colo.Rev.Stat. § 18-1-707 (1978); Del.Code Ann., Tit. 11, § 467 (1979) (felony involving physical force *and* a substantial risk that the suspect will cause death or serious bodily injury *or* will never be recaptured); Ga.Code § 16-3-21(a) (1984); Ill.Rev.Stat., ch. 38, ¶ 7–5 (1984); Iowa Code § 804.8 (1983) (suspect has used or threatened deadly force in commission of a felony, or would use deadly force if not caught); Ky.Rev.Stat. § 503.090 (1984) (suspect committed felony involving use or threat of physical force likely to cause death or serious injury, *and* is likely to endanger life unless apprehended without delay); Me.Rev.Stat.Ann., Tit. 17-A, § 107 (1983) (commentary notes that deadly force may be used only "where the person to be arrested poses a threat to human life"); Minn.Stat. § 609.066 (1984); N.H.Rev.Stat.Ann. § 627:5(II) (Supp. 1983); N.J.Stat.Ann. § 2C-3-7 (West 1982); N.Y.Penal Law § 35.30 (McKinney Supp. 1984–1985); N.C.Gen.Stat. § 15A–401 (1983); N.D.Cent.Code § 12.1-05-07.2.d (1976); 18 Pa.Cons.Stat. § 508 (1982); Tex.Penal Code Ann. § 9.51(c) (1974); Utah Code Ann. § 76-2-404 (1978).

[18]See La.Rev.Stat.Ann. § 14:20(2) (West 1974); Vt.Stat.Ann., Tit. 13, § 2305 (1974 and Supp.1984). A Federal District Court has interpreted the Louisiana statute to limit the use of deadly force against fleeing suspects to situations where "life itself is endangered or great bodily harm is threatened." *Sauls v. Hutto,* 304 F.Supp. 124, 132 (ED La.1969).

[19]These are Maryland, Montana, South Carolina, and Wyoming. A Maryland appellate court has indicated, however, that deadly force may not be used against a felon who "was in the process of fleeing and, at the time, presented no immediate danger to . . . anyone. . . . " *Giant Food, Inc. v. Scherry,* 51 Md.App. 586, 589, 596, 444 A.2d 483, 486, 489 (1982).

[20]In adopting its current statute in 1979, for example, Alabama expressly chose the common-law rule over more restrictive provisions. Ala.Code 13A-3-27, Commentary, pp. 67–68 (1982). Missouri likewise considered but rejected a proposal akin to the Model Penal Code rule. See *Mattis v. Schnarr,* 547 F.2d 1007, 1022 (CA8 1976) (Gibson, C.J., dissenting), vacated as moot *sub nom. Ashcroft v. Mattis,* 431 U.S. 171, 97 S.Ct. 1739 52 L.Ed.2d 219 (1977). Idaho, whose current statute codifies the common-law rule, adopted the Model Penal Code in 1971, but abandoned it in 1972.

permit the use of deadly force against any felon; 86.8% explicitly do not. K. Matulia, A Balance of Forces: A Report of the International Association of Chiefs of Police 161 (1982) (table). See also Record 1108–1368 (written policies of 44 departments). See generally W. Geller & K. Karales, Split-Second Decisions 33–42 (1981); Brief for Police Foundation et al. as *Amici Curiae*. In light of the rules adopted by those who must actually administer them, the older and fading common-law view is a dubious indicium of the constitutionality of the Tennessee statute now before us.

Actual departmental policies are important for an additional reason. We would hesitate to declare a police practice of long standing "unreasonable" if doing so would severely hamper effective law enforcement. But the indications are to the contrary. There has been no suggestion that crime has worsened in any way in jurisdictions that have adopted, by legislation or departmental policy, rules similar to that announced today. *Amici* noted that "[a]fter extensive research and consideration, [they] have concluded that laws permitting police officers to use deadly force to apprehend unarmed, non-violent fleeing felony suspects actually do not protect citizens or law enforcement officers, do not deter crime or alleviate problems caused by crime, and do not improve the crime-fighting ability of law enforcement agencies." *Id.,* at 11. The submission is that the obvious state interests in apprehension are not sufficiently served to warrant the use of lethal weapons against all fleeing felons. See *supra,* at 1700–1701, and n. 10.Nor do we agree with petitioners and appellant that the rule we have adopted requires the police to make impossible, split-second evaluations of unknowable facts. See Brief for Petitioners 25; Brief for Appellant 11. We do not deny the practical difficulties of attempting to assess the suspect's dangerousness. However, similarly difficult judgments must be made by the police in equally uncertain circumstances. See, e.g., *Terry v. Ohio,* Nor is there any indication that in States that allow the use of deadly force only against dangerous suspects, see nn. 15, 17–19, *supra,* the standard has been difficult to apply or has led to a rash of litigation involving inappropriate second-guessing of police officers' split-second decisions. Moreover, the highly technical felony/misdemeanor distinction is equally, if not more, difficult to apply in the field. An officer is in no position to know, for example, the precise value of property stolen, or whether the crime was a first or second offense. Finally, as noted above, this claim must be viewed with suspicion in light of the similar self-imposed limitations of so many police departments.

The (trial judge) concluded that Hymon was justified in shooting Garner because state law allows, and the Federal Constitution does not forbid, the use of deadly force to prevent the escape of a fleeing felony suspect if no alternative means of apprehension is available. See App. to Pet. for Cert. A9–A11, A38. This conclusion made a determination of Garner's apparent dangerousness unnecessary. The court did find, however, that Garner appeared to be unarmed, though Hymon could not be certain that was the case. *Id.,* at A4, A23. See also App. 41, 56; Record 219. *Restated in Fourth Amendment terms, this means Hymon had no articulable basis to think Garner was armed.*

*In reversing, the Court of Appeals accepted the District Court's factual conclusions and held that "the facts, as found, did not justify the use of deadly force" <u>710 F.2d, at 246.</u> We agree. Officer Hymon could not reasonably have believed that Garner-young, slight, and unarmed-posed any threat. Indeed, Hymon never attempted to justify his actions on any basis other than the need to prevent an escape.

The District Court stated in passing that "[t]he facts of this case did not indicate to Officer Hymon that Garner was 'non-dangerous.'" App. to Pet. for Cert. A34. This conclusion is not explained, and seems to be based solely on the fact that Garner had broken into a house at night. However, the fact that Garner was a suspected burglar could not, without regard to the other circumstances, automatically justify the use of deadly force. Hymon did not have probable cause to believe that Garner, whom he correctly believed to be unarmed, posed any physical danger to himself or others.

The dissent argues that the shooting was justified by the fact that Officer Hymon had probable cause to believe that Garner had committed a nighttime burglary. *Post*, at 1711, 1712. While we agree that burglary is a serious crime, we cannot agree that it is so dangerous as automatically to justify the use of deadly force. The FBI classifies burglary as a "property" rather than a "violent" crime. See Federal Bureau of Investigation, Uniform Crime Reports, Crime in the United States 1 (1984).[21] Although the armed burglar would present a different situation, the fact that an unarmed suspect has broken into a dwelling at night does not automatically mean he is physically dangerous. This case demonstrates as much. In fact, the available statistics demonstrate that burglaries only rarely involve physical violence. During the 10-year period from 1973–1982, only 3.8% of all burglaries involved violent crime. Bureau of Justice Statistics, Household Burglary 4 (1985).[22] See also T. Reppetto, Residential Crime 17, 105 (1974); Conklin & Bittner, Burglary in a Suburb, 11 Criminology 208, 214 (1973).

We wish to make clear what our holding means in the context of this case. The complaint has been dismissed as to all the *individual* defendants. The State is a party only by virtue of 28 U.S.C. § 2403(b) and is not subject to liability. The possible liability of the remaining defendants—the Police Department and the city of Memphis—hinges on *Monell v. New York City Dept. of Social Services*, 436 U.S. 658 (1978), and is left for remand. We hold that the statute is invalid insofar as it purported to give Hymon the authority to act as he did. As for the policy of the Police Department, the absence of any discussion of this issue by the courts below, and the uncertain state of the record, preclude any consideration of its validity.

The judgment of the Court of Appeals is affirmed, and the case is remanded for further proceedings consistent with this opinion.
So ordered.

Justice O'CONNOR, with whom THE CHIEF JUSTICE and Justice REHNQUIST join, dissenting.

The Court today holds that the Fourth Amendment prohibits a police officer from using deadly force as a last resort to apprehend a criminal suspect who refuses to halt when fleeing the scene of a nighttime burglary. This conclusion rests on the majority's balancing of the interests of the suspect and the public interest in effective

---

[21]In a recent report, the Department of Corrections of the District of Columbia also noted that "there is nothing inherently dangerous or violent about the offense," which is a crime against property. D.C. Department of Corrections, Prisoner Screening Project 2 (1985).

[22]The dissent points out that three-fifths of all rapes in the home, three-fifths of all home robberies, and about a third of home assaults are committed by burglars. *Post*, at 1709. These figures mean only that if one knows that a suspect committed a rape in the home, there is a good chance that the suspect is also a burglar.

law enforcement. Notwithstanding the venerable common-law rule authorizing the use of deadly force if necessary to apprehend a fleeing felon, and continued acceptance of this rule by nearly half the States, the majority concludes that Tennessee's statute is unconstitutional inasmuch as it allows the use of such force to apprehend a burglary suspect who is not obviously armed or otherwise dangerous. Although the circumstances of this case are unquestionably tragic and unfortunate, our constitutional holdings must be sensitive both to the history of the Fourth Amendment and to the general implications of the Court's reasoning. By disregarding the serious and dangerous nature of residential burglaries and the long-standing practice of many States, the Court effectively creates a Fourth Amendment right allowing a burglary suspect to flee unimpeded from a police officer who has probable cause to arrest, who has ordered the suspect to halt, and who has no means short of firing his weapon to prevent escape. I do not believe that the Fourth Amendment supports such a right, and I accordingly dissent.

The facts below warrant brief review because they highlight the difficult, split-second decisions police officers must make in these circumstances. Memphis Police Officers Elton Hymon and Leslie Wright responded to a late-night call that a burglary was in progress at a private residence. When the officers arrived at the scene, the caller said that "they" were breaking into the house next door. The officers found the residence had been forcibly entered through a window and saw lights on inside the house. Officer Hymon testified that when he saw the broken window he realized "that something was wrong inside," but that he could not determine whether anyone-either a burglar or a member of the household-was within the residence. As Officer Hymon walked behind the house, he heard a door slam. He saw Edward Eugene Garner run away from the house through the dark and cluttered backyard. Garner crouched next to a 6-foot-high fence. Officer Hymon thought Garner was an adult and was unsure whether Garner was armed because Hymon *"had no idea what was in the hand [that he could not see] or what he might have had on his person."* In fact, Garner was 15 years old and unarmed. Hymon also did not know whether accomplices remained inside the house. The officer identified himself as a police officer and ordered Garner to halt. Garner paused briefly and then sprang to the top of the fence. Believing that Garner would escape if he climbed over the fence, Hymon fired his revolver and mortally wounded the suspected burglar.

The deceased's father, filed a <u>42 U.S.C. § 1983</u> action in federal court against Hymon, the city of Memphis, and other defendants, for asserted violations of Garner's constitutional rights. The District Court for the Western District of Tennessee held that Officer Hymon's actions were justified by a Tennessee statute that authorizes a police officer to "use all the necessary means to effect the arrest," if "after notice of the intention to arrest the defendant, he either flee or forcibly resist." <u>Tenn.Code Ann. § 40-7-108</u> (1982). As construed by the Tennessee courts, this statute allows the use of deadly force only if a police officer has probable cause to believe that a person has committed a felony, the officer warns the person that he intends to arrest him, and the officer reasonably believes that no means less than such force will prevent the escape. See, e.g., <u>*Johnson v. State,* 173 Tenn. 134.</u> The District Court held that the Tennessee statute is constitutional and that Hymon's actions as authorized by that statute did not violate Garner's constitutional rights. The Court of Appeals for the Sixth Circuit reversed on the grounds that the Tennessee statute "authorizing the killing of an unarmed, nonviolent fleeing felon by police in order to prevent escape" violates the Fourth Amendment and the Due Process Clause of the Fourteenth Amendment. 710 F.2d 240, 244 (1983).

The Court affirms on the ground that application of the Tennessee statute to authorize Officer Hymon's use of deadly force constituted an unreasonable seizure in violation of the Fourth Amendment. The precise issue before the Court deserves emphasis, because both the decision below and the majority obscure what must be decided in this case. The issue is not the constitutional validity of the Tennessee statute on its face or as applied to some hypothetical set of facts. Instead, the issue is whether the use of deadly force by Officer Hymon under the circumstances of this case violated Garner's constitutional rights. Thus, the majority's assertion that a police officer who has probable cause to seize a suspect "may not always do so by killing him," is unexceptionable but also of little relevance to the question presented here. The same is true of the rhetorically stirring statement that "[t]he use of deadly force to prevent the escape of all felony suspects, whatever the circumstances, is constitutionally unreasonable." The question we must address is whether the Constitution allows the use of such force to apprehend a suspect who resists arrest by attempting to flee the scene of a nighttime burglary of a residence.

For purposes of Fourth Amendment analysis, I agree with the Court that Officer Hymon "seized" Garner by shooting him. Whether that seizure was reasonable and therefore permitted by the Fourth Amendment requires a careful balancing of the important public interest in crime prevention and detection and the nature and quality of the intrusion upon legitimate interests of the individual. *United States v. Place.* In striking this balance here, it is crucial to acknowledge that police use of deadly force to apprehend a fleeing criminal suspect falls within the "rubric of police conduct . . . necessarily [involving] swift action predicated upon the on-the-spot observations of the officer on the beat" *Terry v. Ohio.* The clarity of hindsight cannot provide the standard for judging the reasonableness of police decisions made in uncertain and often dangerous circumstances. Moreover, I am far more reluctant than is the Court to conclude that the Fourth Amendment proscribes a police practice that was accepted at the time of the adoption of the Bill of Rights and has continued to receive the support of many state legislatures. Although the Court has recognized that the requirements of the Fourth Amendment must respond to the reality of social and technological change, fidelity to the notion of *constitutional*—as opposed to purely judicial—limits on governmental action requires us to impose a heavy burden on those who claim that practices accepted when the Fourth Amendment was adopted are now constitutionally impermissible.

The public interest involved in the use of deadly force as a last resort to apprehend a fleeing burglary suspect relates primarily to the serious nature of the crime. Household burglaries not only represent the illegal entry into a person's home, but also "pos[e] real risk of serious harm to others." Solem v. Helm, 463 U.S. 277, 315–316 (1983) (BURGER, C.J., dissenting). According to recent Department of Justice statistics, "[t]hree-fifths of all rapes in the home, three-fifths of all home robberies, and about a third of home aggravated and simple assaults are committed by burglars." Bureau of Justice Statistics Bulletin, Household Burglary 1 (January 1985). During the period 1973–1982, 2.8 million such violent crimes were committed in the course of burglaries. Victims of a forcible intrusion into their home by a nighttime prowler will find little consolation in the majority's confident assertion that "burglaries only rarely involve physical violence." Moreover, even if a particular burglary, when viewed in retrospect, does not involve physical harm to others, the "harsh potentialities for violence" inherent in the forced entry into a home preclude characterization of the crime as "innocuous, inconsequential, minor, or 'nonviolent.'" *Solem v. Helm, supra,* See also Restatement of Torts § 131, Comment *g* (1934) (burglary is among felonies that normally cause or threaten death or serious bodily harm); R. Perkins & R. Boyce, Criminal Law 1110 (3rd ed. 1982) (burglary is dangerous felony that creates unreasonable risk of great personal harm).

Because burglary is a serious and dangerous felony, the public interest in the prevention and detection of the crime is of compelling importance. Where a police officer has probable cause to arrest a suspected burglar, the use of deadly force as a last resort might well be the only means of apprehending the suspect. With respect to a particular burglary, subsequent investigation simply cannot represent a substitute for immediate apprehension of the criminal suspect at the scene. See President's Commission on Law Enforcement and Administration of Justice, Task Force Report: The Challenge of Crime in a Free Society 97 (1967). Indeed, the Captain of the Memphis Police Department testified that in his city, if apprehension is not immediate, it is likely that the suspect will not be caught. Although some law enforcement agencies may choose to assume the risk that a criminal will remain at large, the Tennessee statute reflects a legislative determination that the use of deadly force in prescribed circumstances will serve generally to protect the public. Such statutes assist the police in apprehending suspected perpetrators of serious crimes and provide notice that a lawful police order to stop and submit to arrest may not be ignored with impunity.

Against the strong public interests justifying the conduct at issue here must be weighed the individual interests implicated in the use of deadly force by police officers. The majority declares that "[t]he suspect's fundamental interest in his own life need not be elaborated upon." This blithe assertion hardly provides an adequate substitute for the majority's failure to acknowledge the distinctive manner in which the suspect's interest in his life is even exposed to risk. For purposes of this case, we must recall that the police officer, in the course of investigating a nighttime burglary, had reasonable cause to arrest the suspect and ordered him to halt. The officer's use of force resulted because the suspected burglar refused to heed this command and the officer reasonably believed that there was no means short of firing his weapon to apprehend the suspect. Without questioning the importance of a person's interest in his life, *I do not think this interest encompasses a right to flee unimpeded from the scene of a burglary.* [T]he policeman's hands should not be tied merely because of the possibility that the suspect will fail to cooperate with legitimate actions by law enforcement personnel. The legitimate interests of the suspect in these circumstances are adequately accommodated by the Tennessee statute: *to avoid the use of deadly force and the consequent risk to his life, the suspect need merely obey the valid order to halt.*

A proper balancing of the interests involved suggests that use of deadly force as a last resort to apprehend a criminal suspect fleeing from the scene of a nighttime burglary is not unreasonable within the meaning of the Fourth Amendment. Admittedly, the events giving rise to this case are in retrospect deeply regrettable. No one can view the death of an unarmed and apparently nonviolent 15-year-old without sorrow, much less disapproval. Nonetheless, the reasonableness of Officer Hymon's conduct for purposes of the Fourth Amendment cannot be evaluated by what later appears to have been a preferable course of police action. The officer pursued a suspect in the darkened backyard of a house that from all indications had just been burglarized. *The police officer was not certain whether the suspect was alone or unarmed;* nor did he know what had transpired inside the house. He ordered the suspect to halt, and when the suspect refused to obey and attempted to flee into the night, the officer fired his weapon to prevent escape. The reasonableness of this action for purposes of the Fourth Amendment is not determined by the unfortunate nature of this particular case; instead, the question is whether it is constitutionally impermissible for police officers, as a last resort, to shoot a burglary suspect fleeing the scene of the crime.

Whatever the validity of Tennessee's statute in other contexts, I cannot agree that its application in this case resulted in a deprivation "without due process of law." Nor do I believe that a criminal suspect who is shot while trying to avoid apprehension has a cognizable claim of a deprivation of his Sixth Amendment right to trial by jury. Finally, because there is no indication that the use of deadly force was intended to punish rather than to capture the suspect, there is no valid claim under the Eighth Amendment. Accordingly, I conclude that the District Court properly entered judgment against (Garner), and I would reverse the decision of the Court of Appeals.

The Court's opinion sweeps broadly to adopt an entirely new standard for the constitutionality of the use of deadly force to apprehend fleeing felons. Thus, *the Court lightly brushe[s] aside a long-standing police practice that predates the Fourth Amendment and continues to receive the approval of nearly half of the state legislatures.* I cannot accept the majority's creation of a constitutional right to flight for burglary suspects seeking to avoid capture at the scene of the crime. Whatever the constitutional limits on police use of deadly force in order to apprehend a fleeing felon, I do not believe they are exceeded in a case in which a police officer has probable cause to arrest a suspect at the scene of a residential burglary, orders the suspect to halt, and then fires his weapon as a last resort to prevent the suspect's escape into the night. I respectfully dissent.

United States Court of Appeals
Eleventh Circuit
Stacy Allen DRAPER, Plaintiff-Appellant
v.
Clinton D. REYNOLDS, Deputy, Defendant-Appellee
369 F.3d 1270

May 17, 2004

Appeal from the United States District Court for the Northern District of Georgia.

Before <u>EDMONDSON</u>, Chief Judge, <u>HULL</u>, Circuit Judge, and EDENFIELD, District Judge.

<u>HULL</u>, Circuit Judge:

Plaintiff Stacy Allen Draper sued Defendant Deputy Sheriff Clinton D. Reynolds, under <u>42 U.S.C. § 1983</u>, for civil rights violations arising out of a traffic stop and arrest. The district court granted summary judgment for Reynolds on the federal claims.We affirm.

I. Background

A. The Traffic Stop

At approximately 11:30 p.m. on July 19, 2001, Deputy Sheriff Clinton D. Reynolds ("Reynolds") stopped a tractor trailer truck (the "truck") driven by Plaintiff Stacy Allen Draper ("Draper"). While on patrol for the Sheriff's Office of Coweta County, Georgia, Reynolds observed Draper's truck traveling northbound on I-85 and stopped the truck allegedly because its tag light was not appropriately illuminated under Georgia law.

After Draper pulled his truck to the side of the interstate, Reynolds stopped his patrol car directly behind the truck. Reynolds on foot approached the passenger side of the truck cab, as was his practice in all roadside stops. When Reynolds reached the truck cab, the engine was running, the passenger window was closed, and the cab was illuminated briefly by an interior light but then became dark. Draper observed Reynolds at the passenger side and believed that Reynolds was performing an inspection of the vehicle. From the passenger side, Reynolds shined his flashlight at the truck cab twice.

For summary judgment purposes, we accept Draper's version of what happened.[1] Draper was blinded by the flashlight the second time Reynolds shined it in the cab. Draper rolled down the passenger window and politely asked Reynolds to stop shining the flashlight at him. Reynolds then "said something like god dammit, you don't worry about what I'm doing over here." Draper again politely

---

[1] We recite the facts in the light most favorable to Plaintiff Draper. However, Reynolds hotly disputes Draper's version of the facts. Reynolds contends that he quickly "blinked" the flashlight into the cab twice in an attempt to "let [Draper] know that I was standing over there on the side for him to meet me over there, to know where I was at." According to Reynolds, Draper then rolled down the passenger window and said, "[W]hy the fuck are you shining that god damn flashlight in my eyes[?]"

asked Reynolds to stop shining the light at him. Reynolds replied, "I told you to get your fucking ass over here two times." Draper then told Reynolds to get his "god darn flashlight" out of his eyes.

Reynolds then instructed Draper to meet him behind the truck, a location in view of a police camera that Reynolds had activated in his patrol car.[2] Reynolds also unholstered his TASER International ADVANCED TASER M26 ("taser gun"),[3] which he kept in his hand through the remainder of the encounter. Draper got out of the truck cab and walked to the back of the truck.

The video camera in the patrol car recorded Draper's and Reynolds's speech and actions behind the truck.[4] Upon arrival behind the truck, Draper immediately began shouting and complaining about Reynolds's shining the flashlight in his face. Reynolds calmly asked Draper for his driver's license, but Draper continued to complain about Reynolds's prior use of the flashlight. Draper also insisted that he had done nothing wrong. During the encounter, Draper was belligerent, gestured animatedly, continuously paced, appeared very excited, and spoke loudly.

Reynolds repeatedly asked Draper to stop yelling and informed Draper that he would be taken to jail if he continued to yell. Reynolds told Draper that he also needed Draper's log book and bill of lading. Draper began to walk toward the truck cab while asking Reynolds if he needed anything else, but then turned around and loudly accused Reynolds of harassing him. Reynolds replied that he needed Draper's license and insurance.

Draper handed his license to Reynolds and again began walking to the truck cab, but turned around when Reynolds told him for the second time to retrieve his bill of lading, proof of insurance, and log book. Draper still did not go to the truck cab but instead walked back toward Reynolds and accused him again of harassment. For the third time, Reynolds told Draper to get the requested items, and Draper responded by exclaiming, "How 'bout you just go ahead and take me to fucking jail, then, man, you know, because I'm not going to kiss your damn ass because you're a police officer." Reynolds instructed Draper to calm down, but Draper protested loudly that he was calm. Reynolds explained that he believed Draper's actions were "threatening" and "putting [Reynolds] on the defensive."

For the fourth time, Reynolds told Draper to retrieve the requested documents. Draper did not move to the truck cab to get them and loudly complained that Reynolds was treating him like a "child" and disrespecting him. Reynolds replied that he had not disrespected Draper, and then he signaled to his back up, which had just arrived, with his flashlight. Draper continued to yell and accuse Reynolds of

---

[2]The police camera was located in Reynolds's car parked behind the truck. Because of the camera's location, the encounter at the truck cab is not clearly visible and no sound is heard. The police camera, however, recorded the actions and sound from the encounter behind the truck.

[3]Reynolds's taser gun is a Conducted Energy Weapon that uses propelled wire to conduct energy to a remote target, thereby controlling and overriding the body's central nervous system. The taser gun fires two probes up to a distance of 21 feet from a replaceable cartridge. These probes are connected to the taser gun by high-voltage insulated wire. When the probes make contact with the target, the taser gun transmits electrical pulses along the wires and into the body of the target, through up to two inches of clothing.

[4]See Appendix 1 for a transcript of the conversation between Draper and Reynolds at the back of the truck captured by the police video camera.

disrespecting him. For the fifth time, Reynolds told Draper to retrieve the documents and then promptly discharged his taser gun at Draper's chest. Draper fell to the ground out of the police camera's view. Reynolds told Draper to stay on the ground and threatened to discharge the taser gun again if Draper did not comply. Reynolds then yelled to his back-up officer who had just arrived: "Handcuff this son of a bitch." Draper was handcuffed, searched, and placed in the back of the police car.[5] The police also searched Draper's truck at the arrest site.

After the other officers arrived and Draper was arrested, Reynolds stated to the officers that he thought Draper was going "to fight me" and that he pulled Draper over for a tag light violation. At the end of the video, the police camera focused on the area of the tag, while Reynolds again explained that he pulled Draper over for a tag light violation. Draper properly points out that at the end of the video, *all* of his truck's rear lights were turned off and were not shining, and thus the video does not establish conclusively that his tag light was out. As noted in his incident report, Reynolds charged Draper with obstruction of an officer, in violation of several Georgia statutes.

B. Procedural History

Draper filed suit against Reynolds individually in the State Court of Coweta County, Georgia under 42 U.S.C. § 1983 and state law. Draper's complaint contends that Reynolds improperly stopped him, falsely arrested him, and used excessive force in his arrest, all in violation of his constitutional rights and state law. Reynolds removed the case to the United States District Court for the Northern District of Georgia. Reynolds moved for summary judgment based on qualified immunity. The district court granted Reynolds's motion for summary judgment with regard to the federal claims. Draper appeals the district court's grant of summary judgment.

II. Standard of Review

We review *de novo* a district court's grant of summary judgment based on qualified immunity and apply the same legal standards as the district court. *Durruthy v. Pastor,* 351 F.3d 1080, 1084 (11th Cir.2003). "We resolve all issues of material fact in favor of the plaintiff, and then determine the legal question of whether the defendant is entitled to qualified immunity under that version of the facts." *Id.*

III. Discussion

A. Qualified Immunity

To determine whether Reynolds is entitled to qualified immunity, we apply a two-part inquiry. First, applying the facts in the light most favorable to Draper, we must

---

[5]While handcuffing Draper, one back-up officer placed a knee in Draper's back, which Draper claims forced a taser gun probe into his skin in the chest area. This back-up officer is not a defendant. Draper states that this area (approximately one quarter of an inch in size) became infected. Draper admits that he did not request medical treatment while in the Coweta County jail but still claims that Reynolds was deliberately indifferent to Draper's medical needs. Further, Draper raises this medical needs claim for the first time on appeal, and thus we consider it waived.

ascertain whether Reynolds violated Draper's constitutional rights. Second, if we decide that a constitutional violation occurred, we then must determine whether the rights violated were "clearly established." We thus begin by analyzing whether Reynolds violated Draper's constitutional rights.

B. Probable Cause for Traffic Stop

Draper sues Reynolds for stopping his truck in violation of the Fourth Amendment. Draper contends that Reynolds's reason for stopping Draper—that the tag light on Draper's truck was not adequately illuminated—was pretextual, (and alleges that) Reynolds wanted to search vehicles for drugs with the hope of having vehicles forfeited to the Sheriff of Coweta County.

As the district court correctly noted, the Supreme Court and this Court previously rejected the use of such pretextual-stop analysis and concluded that ulterior motives will not invalidate police conduct based on probable cause to believe a violation of the law occurred. _Whren v. United States_, 517 U.S. 806 (1996) (The _Whren_ case held that if there is PC to make a stop, the alleged reason behind the stop is immaterial).

Thus, the only question for purposes of examining the constitutionality of Reynolds' stop is: Did Reynolds have probable cause to believe that a traffic violation had occurred? Under Georgia law, a tag must be illuminated with a white light so that it is legible from 50 feet to the rear. At his deposition, Reynolds testified that he stopped Draper because he observed that Draper's tag light was out. At his deposition, Draper testified that he picked up his truck at the wrecker yard between eleven a.m. and noon the next day and that his tag light was working. That the tag light was working to an unknown extent during daylight does not directly contradict Reynolds's position that the registration plate was not clearly legible from fifty feet away on the night of the stop and is insufficient to create a genuine issue of material fact in this record. We thus conclude that Reynolds had probable cause to stop Draper's truck.

C. Probable Cause to Arrest Draper

Even if the stop was constitutional, Draper contends that Reynolds violated his Fourth Amendment rights by arresting him. Probable cause to arrest exists "when the facts and circumstances within the officer's knowledge, of which he or she has reasonably trustworthy information, would cause a prudent person to believe, under the circumstances shown, that the suspect has committed, is committing, or is about to commit an offense." _Durruthy_, 351 F.3d at 1088 (quoting _McCormick v. City of Fort Lauderdale_, 333 F.3d 1234, 1243 (11th Cir.2003)). As discussed earlier, Reynolds had probable cause to stop Draper for a tag light violation, and that probable cause was also sufficient to permit Reynolds to arrest Draper for that violation. Thus, we now focus on the obstruction-of-justice charge.[6]

Under Georgia law, it is unlawful to knowingly and willfully obstruct or hinder any law enforcement officer in the lawful discharge of his official duties.[7]

---

[6]The parties do not dispute that a custodial arrest may be made for both a misdemeanor offense and traffic violations. _See Atwater v. City of Lago Vista_, 532 U.S. 318 (2001).

[7]Section 16-10-24(a) states in relevant part: "[A] person who knowingly and willfully obstructs or hinders any law enforcement officer in the lawful discharge of his official duties is guilty of a misdemeanor." Ga.Code Ann. § 16-10-24(a).

The undisputed facts in this case show that at least five times Reynolds instructed Draper to retrieve certain relevant documents. Each time Reynolds requested these items, Draper failed to comply with the request. Instead, Draper accused Reynolds of harassing him and even yelled at Reynolds, "How 'bout you just go ahead and take me to fucking jail. . . . " Draper acted in a confrontational and agitated manner, paced back and forth, and repeatedly yelled at Reynolds while they were at the back of the truck. By repeatedly refusing to comply with Reynolds's reasonable instructions, and by acting belligerently and confrontationally, Draper hindered Reynolds in completing the traffic stop.[8] Thus, Reynolds had ample probable cause to arrest Draper for violating (Georgia law).

D. Excessive Force

Draper also asserts that Reynolds used excessive force in effectuating the arrest by discharging a taser gun at Draper's chest. Draper argues that Reynolds did not need to use any force in arresting him because Draper gladly would have complied with Reynolds's arrest requests if Reynolds had just verbally told him he was under arrest.

"The Fourth Amendment's freedom from unreasonable searches and seizures encompasses the plain right to be free from the use of excessive force in the course of an arrest." _Lee v. Ferraro_, 284 F.3d 1188 at 1197 (11th Cir.2002) (citing _Graham v. Connor_, 490 U.S. 386, 394–395 (1989). A court looks to the "totality of circumstances" to determine whether the manner of arrest was reasonable. _See Tennessee v. Garner_, 471 U.S. 1, 8–9 (1985). "[I]n determining if force was reasonable, courts must examine (1) the need for the application of force,[9] (2) the relationship between the need and amount of force used, and (3) the extent of the injury inflicted" _Lee_, 284 F.3d at 1198. It is well settled that the right to make an arrest "necessarily carries with it the right to use some degree of physical coercion or threat thereof to effect it " _Graham_, 490 U.S. at 396. Moreover, "[t]he calculus of reasonableness must embody allowance for the fact that police officers are often forced to make split-second judgments—in circumstances that are tense, uncertain, and rapidly evolving—about the amount of force that is necessary in a particular situation" _Graham_, 490 U.S. at 396–397.

*In the circumstances of this case, Reynolds's use of the taser gun to effectuate the arrest of Draper was reasonably proportionate to the difficult, tense and uncertain situation that Reynolds faced in this traffic stop, and did not constitute excessive

---

[8]_Pinchon v. State_, 237 Ga.App. 675, 676, 516 S.E.2d 537 (1999) ("Argument, flight, stubborn obstinance, and lying are all examples of conduct that may satisfy the obstruction element"); _Johnson v. State_, 234 Ga.App. 218, 507 S.E.2d 13 (1998) (affirming obstruction conviction where defendant refused to obey police officer's command to exit vehicle); _Carter v. State_, 222 Ga.App. 397, 397–98, 474 S.E.2d 228 (1996) (concluding that whether defendant's making "loud, unruly statements and using profane language" when police questioned her in her home constituted misdemeanor obstruction was a question for the trier of fact); _Duke v. State_, 205 Ga.App. 689, 689–90, 423 S.E.2d 427 (1992) (concluding that misdemeanor obstruction does not require "evidence of forcible resistence or opposition"); _Hall v. State_, 201 Ga.App. 328, 411 S.E.2d 274 (1991) (refusing to produce drivers' license and beginning to walk toward car were sufficient for obstruction conviction); _Bailey v. State_, 190 Ga.App. 683, 683–84, 379 S.E.2d 816 (1989) (stating that defendant's refusal to identify himself was not merely discourteous but was sufficient for obstruction conviction).

[9]As this Court recently explained in _Lee v. Ferraro_, the need for the application of force is measured by this test: "the force used by a police officer in carrying out an arrest must be reasonably proportionate to the need for that force, which is measured by the severity of the crime, the danger to the officer, and the risk of flight " 284 F.3d at 1198 (interpreting _Graham_).

force. From the time Draper met Reynolds at the back of the truck, Draper was hostile, belligerent, and uncooperative. No less than five times, Reynolds asked Draper to retrieve documents from the truck cab, and each time Draper refused to comply. Rather, Draper accused Reynolds of harassing him and blinding him with the flashlight. Draper used profanity, moved around and paced in agitation, and repeatedly yelled at Reynolds. Because Draper repeatedly refused to comply with Reynolds's verbal commands, starting with a verbal arrest command was not required in these particular factual circumstances. More importantly, a verbal arrest command accompanied by attempted physical handcuffing, in these particular factual circumstances, may well have, or would likely have, escalated a tense and difficult situation into a serious physical struggle in which either Draper or Reynolds would be seriously hurt. Thus, there was a reasonable need for some use of force in this arrest.

Although being struck by a taser gun is an unpleasant experience, the amount of force Reynolds used—a single use of the taser gun causing a one-time shocking— was reasonably proportionate to the need for force and did not inflict any serious injury. Indeed, the police video shows that Draper was standing up, handcuffed, and coherent shortly after the taser gun stunned and calmed him. The single use of the taser gun may well have prevented a physical struggle and serious harm to either Draper or Reynolds. Under the "totality of the circumstances," Reynolds's use of the taser gun did not constitute excessive force, and Reynolds did not violate Draper's constitutional rights in this arrest.

IV. Conclusion

For all these reasons, we affirm the district court's grant of summary judgment in favor of Reynolds on Draper's federal claims.

AFFIRMED.

Petition for writ of certiorari to the United States Court of Appeals for the Eleventh Circuit denied. (What this means is that the Supremes decided not to review the case.) U.S., 2004 **Draper** v. **Reynolds** 125 S.Ct. 507.

Appendix 1

Draper: [Inaudible] Man, I don't know. I can't see no more.

Reynolds: Got your driver's license?

Draper: Yeah. I got my driver's license.

Reynolds: What's wrong?

Draper: Man, you're shining and blinding me, you know. . . . [Inaudible]

Reynolds: I'm shining at you to come out.

Draper: You ain't saying nothing. You just. . . .

Reynolds: You got the window up.

Draper: Whatever. Of course I can't. All I see is somebody standing there.

Reynolds: Look, you got the wrong answers out here, sir.

Draper: No I don't . . . [Inaudible] I just got . . . [Inaudible] in my eyes . . .

Reynolds: Quit yelling at me. Quit yelling at me.

Draper: I ain't doing nothing wrong. I'm just going down the road, minding my own business.

Reynolds: You don't know why I stopped you. And if you keep yelling at me, you're going to be in jail.

Draper: Oh, for what? Now I'm going to go to jail for what?

Reynolds: Cause of the way you're acting out here . . .

Draper: Answer my question.

Reynolds: . . . You're not going to sit here and yell at me, sir. I'm going to tell you that right now.

Draper: Oh, but you'll let another guy . . . [Inaudible] with a . . . I ain't even going to go there . . . [Inaudible] all right . . . here . . .

Reynolds: Now I need your log book. I need your bill of lading.

Draper: [Begins to walk toward truck cab, then turns back.] You need anything else? I don't know why you're harassing me. You're, first of all, I guess you're . . . [Inaudible]

Reynolds: Let me see your driver's license and your insurance.

Draper: . . . Picking on me or something . . . I don't know . . . [Inaudible] Maybe, what . . . [Inaudible] I don't know what your problem is . . . [Inaudible]

Reynolds: Sir, you need to go get your bill of lading and your proof of insurance. And bring it back to me. I also need your log book.

Draper: I think this is . . . [Inaudible]

Reynolds: I also need your log book, sir.

Draper: [Inaudible] . . . I'll bring everything you need, okay?

Reynolds: Sir, you're going to. Thanks.

Draper: Oh, I know, and I will. But I don't understand what your problem is with me. You see, because I think you're harassing me.

Reynolds: I think you need to go get what I asked you to get, sir.

Draper: How bout you just go ahead and take me to fucking jail, then, man, you know, because I'm not going to kiss your damn ass because you're a police officer. I'm a law abiding . . . [Inaudible]

Reynolds: You need to calm down, sir.

Draper: I am calm. I am calm.

Reynolds: No you're not.

Draper: I am calm.

Reynolds: No you're not. You're . . . [Inaudible] yelling at me and you're threatening me.

Draper: No, I'm not threatening you . . . [Inaudible] Why you saying I'm threatening you? Did I say I was going to hurt you or something?

Reynolds: You ain't going to. I'm not worried about that.

Draper: [Inaudible]

Reynolds: Cause of the way you're acting. You're putting me on the defensive.

Draper: How am I acting? I'm . . . [Inaudible]

Reynolds: I asked you to go get what I asked you to get, sir.

Draper: [Inaudible] . . . talking to me as if I'm a little child or something . . . [Inaudible] That's what I'm talking about . . . [Inaudible] have no respect for the public out here or something . . . [Inaudible]

Reynolds: I haven't disrespected you, sir.

Draper: You did. You . . . [Inaudible] shining a light in my face . . .

Reynolds: Sir . . .

Draper: . . . get out of the truck . . .

Reynolds: Go get what I asked you to get now, sir.

C.A.11 (Ga.), 2004
Draper v. Reynolds
369 F.3d 1270

APPENDIX B

Actual Search Warrants and Affidavits

SEARCH WARRANT AFFIDAVIT 1

This search warrant affidavit, written for 2436 NW 42 St., in Miami, Florida, was to remove the dead body of its occupant and to search the apartment for evidence of the homicide. As is evident from reading the affidavit, the victim returned home with a friend, a day or two earlier, and that person was not present when the body was found. This friend may have had Fourth Amendment standing to object to any search, so in an abundance of caution, the author prepared this warrant for the Homicide detectives of the Metro Dade Police Department.

IN THE CIRCUIT COURT OF THE ELEVENTH JUDICIAL CIRCUIT
IN AND FOR DADE COUNTY, FLORIDA

STATE OF FLORIDA)
) SS
COUNTY OF DADE)

AFFIDAVIT FOR SEARCH WARRANT

Before me, _Jeffrey Rosinek_ , a Judge of the Circuit Court
of the Eleventh Judicial Circuit of Florida, personally appeared Detective
Thomas Dean Surman of the Metro-Dade Police Department, Homicide Bureau, who
being by me first duly sworn, deposes and says that he has probable cause to
believe and does believe that in the premises described as:

2436 Northwest 42nd Street, first floor apartment, being in
unincorporated Dade County, Florida. The premises is a two-story CBS
constructed building which is located on the south side of Northwest 42nd
Street facing north. The front (north) side of the building has a main entry
door which opens out and is painted tan on the outside and green on the
inside, the remainder of the building is tan in color. The front (north) side
also has three windows on the first floor and two on the second. The west end
of the building is occupied by an external staircase rising to the second
floor of the building. The location to be searched is the first floor
apartment of the deceased which occupies the entire first floor of the above-
described premises, hereinafter referred to as "The Premises", a weapon,
instrumentality, or means by which a felony, to wit: murder, in violation of
Florida Statutes 782.04, has been committed, or evidence relevant to proving
said felony has been committed, is contained therein, to wit: blood droppings
and other body fluids, fingerprints, knives, hairs, and other items of
evidentiary value, hereinafter referred to as "The Property".

Affiant's reasons for the belief that "The Premises" are being used as
stated above and that the felony aforesaid has been committed and that "The
Property" above-mentioned is being concealed and stored at "The Premises"
above-described and the facts establishing the grounds for this affidavit and
the probable cause for believing that such facts exist, are as follows:

Your Affiant and his team members have been assigned the investigation
into the death of Edward Singleton whose body was found at 2436 Northwest 42nd
Street, Miami, Dade County, Florida, on Sunday, February 13, 1994, at
approximately 10:15 p.m.

Judge's Initials _____   Page 1

Neighbors of the deceased, upon hearing sounds of a fight, called police. Metro-Dade Police officers and Metro-Dade Fire Rescue arrived on the scene and the victim was pronounced dead by paramedics.

While the autopsy as of this writing has not been completed, once the victim's clothing was removed, an examination of his body revealed a stab wound to the side.

In order to fully investigate this death, a crime scene examination of the deceased's apartment must be undertaken.

The neighbors who originally called the police told officers that the victim had a part-time, live-in female companion whose whereabouts are presently unknown. As she is unable to give consent to a search to this joint premises, and is a person who may be eventually implicated in this investigation, she has Fourth Amendment Rights which must be respected.

WHEREFORE, Affiant prays for an order from this Court allowing him and his team members to enter the dwelling of the deceased and conduct an examination into his death.

WHEREFORE, Affiant prays that a Search Warrant be issued commanding the Director of the Metro-Dade Police Department, Dade County, Florida, who is also known as the Sheriff of Metropolitan Dade County, Florida, or his Deputies, and the Commissioner of the Florida Department of Law Enforcement, or any of his duly constituted agents, and all Investigators of the State Attorney of the Eleventh Judicial Circuit of Florida, Dade County, Florida, with the proper and necessary assistance, to search "The Premises" above-described, and all spaces therein, and the curtilage thereof, for "The Property" above-described, making the search in the Daytime or the Nighttime, as the exigencies may demand or require, or on Sunday, and if the same be found on "The Premises" to seize the same as evidence and to arrest any person in the unlawful possession thereof.

_____
AFFIANT

SWORN TO AND SUBSCRIBED before me this the 14ᵗʰ day of

_____, 1994.

_____
JUDGE OF THE CIRCUIT COURT OF
THE ELEVENTH JUDICIAL CIRCUIT
OF FLORIDA

Judge's Initials _____   Page 2

IN THE CIRCUIT COURT OF THE ELEVENTH JUDICIAL CIRCUIT
IN AND FOR DADE COUNTY, FLORIDA

STATE OF FLORIDA)
) SS
COUNTY OF DADE)

$$\langle \text{ SEARCH WARRANT } \rangle$$

IN THE NAME OF THE STATE OF FLORIDA, TO ALL AND SINGULAR:

The Director of the Metro-Dade Police Department, Dade County, Florida, who is also known as the Sheriff of Metropolitan Dade County, Florida, or his Deputies, and the Commissioner of the Florida Department of Law Enforcement, or any of his duly constituted Agents, and all Investigators of the State Attorney of the Eleventh Judicial Circuit of Florida, or any of his duly qualified officers, Dade County, Florida.

Affidavit having been made before me by Detective Thomas Dean Surman of the Metro-Dade Police Department Homicide Bureau, alleging that he has probable cause to believe and does believe that in the premises described as:

2436 Northwest 42nd Street, first floor apartment, being in unincorporated Dade County, Florida. The premises is a two-story CBS constructed building which is located on the south side of Northwest 42nd Street facing north. The front (north) side of the building has a main entry door which opens out and is painted tan on the outside and green on the inside, the remainder of the building is tan in color. The front (north) side also has three windows on the first floor and two on the second. The west end of the building is occupied by an external staircase rising to the second floor of the building. The location to be searched is the first floor apartment of the deceased which occupies the entire first floor of the above-described premises, hereinafter referred to as "The Premises", a weapon, instrumentality, or means by which a felony, to wit: murder, in violation of Florida Statutes 782.04, has been committed, or evidence relevant to proving said felony has been committed, is contained therein, to wit: blood droppings and other body fluids, fingerprints, knives, hairs, and other items of evidentiary value, hereinafter referred to as "The Property".

And as I am satisfied that there is probable cause to believe that "The Premises" are being used as aforesaid and that the felony aforesaid has been committed and that "The Property" above-mentioned is being concealed and stored at "The Premises" above-described, I expressly find probable cause for the issuance of this Search Warrant.

YOU ARE HEREBY COMMANDED to enter and search forthwith "The Premises" above described, and the curtilage thereof, for "The Property" above-described, serving this Warrant and making the search in the Daytime or Nighttime, as the exigencies may demand or require, or on Sunday, with the proper and necessary assistance, and if "The Property" above-described be found there, to seize it and to arrest all persons in the unlawful possession thereof, leaving a copy of this Warrant and a receipt for the property taken and prepare a written Inventory of the property seized and return this Warrant and bring the property and all persons arrested before a court having competent jurisdiction of the offense within ten (10) days from the date of issuance as required by law.

WITNESS MY HAND and seal this the _14ᵗʰ_ day of _February_ , 1994.

_____

JUDGE OF THE CIRCUIT COURT OF
THE ELEVENTH JUDICIAL CIRCUIT
OF FLORIDA

Judge's Initials   Page 2

SEARCH WARRANT AFFIDAVIT 2

This search warrant affidavit, for 710 N.E. 145 St., in North Miami, Florida, was prepared for a different purpose than the previous one. In this case, a mother and her two children had been missing for several days. Her husband had given conflicting accounts of their absence to different people. As police officers were walking around the outside of house looking for any signs of foul play, they detected a strange odor coming from an open window. The Fire Department was requested to force an entry due to the nature of the odor.

Entering police officers saw in the garage, a recently made coffin-shaped box made from CBS blocks and concrete. Near the box were construction tools and Voodoo paraphernalia. Seeping from within the box were apparent body fluids.

One search warrant was for the home, to break open the box to search for the missing people and any evidence of the crime. Another warrant, supported by the same affidavit, was requested for the missing family car.

IN THE CIRCUIT COURT OF THE ELEVENTH JUDICIAL CIRCUIT
IN AND FOR DADE COUNTY, FLORIDA

STATE OF FLORIDA)
) SS
COUNTY OF DADE)

AFFIDAVIT FOR SEARCH WARRANT

Before me, _Jeffrey Rosinek_, a Judge of the Circuit Court
of the Eleventh Judicial Circuit of Florida, personally appeared Detective
Kenneth Bethel of the North Miami Police Department, who being by me first
duly sworn, deposes and says that he has probable cause to believe and does
believe that in the premises described as:

710 Northeast 145th Street, North Miami, being in Dade County, Florida, a
single family home, yellow with dark brown trim, gray shingle roof, with steel
gratings over the windows, with a solid wood front door. A marker on the
front of the house shows a number of 710. The house is facing north and is
surrounded by a chain fence partially painted green. A TV satellite dish
attached to the rear of the house is visible from the front yard. Parked in
the driveway is 1985 Isuzu four-door sedan, red in color, tag #TWC66Y.
Stacked in the driveway are construction materials, i.e. CBS block, sand and
empty chlorine containers, hereinafter referred to as "The Premises", a
weapon, instrumentality, or means by which a felony, to wit: Homicide or
Kidnapping, in violation of Florida Statutes 782.04 and 787.01, has been
committed, or evidence relevant to proving said felony has been committed, is
contained therein, to wit: human bodies, body fluids, construction materials,
construction tools, latent fingerprints, weapons including machetes, knives,
guns, restraining devices and any other items of evidentiary value as well as
any documents that might assist your Affiant in locating Esnel Jean or persons
who may know where he may be, hereinafter referred to as "The Property".

Affiant's reasons for the belief that "The Premises" are being used as
stated above and that the felony aforesaid has been committed and that "The
Property" above-mentioned is being concealed and stored at "The Premises"
above-described and the facts establishing the grounds for this affidavit and
the probable cause for believing that such facts exist, are as follows:

Your Affiant is Detective Kenneth Bethel of the North Miami Police
Department. He has been a police officer for seven years and is currently
assigned to the Crimes Against Persons Unit. He has been assigned with his

Judge's Initials _____

Post-It® Fax Note	7671	Date 7-7-97	# of pages ▶ 7
To ASA WAKSMAN		From D. SLOVONIC	
Co./Dept.		Co. NMPD	
Phone # 547-0310		Phone # 891-0294,X3118	
Fax # 547-0313		Fax #	

team members to investigate a missing persons report filed by Archie Accius.
He reported on March 27, 1996, that his sister, Wilda Pierre, and her two
children, Evans Pierre and Melinda Juste, are missing. They were last seen on
Saturday, March 23, 1996. The North Miami Police Department has contacted the
school of one of the children and has learned that the child has not been
present since Friday, March 22, 1996. When investigators came to the house on
March 28, 1996, no one was home and the the family car, a 1989 Toyota Camry
four-door, blue in color with tag #RBR08S was missing. The brother stated
that his sister and her children live with Esnel Jean, who is a black Haitian
male. Investigators observed sand and CBS block and empty chlorine containers
at the front of the house. On March 29, 1996, Archie Accius responded to
North Miami Police Department and requested additional assistance. Missing
Persons Detective Ruggiero returned to the premises with Mr. Accius and
observed the house locked, the aforementioned car missing, and after walking
to the side of the house near an open window detected a foul odor coming from
within. Fearing that the missing persons may be dead, injured or in another
form of distress, she requested Metro-Dade Fire Department to force entry in
order to see whether medical attention was necessary. Other members of your
Affiant's team responded to the premises and entered and began to search for
anyone who might need medical attention and the cause of the foul odor. The
odor drew their attention to the garage area. In the garage a recently made
coffin-like box constructed of CBS block and concrete was observed. Next to
the box were similar CBS construction materials and tools including a trowel,
hammer, levels, etc. Seen emanating from the box was apparent body fluids
from two separate areas of the box. The box was sealed with concrete and has
not been opened. Before leaving the house officers made a search of the rest
of the house for any injured or missing persons and found none. The husband
of Wilda Pierre is still missing as is the aforesaid vehicle which is
registered in both their names. Your Affiant has learned from Wilda Pierre's
neighbors that her husband Esnel Jean is a Voodoo Priest and practices his
rituals at the premises. A dead animal skin believed to be a goat was found
in the backyard. Also, hanging over the coffin-like box are various Voodoo
paraphernalia including a machete, dolls, ribbons, etc. A person with
knowledge of Haitian Voodoo practices advised your Affiant that those types of
items are indicative of a Voodoo chapel. As Wilda Pierre's husband is not
available to give consent for your Affiant to open the box and do a full crime
scene search of the house and Wilda Pierre is also currently unavailable to

give consent, your Affiant prays that this Honorable Court will enter its Order demanding he and his team members conduct a full and complete crime scene examination of the premises. Items to be looked for and removed include human bodies, body fluids, construction materials, construction tools, latent fingerprints, weapons, including machetes, knives, guns, restraining devices, and any other items of evidentiary value as well as any documents that might assist your Affiant in locating Mr. Jean or persons who know where he may be. As the aforementioned family vehicle is missing, your Affiant believes Mr. Esnel Jean may have fled in it with other items of evidentiary value.

Your Affiant has learned that approximately two weeks ago Esnel Jean sold that vehicle for one thousand two hundred dollars ($1,200) but that Ms. Pierre had since recovered the vehicle and regained possession of it. That vehicle is presently missing.

WHEREFORE, Affiant prays that a Search Warrant be issued commanding the Director of the Metro-Dade Police Department, Dade County, Florida, who is also known as the Sheriff of Metropolitan Dade County, Florida, or his Deputies, and the Commissioner of the Florida Department of Law Enforcement, or any of his duly constituted agents, and all Investigators of the State Attorney of the Eleventh Judicial Circuit of Florida, and Chief of Police of the City of North Miami, or any of his duly qualified officers, Dade County, Florida, with the proper and necessary assistance, to search "The Premises" above-described, and all spaces therein, and the curtilage thereof, for "The Property" above-described, making the search in the Daytime or the Nighttime, as the exigencies may demand or require, or on Sunday, and if the same be found on "The Premises" to seize the same as evidence and to arrest any person in the unlawful possession thereof.

DET. _____
AFFIANT

SWORN TO AND SUBSCRIBED before me this the 27 day of MARCH , 1996.

_____
JUDGE OF THE CIRCUIT COURT OF
THE ELEVENTH JUDICIAL CIRCUIT
OF FLORIDA

Judge's Initials _____ Page 3

IN THE CIRCUIT COURT OF THE ELEVENTH JUDICIAL CIRCUIT
IN AND FOR DADE COUNTY, FLORIDA

STATE OF FLORIDA)
) SS
COUNTY OF DADE   )

SEARCH WARRANT

IN THE NAME OF THE STATE OF FLORIDA, TO ALL AND SINGULAR:

The Director of the Metro-Dade Police Department, Dade County, Florida, who is also known as the Sheriff of Metropolitan Dade County, Florida, or his Deputies, and the Commissioner of the Florida Department of Law Enforcement, or any of his duly constituted Agents, and all Investigators of the State Attorney of the Eleventh Judicial Circuit of Florida, and Chief of Police of the City of North Miami, or any of his duly qualified officers, Dade County, Florida.

Affidavit having been made before me by Detective Kenneth Bethel, that he has probable cause to believe and does believe that in the premises described as:

710 Northeast 145th Street, North Miami, being in Dade County, Florida, a single family home, yellow with dark brown trim, gray shingle roof, with steel gratings over the windows, with a solid wood front door. A marker on the front of the house shows a number of 710. The house is facing north and is surrounded by a chain fence partially painted green. A TV satellite dish attached to the rear of the house is visible from the front yard. Parked in the driveway is 1985 Isuzu four-door sedan, red in color, tag #TWC66Y. Stacked in the driveway are construction materials, i.e. CBS block, sand and empty chlorine containers, hereinafter referred to as "The Premises", a weapon, instrumentality, or means by which a felony, to wit: Homicide or Kidnapping, in violation of Florida Statutes .782.04 and 787.01, has been committed, or evidence relevant to proving said felony has been committed, is contained therein, to wit: human bodies, body fluids, construction materials, construction tools, latent fingerprints, weapons including machetes, knives, guns, restraining devices and any other items of evidentiary value as well as any documents that might assist your Affiant in locating Esnel Jean or persons who may know where he may be, hereinafter referred to as "The Property".

Judge's Initials _____   Page 1

YOU ARE HEREBY COMMANDED to enter and search forthwith "The Premises" above described, and the curtilage thereof, for "The Property" above-described, serving this Warrant and making the search in the Daytime or Nighttime, as the exigencies may demand or require, or on Sunday, with the proper and necessary assistance, and if "The Property" above-described be found there, to seize it and to arrest all persons in the unlawful possession thereof, leaving a copy of this Warrant and a receipt for the property taken and prepare a written Inventory of the property seized and return this Warrant and bring the property and all persons arrested before a court having competent jurisdiction of the offense within ten (10) days from the date of issuance as required by law.

WITNESS MY HAND and seal this the _25_ day of _____ , 1996.

_____
JUDGE OF THE CIRCUIT COURT OF
THE ELEVENTH JUDICIAL CIRCUIT
OF FLORIDA

Judge's Initials _____   Page 2

IN THE CIRCUIT COURT OF THE ELEVENTH JUDICIAL CIRCUIT
IN AND FOR DADE COUNTY, FLORIDA

STATE OF FLORIDA   )
) SS
COUNTY OF DADE   )

SEARCH WARRANT

IN THE NAME OF THE STATE OF FLORIDA, TO ALL AND SINGULAR:

The Director of the Metro-Dade Police Department, Dade County, Florida,
who is also known as the Sheriff of Metropolitan Dade County, Florida, or his
Deputies, and the Commissioner of the Florida Department of Law Enforcement,
or any of his duly constituted Agents, and all Investigators of the State
Attorney of the Eleventh Judicial Circuit of Florida, and Chief of Police of
the City of North Miami, or any of his duly qualified officers, Dade County,
Florida.

Affidavit having been made before me by Detective Kenneth Bethel, that he
has probable cause to believe and does believe that in the premises described
as:

A 1989 Toyota Camry four-door, blue in color with tag #RBR08S,
hereinafter referred to as "The Premises", a weapon, instrumentality, or means
by which a felony, to wit: Homicide or Kidnapping, in violation of Florida
Statutes 782.04 and 787.01, has been committed, or evidence relevant to
proving said felony has been committed, is contained therein, to wit: human
bodies, body fluids, construction materials, construction tools, latent
fingerprints, weapons including machetes, knives, guns, restraining devices
and any other items of evidentiary value as well as any documents that might
assist your Affiant in locating Esnel Jean or persons who may know where he
may be, hereinafter referred to as "The Property".

And as I am satisfied that there is probable cause to believe that "The
Premises" are being used as aforesaid and that the felony aforesaid has been
committed and that "The Property" above-mentioned is being concealed and
stored at "The Premises" above-described, I expressly find probable cause for
the issuance of this Search Warrant.

Judge's Initials _____   Page 1

And as I am satisfied that there is probable cause to believe that "The Premises" are being used as aforesaid and that the felony aforesaid has been committed and that "The Property" above-mentioned is being concealed and stored at "The Premises" above-described, I expressly find probable cause for the issuance of this Search Warrant.

YOU ARE HEREBY COMMANDED to enter and search forthwith "The Premises" above described, and the curtilage thereof, for "The Property" above-described, serving this Warrant and making the search in the Daytime or Nighttime, as the exigencies may demand or require, or on Sunday, with the proper and necessary assistance, and if "The Property" above-described be found there, to seize it and to arrest all persons in the unlawful possession thereof, leaving a copy of this Warrant and a receipt for the property taken and prepare a written Inventory of the property seized and return this Warrant and bring the property and all persons arrested before a court having competent jurisdiction of the offense within ten (10) days from the date of issuance as required by law.

WITNESS MY HAND and seal this the 29² day of _____March_____, 1996.

_____

JUDGE OF THE CIRCUIT COURT OF
THE ELEVENTH JUDICIAL CIRCUIT
OF FLORIDA

Judge's Initials _____   Page 2

SEARCH WARRANT AFFIDAVIT 3

This is a blank search warrant and affidavit used in the author's jurisdiction. Feel free to use it as a template; just insert your jurisdiction's county, state, and police department. Above and beyond the Fourth Amendment's requirements, your state probably has a statute setting forth how the warrant must be executed. Be aware of that, as suppression may lie for faulty execution. Good luck.

IN THE CIRCUIT COURT OF THE ELEVENTH JUDICIAL CIRCUIT
IN AND FOR MIAMI-DADE COUNTY, FLORIDA

STATE OF FLORIDA   )
)   SS
COUNTY OF MIAMI-DADE   )

AFFIDAVIT FOR SEARCH WARRANT

Before me,_____ , a judge of the Circuit Court of the Eleventh Judicial Circuit of Florida, personally appeared _____, who being by me first duly sworn, deposes and says that he has probable cause to believe and does believe that the premises described as:

_____, being in (the city of) Miami-Dade County, Florida, hereinafter referred to as "The Premises," contains a weapon, instrumentality, or means by which a felony, to wit: _____, in violation of Florida Statutes, has been committed, or evidence relevant to proving said felony has been committed, to wit: _____, hereinafter referred to as "The Property."

Affiant's reasons for the belief that "The Premises" are being used as stated above and that the felony aforesaid has been committed and that "The Property" above-mentioned is being concealed and stored at "The Premises" above-described and the facts establishing the grounds for this affidavit and the probable cause for believing that such facts exist, are as follows:

_____

WHEREFORE, Affiant prays that a Search Warrant be issued commanding the Director of the Miami-Dade Police Department, Miami-Dade County, Florida, who is also known as the Sheriff of Metropolitan Miami-Dade County, Florida, or his Deputies, and the Commissioner of the Florida Department of Law Enforcement, or any of his duly constituted agents, and all Investigators of the State Attorney of the Eleventh Judicial Circuit of Florida, and the Chief of Police for the City of _____, or any of his duly qualified officers, Miami-Dade County, Florida, with the proper and necessary assistance, to search "The Premises" above-described, and all spaces therein, and the curtilage thereof, for "The Property" above-described, making the search in the Daytime or the Nighttime, as the exigencies may demand or require, or on Sunday, and if the same be found on "The Premises" to seize the same as evidence and to arrest any person in the unlawful possession thereof.

_____
AFFIANT

SWORN TO AND SUBSCRIBED before me this the _____ day of _____, 2008.

_____
JUDGE OF THE CIRCUIT COURT OF THE
ELEVENTH JUDICIAL CIRCUIT OF
FLORIDA

Judge's Initials _____

IN THE CIRCUIT COURT OF THE ELEVENTH JUDICIAL CIRCUIT
IN AND FOR MIAMI-DADE COUNTY, FLORIDA

STATE OF FLORIDA   )
)   SS

COUNTY OF MIAMI-DADE   )

SEARCH WARRANT

IN THE NAME OF THE STATE OF FLORIDA, TO ALL AND SINGULAR:

The Director of the Miami-Dade Police Department, Miami-Dade County, Florida, who is also known as the Sheriff of Metropolitan Miami-Dade County, Florida, or his Deputies, and the Commissioner of the Florida Department of Law Enforcement, or any of his duly constituted Agents, and all Investigators of the State Attorney of the Eleventh Judicial Circuit of Florida, and the Chief of Police for the City of _____, or any of his duly qualified officers, Miami-Dade County, Florida.

Affidavit having been made before me by _____, that he has probable cause to believe and does believe that the premises described as:

_____, being in (the city of) Miami-Dade County, Florida, hereinafter referred to as "The Premises," contains a weapon, instrumentality, or means by which a felony, to wit: _____, in violation of Florida Statutes, has been committed, or evidence relevant to proving said felony has been committed, to wit: _____, hereinafter referred to as "The Property."

And as I am satisfied that there is probable cause to believe that "The Premises" are being used as aforesaid and that the felony aforesaid has been committed and that "The Property" above-mentioned is being concealed and stored at "The Premises" above-described, I expressly find probable cause for the issuance of this Search Warrant.

YOU ARE HEREBY COMMANDED to enter and search forthwith "The Premises" above described, and the curtilage thereof, for "The Property" above-described, serving this Warrant and making the search in the Daytime or Nighttime, as the exigencies may demand or require, or on Sunday, with the proper and necessary assistance, and if "The Property" above-described be found there, to seize it and to arrest all persons in the unlawful possession thereof, leaving a copy of this Warrant and a receipt for the property taken and prepare a written Inventory of the property seized and return this Warrant and bring the property and all persons arrested before a court having competent jurisdiction of the offense within ten (10) days from the date of issuance as required by law.

WITNESS MY HAND and seal this the _____ day of _____, 2008.

                                     _____
                                     JUDGE OF THE CIRCUIT COURT OF THE
                                     ELEVENTH JUDICIAL CIRCUIT OF
                                                   FLORIDA

Judge's Initials _____

STATE OF FLORIDA   )
) SS

COUNTY OF MIAMI-DADE   )

RETURN AND INVENTORY

I, _____, received the attached Search Warrant on _____, 2008, and duly executed it as follows:

On _____, 2008, at _____ o'clock _____.M., I searched the premises described in the Search Warrant and left a copy of the Search Warrant with: _____, together with an inventory of property taken pursuant to the Search Warrant:

(USE REVERSE SIDE FOR CONTINUATION)

I, _____, the officer by whom the warrant was executed, do swear that the above Inventory contains a true and detailed account of all the property taken by me on said Warrant.

_____

APPENDIX C

Consent to be Searched Forms, English and Spanish

HOUSE AND VEHICLE

METRO-DADE POLICE DEPARTMENT

WAIVER OF CONSTITUTIONAL RIGHTS: CONSENT TO SEARCH

BEFORE ANY SEARCH IS MADE, YOU MUST UNDERSTAND YOUR RIGHTS:

(1) You may refuse to consent to a search and may demand that a search warrant be obtained prior to any search of the premises or vehicle described below.

(2) If you consent to a search, anything of evidentiary value seized in the course of the search can be introduced into evidence in court.

I HAVE READ THE ABOVE STATEMENT OF MY RIGHTS AND I AM FULLY AWARE OF THE SAID RIGHTS.

I HEREBY CONSENT TO A SEARCH WITHOUT WARRANT BY OFFICERS OF THE METRO-DADE POLICE DEPARTMENT OF ALL AREAS AND CONTENTS OF THE BELOW DESCRIBED PREMISES, VEHICLE, VESSEL, OR AIRCRAFT.

_____

_____

_____

I HEREBY AUTHORIZE THE SAID OFFICERS TO SEIZE ANY ARTICLE WHICH THEY MAY DEEM TO BE OF EVIDENTIARY VALUE.

THIS STATEMENT IS SIGNED OF MY OWN FREE WILL WITHOUT ANY THREATS OR PROMISES HAVING BEEN MADE TO ME.

_____

Signature of Consenting Individual

_____

Date   Time

_____

Witness: DATE/TIME

_____

Witness: DATE/TIME

Original - Case File
Copy - State Attorney's Office

RENUNCIA A LOS DERECHOS CONSTITUCIONALES: CONSENTIMIENTO PARA EFECTUAR UN REGISTRO O PESQUISAS.

ESTE CONSENTIMIENTO (O PERMISO) DEBE OBTENERSE DE LA PERSONA QUE ESTE BAJO LA CUSTODIA DE LA POLICIA.

(1) Usted puede negarse a consentir que se lleven a cabo las pesquisas o los registros, y puede exigir que se obtenga un permiso para efectuar un registro o pesquisas antes de llevar a cabo tales, en el lugar o en el vehículo que se describe a continuación.

(2) Si usted da su consentimiento para efectuar pesquisas o registros, cualquier objeto o dato que sirva como evidencia y decomisado en el curso de dicho registros o pesquisas, podrá y será presentado en la corte como prueba contra usted.

HE LEIDO LA DESCRIPCION DE MIS DERECHOS CONSTITUCIONALES TAL COMO SE EXPONEN ARRIBA Y COMPRENDO PERFECTAMENTE DICHOS DERECHOS.

POR ESTE MEDIO DOY MI CONSENTIMIENTO PARA QUE LOS OFICIALES DEL DEPARTAMENTO DE SEGURIDAD PUBLICA DEL CONDADO DE DADE (METROPOLITANO) EFECTUEN REGISTROS Y PESQUISAS SIN NECESIDAD DE UNA ORDEN O MANDATO EN LO SIGUIENTE: (Describa el lugar o el Vehículo).

POR ESTE MEDIO YO AUTHORIZO A DICHOS OFICIALES A DECOMISAR CUALQUIER ARTICULO O DATO QUE ELLOS CONSIDEREN PUEDAN SERVIR COMO EVIDENCIA. FIRMO LA PRESENTE DECLARACION VOLUNTARIAMENTE, PARA CONSTANCIA DE QUE NO HE SIDO AMENAZADO, NI SE ME HA HECHO NINGUN OFRECIMIENTO.

_____
Firma

_____
Fecha y Hora

_____
Testigo   Fecha y Hora

_____
Testigo   Fecha y Hora

11 1.21-78A

HIALEAH POLICE DEPARTMENT

CONSENT TO SEARCH

You may refuse to consent to a search and may demand that a search warrant be obtained prior to any search of the premises or vehicle described below.

If you consent to a search, anything of evidentiary value seized in the course of the search, can and will be introduced into evidence in court against you.

I have read the above statement and I am fully aware of the said rights.

I hereby consent to a search without warrant by officers of the City of Hialeah Police Department of the following:

Jessica Ramos

_10090 N.W.____ Ave   786-386-____

This statement is signed of my own free will without any threats or promises having been made to me.

Jessica Ramos

5-6-08   6:45
Date   **Time**

[signature]   1191
Witness

[signature]   0882
Witness

08-17580
Hialeah Police Department Case Number

CONSENTIMIENTO PARA REGISTRO

08-17580
Número del Caso

Usted puede negar consentimiento a un registro y demandar que se obtenga una orden de registro antes de cualquier registro del local, vehículo, u otra propiedad descrito abajo.

Si usted da el consentimiento para un registro, cualquier artículo que tenga valor como evidencia que se obtenga durante el registro puede ser y será introducido como evidencia encontra suya en la corte.

Yo he leído esta declaración y estoy completamente consiente de mis derechos. Yo doy mi consentimiento a un registro sin una orden de registro por los oficiales de la Policía de Hialeah a lo siguiente:

WHITE COLORED

1999 FORD EXPLORER

FL TAG # RS61

VIN: 1FMZU32X3XUC560

Esta declaración es firmada por mi voluntariamente sin que me hayan hecho ni promesas ni amenazas.

Firma: X _____

Fecha: 5-06-08   Hora: 7.15PM

Oficial: NOEL TORRES   ID# 1036

Firma del Oficial: _____

Fecha: 050608   Hora: 1915